CHAPTER I
AZTECLAND

Prescott says: "Of all that extensive empire which once acknowledged the authority of Spain in the New World, no portion for interest and importance, can be compared with Mexico;—and this equally, whether we consider the variety of its soil and climate; the inexhaustible stores of its mineral wealth; its scenery, grand and picturesque beyond example; the character of its ancient inhabitants, not only far surpassing in intelligence that of the other North American races, but reminding us, by their monuments, of the primitive civilization of Egypt and Hindoostan; or, lastly, the peculiar circumstances of its conquest, adventurous and romantic as any legend devised by Norman or Italian bard of chivalry."

Mexico is a country in which the old predominates. The American visitor will bring back more distinct recollections of the Egyptian carts and plows, the primitive manners and customs, than he will of the evidences of modern civilization. An educated Mexican whom I met, chided the Americans for this tendency, for, said he, "all that is written of Mexico is descriptive of the Indians and their habits, while progressive Mexico is ignored." This is to a great extent true, for it is the unique and ancient that attracts and holds the attention of the traveller. For this reason tourists go to Egypt to see the pyramids, sphinx and tombs of the Pharaohs.

It is not necessary for the traveller to venture out upon perilous seas to see mute evidences of a life older than printed record. In this land of ancient civilization and primitive customs, there are cities which stand out like oriental pearls transplanted to the Occident from the shores of the Red Sea. Here in Mexico can be found pyramids which are no mean rivals to those great piles on the Egyptian deserts; crumbling ruins of tombs, and palaces, and temples, ornamented in arabesque and grecque designs, not unlike the structures along the banks of the mighty Nile; and the same primitive implements of husbandry which we have viewed so often in the pages of the large family Bible. Then, as an additional attraction, there is the actual presence of the aborigines, Aztec, Zapotec, and Chichimec, speaking the same language, observing the same ceremonies, and following the same customs which were old when the foreigners came.

There is no history to enlighten us as to the age of these monuments, and there are few hieroglyphics to be deciphered upon which a Rosetta Stone might shed light. The student is led to wonder whether the Egyptian civilization antedated the Mexican, or whether the former is simply the Mexican learning and skill transplanted to the Orient and there modified and improved. It is quite possible, that, while our own ancestors were still barbarians, and little better than savages, swarming over northern Europe, the early races in Mexico had developed a civilization advanced and progressive. They knew how to build monuments which in masonry and carving teach us lessons to-day. They made beautiful pottery and artistic vessels, and they used gold for money and ornaments.

Notwithstanding the fact that for a thousand miles the republics of Mexico and the United States join, the average American knows less concerning Mexico than he does of many European countries; and it is much misunderstood as well as misrepresented. Mexico possesses the strongest possible attractions for the tourist. Its scenic wonders are unsurpassed in any other part of the globe in natural picturesqueness; and no country in Europe presents an aspect more unfamiliar and strange to American eyes, or exceeds it in historic interest.

Vast mountains including snow-capped Popocatapetl and Ixtaccihuatl, the loftiest peaks on the American continent, are seen here amid scenes of tropical beauty and luxuriance. Great cities are found with their customs and characteristics almost unchanged since they were built by the Spaniards; and there are still more ancient cities and temples which were built by prehistoric races.

SNOW-CAPPED POPOCATAPETL

It is a land of tradition and romance, and of picturesque contrasts. At almost every turn there is something new, unique, interesting, and even startling. It has all the climates from the torrid zone to regions of perpetual snow on the summits of the lofty volcanic peaks, and is capable of producing nearly every fruit found between the equator and the Arctic circle. The softness and sweetness of the air; the broken and ever-varying line of rugged hills against a matchless sky; the beautiful views between the mountain ranges; the care-free life which is omnipresent each add their charm to the composite picture. Dirt is everywhere and poverty abounds, but even these are removed from the commonplace by the brilliant colour on every hand.

F. Hopkinson Smith in "A White Umbrella in Mexico" epitomizes this marvellously attractive country as follows: "A land of white sunshine, redolent with flowers; a land of gay costumes, crumbling churches, and old convents; a land of kindly greetings, of extreme courtesy, of open, broad hospitality. It was more than enough to revel in an Italian sun, lighting up a semi-tropical land; to look up to white-capped peaks, towering into blue; to look down upon wind-swept plains, encircled by ragged chains of mountains; to catch the sparkle of miniature cities, jewelled here and there in oases of olive and orange; and to realize that to-day, in its varied scenery, costumes, architecture, street life, canals crowded with flower-laden boats, market plazas thronged with gaily-dressed natives, faded church interiors, and abandoned convents, Mexico is the most marvellously picturesque country under the sun. A tropical Venice! A semi-barbarous Spain! A new Holy Land."

Mexico contains a greater area than is generally understood. It is shaped very much like a cornucopia with an extreme length of nineteen hundred miles, a breadth of seven hundred and fifty miles, and an area of nearly eight hundred thousand square miles. At its narrowest point, the Isthmus of Tehuantepec, it is only one hundred and twenty-five miles across from ocean to ocean. There is a double range of mountains, one near the Pacific coast and the other near the coast of the Gulf of Mexico, between which lie the great table lands, or plateaus, which constitute a large part of the surface.

Transcriber'sNote: The map is clickable for a larger version, if the device you're reading this on supports that.

Three distinct climates are found in Mexico determined by altitude. Those regions six thousand feet or more above sea level are called the *tierras frias*, or cold lands. This is only a relative term, for the cold does not correspond with that of our own northern states. Though termed "cold," the mean temperature is not lower than that of Central Italy. Those lands lying at an altitude of six thousand feet, down to three thousand feet, above sea level are termed the *tierras templadas*, or temperate lands. This is a region of perpetual humidity and is semi-tropical in its vegetation and temperature.

An altitude from four thousand to six thousand feet in Mexico gives a most delightful climate.

Along both the Atlantic and Pacific coasts there is a more or less broad tract called the *tierra caliente*, or hot land, which is a truly tropical region. Forests of dense growth cover the soil, so thick that it is impossible to penetrate them without blazing your way as you go, and in the midst of which tower trees of magnificent size, such as are to be seen only in the tropics. Here it is that nature is over-prodigal in her gifts; and here it is that the *vomito*, as yellow fever is called, lurks with fatal effect. The winds from the sea generally mitigate the fierce heat, especially if one can remain out of the sun during the middle of the day. Sometimes these winds on the Atlantic coast acquire great velocity, and burst forth upon the unprotected shores with terrific fury as the so-called "northers." There is no true winter here, but there is a rainy season from June to October, and a dry season from November to May, the former being the colder.

"In the course of a few hours," says Prescott, "the traveller may experience every gradation of climate, embracing torrid heat and glacial cold, and pass through different zones of vegetation including wheat and the sugar-cane, the ash and the palm, apples, olives, and guavas." The dwellings vary also. In the hot lands the habitations are constructed of bamboo and light poles open to sun and wind, for the only shelter needed is protection from the elements; in the temperate region the huts are made of heavier poles, and are somewhat more durable; in the higher lands they are built of adobe or stone. Sugar cane and coffee, and even the banana, will grow up to four thousand feet. Wheat grows best at six thousand feet and pines commence here too. At seven thousand feet cactus appears, and the *maguey*, ushering in an entirely different zone. Mexico is a country of extremes of heat and cold, poverty and riches, filth and cleanliness, education and extreme ignorance.

Every schoolboy knows of Loch Katrine and Loch Lomond in bonnie Scotland, and most people are familiar with the location of Lago di Como, in Italy. And yet I should not be surprised if fair-sized towns could be found in the United States where no one could tell whether such a body of water as Lake Chapala existed or not. As a matter of fact it is ten times as large as all the lakes of Northern Italy combined; and it embraces islands larger than the entire surface of Loch Lomond. Its steely blue waters and rugged shores need only the magic pen of the novelist or poet to tell of its beauties and invest each nook and glen with romance, and the charming villas of Como to make Chapala as picturesque and fascinating as those better known lakes. It is almost a hundred miles long and thirty-three miles wide at the widest point, and covers fourteen hundred square miles. Patzcuaro and Cuitzeo are also lakes of considerable size near Chapala, and all of them are six thousand feet or more above sea level. They only await development and advertising to become popular resorts.

The vast majority of the inhabitants of Mexico are descendants of Indian races who were found there by the Spanish conquerors, and mixtures of those natives with European settlers. Of the fourteen millions of inhabitants only about nineteen per cent. are white; of the remainder, forty-three per cent. are Indians and thirty-eight per cent. mixed. There is a greater resemblance of the Mexican Indians to the Malay races of Asia than to the American Indians. Their intensely black hair and eyes, brown complexion, small stature, and even a slight obliquity of the eyes bear a strong resemblance to the Japanese. I have seen it stated that, if a Japanese is dressed in Mexican costume, and a Mexican in Japanese dress, it is difficult to tell which is the Jap and which the Mexican. Students of languages say that there is a strong similarity between the Mexican tongues and oriental languages. The different tribes do not mingle much and seldom intermarry, and this fact may contribute to their physical deterioration.

AN INDIAN MAIDEN

Whence came this people? No one can answer. It is generally supposed that the Aztecs came from what are now the south-western states of the Union, and wandered into the Valley of Mexico. They were defeated by the tribes then dwelling there, and sought refuge on the shores of Lake Texcoco. There they beheld a golden eagle of great size and beauty resting on a prickly cactus and devouring a serpent which it held in its talons, and with its wings outstretched toward the rising sun. This was the sign for which they had been looking, and there they proceeded to erect their capital. They first built houses of rushes and reeds in the shallow water and lived upon fish, and constructed floating gardens. As the waters receded somewhat they built more durable structures, including great palaces and temples. They extended their sway over neighbouring races beyond the Valley and conquered tribe after tribe, although never claiming dominion over more than a small portion of the present confines of Mexico. The legend of the eagle and the cactus is still preserved in the coat-of-arms of the present republic.

Of the Aztecs and their history prior to the conquest little is known, except that the country was called Anahuac. Prescott has made his "Conquest of Mexico" as fascinating as a novel, but he has shown the romantic side based upon knowledge of the most fragmentary character. The writings which pass for history were either written by bigoted priests who could not see anything good in an idolatrous people, and who, to please the leaders, painted the Aztecs in blackest colours to justify the cruel measures taken, or they were written by Spaniards who never visited the country of which they presumed to write. As it has been said, "a most gorgeous superstructure of fancy has been raised upon a very meagre foundation of fact." Their civilization was in many respects marvellous and far ahead of that of any other race on the western hemisphere. Under the Montezumas they had grown into a powerful nation, and their rule was one of barbaric splendour and luxury.

The Aztecs succeeded an older race called the Toltecs who were also far advanced in civilization. They were nature worshippers and not only did not indulge in human sacrifices, but were averse to war and detested falsehood and treachery. A Toltec noble is said to have instructed his son after the following manner before sending him away from home: "Never tell a falsehood, because a lie is a grievous sin! Speak ill of nobody. Be not dissolute, for thereby thou wilt incense the gods, and they will cover thee with infamy. Steal not, nor give thyself up to gaming; otherwise thou wilt be a disgrace to thy parents, whom thou oughtest rather to honour, for the education they have given thee. If thou wilt be virtuous, thy example will put the wicked to shame."

Both of these races were also great builders and sculptors and had cultivated the art of picture-writing. They were well housed, decently clothed, made cloth, enjoyed vapour baths, maintained schools, and had a large assortment of household gods. They mined some, and in agriculture, at least, were far ahead of the Mexicans of to-day.

The vandalism of the Spaniards in destroying the writings and other records of the early races is rebuked by Prescott as follows: "We contemplate with indignation the cruelties inflicted by the early conquerors. But indignation is qualified with contempt when we see them thus ruthlessly trampling out the sparks of knowledge, the common boon and property of mankind. We may well doubt which has the strongest claim to civilization, the victor or the vanquished."

The Mexico of to-day cannot be understood without looking for a moment at its settlement and the manner of the conquest. The Spanish *conquistadores* who flocked to these shores with Cortez were a different race from those early settlers, who, persecuted and denied liberty of conscience in the land of their birth, sought a new home on our own hospitable shores. With the union of the crowns of Castille and Aragon by the marriage of Ferdinand and Isabella, and the discovery of the New World, Spain had suddenly leaped to the front, and become, for a time at least, the greatest nation of the day. Ships were constructed in great numbers and sent out, filled with voyagers, "towards that part of the horizon where the sun set."

In the sixteenth century she had practically become the mistress of the seas and the most powerful nation in the world. Her soldiers were brave and the acknowledged leaders of chivalry, but the curse of the Spaniards was their thirst for gold, and her decay was rapid. When Cortez and his band of adventurers came to the court of Montezuma, and saw the lavish display of vessels and ornaments made of the precious metal, they thought they had discovered the land of gold for which they were searching. Attracted by the glowing reports of untold wealth, thousands of Spaniards soon followed the first bands of *conquistadores,* and they rapidly spread over the entire country occupied by the Aztecs, ever searching for the mines from whence this golden harvest came. While the leaders were imprisoning and torturing the Aztec chieftains to force them to give up the hiding places of their treasures, the priests, who everywhere accompanied the soldiers, were baptizing thousands into the new faith and using the confessional for the same end. Thus religious bigotry and the mania for worldly riches went side by side, and ever ringing in the ears of both priest and warrior was the refrain:

"Gold! Gold! Gold! Gold!
Bright and yellow, hard and cold."

Shortly after the conquest all the desirable lands were parcelled out among the invaders and the few Indian *caciques* who had helped, with their powerful influence, in their subjugation. The Spaniards rapidly pacified the country, for the Aztec masses, however warlike they may have been before the coming of the Spaniards, were subdued by one blow. They were soon convinced that opposition to the power of Spain was useless. The priests, also, through their quickly acquired influence, taught submission to those whom God, in His infinite wisdom, had placed over them. Chiefs who would not yield otherwise were bribed to use their power over their vassals in favour of the Spaniards. Thus by force, bribery, intrigue, diplomacy, treachery, and even religion, the Indians were reconciled and the spirit of opposition to the Spaniards broken. The result was a new and upstart nobility who ruled the country with an iron hand in the course of a few decades; and the natives, with the exception of the chiefs, were made vassals of these newly made nobles.

An era of building followed, in which great palaces after the *grandiose* ideas of Spain were constructed by Indian workmen. Churches were built with lavish hand, for these nobles thought to atone for their many misdeeds by constructing and dedicating places of worship to Almighty God, who, according to the teaching of the priest, was the God of the poor, oppressed Indian as well as the God of the haughty Spaniard who had enslaved him. As one writer has said: "When John Smith and his followers were looking for gold mines in Virginia and the Pilgrims were planting corn in Massachusetts, an empire had been founded and built up on the same continent by the Spaniards, and the most stupendous system of plunder the world ever saw was then and there in vigorous operation." Cortez was searching for "a people who had much gold" of which he had heard. It was not God but gold that drew him in his campaign over Mexico. He did not aim to Christianize the natives so much as enrich himself and acquire empire for his sovereign, and religion was a subterfuge plausible and popular in that age.

"I die," said the patriot Hidalgo, when about to be executed in 1811, "but the seeds of liberty will be watered by my blood. The cause will not die; that still lives and will surely triumph." His prediction came true, and freedom from the Spanish yoke of three centuries was secured ten years later after the shedding of much blood. Peace did not follow at once, however, for in the fifty years succeeding the declaration of independence the form of government changed ten times, and there were fifty-four different rulers, including two emperors and a number of dictatorships. Special privileges are difficult to eradicate when established by long usage, and those enjoying them yield only to force. The Church, which had imposed on the people such a vast number of priests, friars, and nuns, and had acquired the most of the wealth of the country, clung with the grip of death to its privileges and property. The changes came gradually, but it has been a half-century since the Church and State were formally separated by constitutional amendment. The bigoted and despotic Romanism, which was allied with the Spanish aristocracy, has at last been subdued. A more tolerant spirit is springing up towards other forms of religious faith through the efforts of a powerful and liberal government. Education is also freeing the people from the superstitious ignorance which has hitherto prevailed in most parts of Mexico. There are occasional outbursts of fanaticism, but they are quickly suppressed, and the government is making an honest effort to preserve freedom of worship to all faiths.

The United States of Mexico is a federation composed of twenty-seven states, three territories, and the federal district in which the capital is located. The states are sovereign within themselves and are held together under a federal constitution very much like our own. This constitution was adopted on the 5th of February, 1857, and its semi-centennial was recently celebrated with a few of the original signers present. There is a congress composed of two bodies, the Senate and Chamber of Deputies which meets twice each year. Each state is represented in the former by two senators and in the latter by one representative for each forty thousand of population. The right of suffrage is restricted so that only a small proportion of the population can exercise that privilege. They have not really reached popular government, and politics, as we know them in the United States, do not exist. A presidential election scarcely caused a ripple on the surface. President Diaz was no doubt the popular choice, but comparatively few votes were cast at his last election. The rule of the Diaz government although decidedly autocratic was beneficial, and has redounded to the good of the country. Though practically an absolute ruler, President Diaz always acted through the regularly organized channels of a complete form of republican government, and outwardly, at least, there was no semblance of a dictatorship.

Mexico is a country of great natural resources and possibilities which have been only partially developed. Its soil is remarkably fertile and could support five times, and, if water could be found on the plateaus, ten times the present population. And I say this notwithstanding the fact that one man has said that Mexico is the poorest country south of Greenland, and north of the south pole. The flora of the country, among which are many useful and medicinal plants, is exceedingly rich and varied. More species of fibre plants are found there than in any other country, and the commercial utility of these plants is not yet fully appreciated. In no country has there been greater waste of natural resources than the Spanish conquerors caused in Mexico. It is as a mining country that Mexico has been best known and the Mexican silver mines have been famous ever since the discovery of the New World, and they are still the greatest single source of wealth. Some of them which have been worked for centuries are still yielding small fortunes in the white metal each year.

The Mexican has his own view of the United States and does not call our boasted progress and much-vaunted civilization, with its hurry, brusque ways and the blotting out of the finer courtesies, an improvement. He appreciates our mechanical contrivances and electrical inventions, but prefers to enjoy life after his own fashion and in the way he thinks that God intended in order to keep men happy. The civilization received by Mexico in the sixteenth century was looked upon as equal to the best in existence, and to this was added an ancient civilization found in the country. From these sources a manner of living has been evolved which bears evidences of culture and refinement. This system has flowed on through the intervening centuries, undisturbed by the march of progress, until the last quarter of a century. Things cannot be changed to Anglo-Saxon standards in a year, or two years, or even a generation. To Americanize Mexico will be a difficult if not impossible undertaking, and there are no signs of such a transition. Americans who live there fall into Mexican ways and moral standards more frequently than Mexicans are converted to the American point of view. The influence of traditions, customs, and climate, and the centuries-old habit of letting the morrow take care of itself is too great to be overcome.

CHAPTER II
ACROSSTHEPLA TEAUS

The traveller going to Mexico by rail will discover that that country begins long before the border is reached. While travelling over the great state of Texas, where the dialect of the natives is as broad as the rolling prairie round about, he is reminded of our southern neighbour by the soft accents of the Spanish language, or by the entrance into the coach of a Mexican cowboy with his great hat and picturesque suit. Leaving beautiful San Antonio, which is a Spanish city modernized, it is but a few hours until the train crosses the muddy Rio Grande at Laredo and, after passing an imaginary line in the centre of the stream, enters the land of burros and *sombreros*, a land of mysterious origin and vast antiquity.

"THE LAND OF BURROS AND *SOMBREROS*"

The custom officials are very polite and soon affix the necessary label "despachado" to the baggage. "*Vamonos*" (we go) replaces the familiar "all aboard," and the train moves out over a country as flat and dreary as a desert. By whichever route the traveller enters Mexico, the journey is very uninteresting for the first half day. There is nothing to relieve the monotony except the telephone and telegraph poles, with their picturesque cross-arms standing out on the desert waste like giant sentinels. There is no vegetation except the prickly pear, cactus, and feather duster palms, for frequently no rain falls for years at a time. It seems almost impossible that anything can get moisture from the parched air of these plains. But nature has strange ways of adapting life to conditions. A good illustration of this is seen in the *ixtle*, a species of cactus whose leaves look as if they could not absorb any moisture because of a hard varnish-like coat. Whenever any water in the form of dew or rain appears, however, this glaze softens and the plant absorbs all the moisture available and then glazes over again as soon as the sun comes out.

There is very little life here. Sometimes at the stations a few adobe huts are seen where dwell the section hands, and a few goats are visible which, no doubt, find the prickly pear and cactus with an occasional railroad spike thrown in for variety, much more satisfying than an unchanging diet of tin cans such as falls to the lot of the city goat. The mountain ranges then appear, and never is the traveller out of sight of them in Mexico. On either side, toward the east and toward the west, is a range with an ever varying outline, sometimes near, then far,—advancing and retreating. At a distance in this clear atmosphere their rough features are mellowed by a soft haze into amethyst and purple; nearer they sometimes rise like a camp of giants and are the most fantastic mountains that earthquakes ever made in sport, looking as if nature had laughed herself into the convulsions in which they were formed.

The Mexican National Railway follows a broad road that was formerly an Indian trail, and the track crosses and recrosses this highway many times. By this same route it is probable that early Mexican races entered that country and marched down toward the Valley of Mexico. It was by this way that General Taylor invaded the country during the Mexican War and several engagements took place along the line of this railroad.

The first town of any size is Monterey, capital of the state of Nuevo Leon, the oldest and one of the most important cities in Northern Mexico. It lies in a lovely valley with high hills on every side. It is at a lower altitude than the cities farther south on this line and enjoys a salubrious climate. Monterey is a very much Americanized town and has great smelters, factories, and breweries, but it also boasts of beautiful gardens and some old churches. The Topo Chico hot springs only a few miles away have a great reputation for healing. Here it was, in 1846, that General Taylor overcame a much superior force of the enemy under General Ampudia in a desperate and stubbornly disputed battle lasting several days, the contest being hotly fought from street to street. The Mexican troops entered the houses and shot at the American soldiers from the windows and roofs. It is now a city of more than fifty thousand people.

Leaving Monterey, the road soon begins a gradual ascent to the higher plateaus and reaches the zone called *tierra fria*, or cold country. This name would seem a misnomer to one who hails from the land of snow and ice, for the mean temperature of this "cold land" is that of a perpetual spring such as is enjoyed north of Mason and Dixon's line. It is properly applied to all that part of Mexico which is six thousand feet or more above the level of the sea and the greater part of the immense central plateaus comes within this designation. These plains which comprise about two-thirds of the entire country, are formed by the great Andes range of mountains which separates into two great *cordillerias* near Oaxaca and gradually grow farther and farther apart as they approach the Rio Grande. The western branch crowds the shore of the Pacific and the eastern follows the coast line of the Gulf of Mexico, but the latter keeps at a greater distance from the sea, thus giving a wider expanse of the hotlands. They are not level tablelands, these *mesas*, as they always slope in some direction. The arid condition follows as a natural course, for the lofty ranges cause the rain to be precipitated on the coast lands except during certain seasons in the year when the winds change. When the rains do come, a miracle is wrought, and the sombre landscape blossoms into a lively green dotted with flowers. It is rare to find such great plains at so high an altitude. Although now almost barren of trees it is probable that in early times these tablelands were covered with a forest growth principally of oak and cypress. This is evidenced by the few groves that yet remain, in which many of the trees are of extraordinary dimensions. The Spaniards completed the spoliation that had been begun by the earlier races.

Saltillo, the next important town, is the capital of the State of Coahuila. It is interesting to Americans, as just a few miles from here and near the railway took place the battle of Buena Vista, at the village of that name. Here the Americans under General Taylor sent double their number of Mexicans under the notorious Santa Anna, flying on February 23rd, 1847.

Still climbing, the road continues toward the capital, passes through a rich mining district, and after the Tropic of Cancer is crossed the traveller is in the Torrid Zone, the spot being marked by a pyramid. Plains, seemingly endless, where for a hundred miles the long stretch of track is without a curve, are traversed, and so dry that wells and water-tanks are objects of interest. It is mostly given up to vast *haciendas*. Some of these estates still remain in the hands of the original families as granted at the time of the conquest.

It was on these vast, seemingly barren plateaus that the *hacienda* reached its highest development. One does not go far south of the Rio Grande before the significance of this institution in Mexican life becomes apparent. Sometimes when the train stops at a little adobe station with a long name, the traveller wonders what is the need of a station; for there is no town and only a few native huts clustered around the depot. However a glance around the horizon will reveal the towers and spire of a *hacienda* nestling at the foot of the hills perhaps several miles away. In the olden times they took the place of the feudal castles of the middle ages in Europe and in these sparsely settled regions they were especially necessary. Within the high walls which often surround them for protection were centralized the residence of the owner and all of his employees and the necessary buildings to store the products of the soil. The *hacendado's* home was a large, roomy building, for, since there were no inns, the traveller must be entertained and hospitality was of the open-handed sort. The travel-worn wayfarer was welcomed and no questions asked. His wants were supplied and at his departure the benediction "Go, and God be with you," followed him. Even yet at some of these great *haciendas*, where the old-time customs prevail, the bell is rung at mealtime and any one who hears it is welcomed at the table.

The term *hacienda* has a double meaning, for it is applied both to the great estates and to the buildings. It is a patriarchal existence that is led by these landed proprietors. A thousand peons and more are frequently attached to the estate. Near the station of Villa Reyes is a great *hacienda* which once controlled twenty thousand peons. These must be provided with homes, but a room fifteen feet square is considered sufficient for a family, no matter how large. Little furniture is needed, for they live out of doors mostly, and mats, which can be removed during the day, take the place of cumbersome beds. The *administrador*, who may be an Indian also, and other heads, live better and are housed in larger quarters. A church is always a part of the estate and a priest must be kept to furnish spiritual solace, as well as a doctor to administer to those whose bodies are infirm. Schools are also maintained by most of the proprietors to-day. The peon must be provided with his provisions each week and a little patch of ground for his own use. Around the buildings lie the cultivated fields, and from early morn until the shades of night have fallen, lines of burros are constantly passing in and out laden with wood, corn, vegetables, poultry, boxes of freight, and all the other items of traffic which are a part of the life of this great household.

After piercing another of the mountain ranges which intersect the country from east to west, and traversing miles of fertile fields and gardens bearing semi-tropical fruits and vegetables, the road enters a valley and the city of San Luis Potosi is reached. Every country has its Saint Louis, but only one has a Saint Louis of the Treasure, and that is San Luis Potosi, the capital of the state of that name. It lies in a spreading plain of great fertility—made so by irrigation—whose gardens extend to the encircling hills that are rich in the mineral treasures which give the city its name. The San Pedro mines near here alone produce an annual output of several millions. These mines were revealed to Spaniards by an Indian who had become converted to Christianity. There is a mint here that coins several millions of dollars each year.

MARKET SCENE IN SAN LUIS POTOSI

San Luis Potosi is not a new city nor has its growth been of the mushroom variety. Founded in the middle of the sixteenth century, it preserves to-day in wood and stone the spirit of old Spain transplanted by the conquerors to the new world. Drawn hither by the reports of gold, the Spanish cavalier stalked through the streets of this town in complete mail before the *Mayflower* landed on the shores of Massachusetts. The priests were chanting the solemn service of the church here long before the English landed at Jamestown. Dust had gathered on the municipal library, which now contains a hundred thousand volumes, centuries before the building of the first little red school house in the United States. Before New York had been thought of, the drama of life was being enacted here daily after Castillian models.

It is a cleanly city and the bright attractive look of its houses is refreshing. A city ordinance compels the citizens to keep up the appearance of their houses, and the colours remind one of Seville. It is pleasant to walk along these streets and through the plazas with their trees and flowers and fountains.

I will never forget my arrival in this city. We reached there about midnight, having been delayed by a wreck; and a number of *mozos* pounced upon the party of Americans who had been dropped by the belated train, each one eager to carry some of the baggage. We were marched through the Alameda, which, for a wonder, adjoins the station, on walks shaded by broad-leaved, tropical plants, down narrow streets and around several corners to the hotel. Arrived here it was only after several minutes of vigorous knocking that a sleepy-looking porter opened the door, and we entered the hotel and walked down the hall through a line of sleeping servants. The room finally assigned to my friend and myself was thirty-four feet long, sixteen feet wide and about twenty-five feet high, and there were four great windows extending nearly from ceiling to floor and protected by heavy iron bars which made them look like the windows of a prison. It had doubtless been some church property at one time, but whether monastery or convent I did not learn.

COCK-FIGHTING IN MEXICO

Not all this city is pretty however, for distance often lends enchantment, and a closer scrutiny takes away much of this charm. I saw filth on the streets here that can only be duplicated in old Spain itself. There are numerous churches and several of them are quite pretentious and contain some fine paintings. On the façade of one church there is a clock presented by the king of Spain in return for the largest piece of gold ever found in America. San Luis is a thrifty city as Mexican towns go and has numerous manufacturing establishments, including a large smelting works, the Compania Metallurgica, and is an important railroad centre. It is distant from the City of Mexico three hundred and sixty-two miles, and has a population of seventy thousand souls.

This city claims quite a number of American families as residents and many of the storekeepers have been somewhat Americanized, for they actually seem to be on the lookout for business. The state capitol is a very interesting building. While looking through this palace I saw the "line up" of petty offenders who were being sent out to sweep the streets. They were the worst looking lot of *pulque*-drinkers I ever saw and were clothed in rags. Each one was given a handful of twigs with which he was obliged to sweep the streets and gutters, and they were sent out in gangs, each under a police officer. The vices of these people are generally more evident than their virtues. They are inveterate gamblers. Wherever one goes (not alone in San Luis Potosi) fighting cocks are encountered tied by the leg to a stake with a few feet of string. Or they may be carried in the arms of young would-be sports who brag of their birds to any one who will listen. One day I saw a man with a cock whose head was one bloody-looking mass. He had just cut off the rooster's comb. When I stopped and looked, the Indian laughed as though it were a great joke and said he was "much sick." This was done so that in a fight his opponent could not catch hold of the comb. Itinerant cock-fighters who travel across the country carrying their birds in hollow straw tubes are popular fellows.

Leaving San Luis Potosi at noontime the traveller catches his last glimpse of this city where

"Upon the whitened city walls
The golden sunshine softly falls,
On archways set with orange trees,
On paven courts and balconies."

The train soon enters a rich agricultural belt and the country becomes more populous. Giant cacti towering straight and tall to a height of fifteen or twenty feet are a common sight.

Dolores Hidalgo where the patriot-priest first sounded the call to liberty and revolution is passed. Then comes Querétero, which occupies a prominent place in Mexican history and is the last city of any size on the way to the capital. Here the treaty of peace between Mexico and the United States was negotiated. In this city Maximilian played the last act in the tragedy of the empire. He was captured while attempting to escape on June 19th, 1867, and was shot on the Cerro de las Campañas, a little hill just outside the city. With him were shot Generals Miramon and Mejia. Maximilian died with the cry of *Viva Mexico* on his lips. There is a magnificent aqueduct here which, because of the high arches, looks like the old ruined aqueduct seen on approaching Rome. The tallest arch is nearly one hundred feet. The entire length of the aqueduct is about five miles and it is still in use. There are a number of factories for cotton goods. Among them is the great Hercules Mill which employs more than two thousand hands. The grounds are laid out in elaborate and beautiful style.

After climbing the mountain range again until an altitude of nearly ten thousand feet has been reached, the descent begins and the beauty of the Valley of Mexico unfolds. Fleeting glimpses of the scene may be caught through little gaps in the mountains until finally the train enters a pass and the traveller has his first view of the City of Mexico. Beyond the glittering towers and domes of the modern city on the site of the ancient Aztec capital lies the bright expanse of the lakes, and still further in the distance is seen the encircling girdle of mountains like a protecting wall around this enchanted scene.

There are many other cities situated on these vast plateaus, for the *tierra fria* has always maintained the bulk of the population in spite of the extraordinary richness of the lowlands. They are growing in size as manufacturing establishments become more numerous. A number of them like Chihuahua, Aguas Calientes, Zacatecas, Guanajuato, Durango, and Leon are interesting cities of from thirty to forty thousand inhabitants and all of them are old. Chihuahua (pronounced Che-wa-wa) is the capital of the state of that name which is the largest state in the republic and is twice as large as the state of Ohio. It has a population of less than four hundred thousand. This will serve to give a little idea of the vastness of these great tablelands and the sparseness of population. It is chiefly devoted to great ranches where hundreds of thousands of cattle are grazed.

It may be interesting to note that cattle ranching originated in this state. All the terms used on the range and roundup are of Spanish origin and are the same that have been employed for centuries. One man here is the owner of a cattle ranch covering seventeen million acres. The traveller might journey for days and cross ranges of mountains and not pass beyond his princely domain. There are a number of cattle ranches of from one to two million acres and a few Americans are now entering the field here since the public domain in the United States has dwindled so much.

Two cities, Guadalajara and Puebla, have long disputed for the honour of second city in the republic. Puebla is situated southeast of the capital and is a city of tiles, for tiles are used everywhere from the domes of churches to floors for the devout to kneel upon. It is the capital of the richest state in the republic and has probably seen more of the vicissitudes of war than any other city. It has been captured and occupied successively by Spaniards, Americans and French and by revolutionists times without number. This city was the scene of General Zaragossa's victory on May 5th, 1862, when he repulsed the French forces just outside the city's gates. This victory is celebrated each year as the "*cinco de Mayo*" (Fifth of May) and is the great anti-foreign day. Formerly foreigners did not show themselves on the street on this day, but that antagonistic sentiment has disappeared. In 1906 because of labour disturbances for which American agitators were blamed trouble was feared on this day, but it passed off without an unpleasant incident. This city was founded as early as 1532. Its history is romantic and full of legends recounting the many visits of the angels. Angels appeared one night and staked out the city. Again, while the cathedral was being built, the angels came after nightfall when the city was wrapped in slumber and built a great part of the tower. At another time the angels were marshalled in mighty hosts just over the city. The people can even point out to you the very places where the angelic visitors roosted. The ecclesiastical records vouch for these appearances of the heavenly visitors and the people devoutly believe in them.

Puebla has wide streets—for Mexico—and many beautiful plazas with flowers and fountains. It is also noted for its bull-fights and has two bull-rings. These are in use nearly every Sunday and frequently for the benefit of or in honour of some church feast or departed saint. The public buildings are very creditable and the city contains good schools and hospitals. A goodly number of foreigners live here, especially Germans. I have noticed that the Germans affiliate with the Mexicans much better than Americans generally do. One reason is that they come here to establish their permanent residence, while Americans, like the Chinese, desire to make their fortunes and then return to the land of their birth to spend their later days.

Puebla has become quite a manufacturing city and especially of cotton goods, paper, flour and soaps. Onyx and marble are quarried near here, and a large number of workmen are employed in the quarries and in the establishments preparing these materials for the market. Several railroads now reach this city, and its importance as an industrial centre is increasing each year.

All kinds of grains that are produced in the temperate zones will grow on the tablelands of Mexico wherever there is sufficient rain or water to be obtained by irrigation. A constantly increasing amount of acreage is being made available through the extension of the irrigation system, but its possibilities are only beginning to be realized. Corn, which is such a great article of food with the Mexicans, is by far the most valuable agricultural product and several hundred million bushels are produced each year. Wheat was first introduced in Mexico by a monk who planted a few grains that he had brought with him. This grain is now raised quite extensively in some districts but frequently there is not enough for even local consumption. Cotton is also produced in a number of the states.

THE *MAGUEY*

Mexico is especially rich in fibre-producing plants and no country in the world has so many different varieties. All of these belong to the great cactus, or *agave*, family. The value of the cactus has never been fully appreciated but new uses are being found for it constantly, and new kinds with valuable qualities are being discovered in Mexico almost yearly. Perhaps the most valuable plant of this family that is being cultivated in Mexico to-day is that species of the *agave* that produces the valuable henequen fibre of commerce. This plant very much resembles the *maguey* and grows on the thin, rocky, limestone soil of Yucatan. From this fibre is made most of the binder twine and much of the rope used in the United States. It has the threefold qualities of strength, pliability and colour. In the past twenty years the cultivation of henequen has grown to enormous proportions, and some of the planters have become millionaires almost rivalling the famous bonanza kings of olden times. The amount of henequen, or sisal, fibre exported to the United States from 1880 to 1905 was nine million, two hundred and nineteen thousand, two hundred and fifteen bales at an estimated value of $300,988,072.66. In 1902 the exports reached a maximum, and amounted to $34,185,275. All of this fibre is exported through the port of Progreso.

Several species of the cactus family are being experimented with, and it is claimed that they will produce an excellent quality of paper pulp. This may help to solve the problem that now bothers paper manufacturers as the forests of spruce disappear before the woodsman's ax. The graceful *maguey*, the *agave americana*, is cultivated almost everywhere on the plateau lands. It also produces a valuable fibre, but this plant is not cultivated primarily for that purpose. The ancient races used the thorns for pins and needles; the leaves furnished a kind of parchment for their writings and thatch for their roofs; and the juice when fermented made a—to them—most delicious drink. On the plains of Apam just east of the Valley of Mexico and north of Puebla the cultivation of the *maguey* has reached the highest development.

The good housewife in the United States who carefully nourishes the century plant, hoping that at least her descendants will have the pleasure of seeing it blossom at the end of a hundred years, would be surprised to see the immense plantations consisting of thousands of this same plant growing here. The plant, commonly called the *maguey*, is a native of Mexico and grows to great size. It flourishes best in rocky and sandy soil and is quite imposing in appearance. Its dark green, spiked leaves which lift themselves up and spread out in graceful curves, sometimes reach a length of fifteen feet, and are a foot in breadth and several inches thick. It requires from six to ten years for the *maguey* to mature on its native heath. When that period arrives a slender stalk springs up from the centre of these great leaves, twenty to thirty feet high, upon which a great mass of small flowers is clustered. This supreme effort exhausts the plant and, its duty to nature having been performed, it withers and dies.

This is not the purpose for which the *maguey* is raised on the big plantations where the rows of graceful century plants stretch out as far as the eye can reach in unwavering regularity. On these plantations the *maguey* is not permitted to flower. The Indians know, by infallible signs, almost the very hour at which it is ready to send up the central stalk, and it is then marked by an overseer with a cross. The stalk is now full of the sap which is the object of its culture. Other Indians follow up the overseer and, making an incision at the base of the plant, extract the central portion, leaving only the rind which forms a natural basin. Into this the sap, which is called *agua miel*, or honey-water, and which is almost as clear as water and as sweet as honey, collects. So quickly does this fluid gather that it is found necessary to remove it two or three times per day. The method of gathering this sap is extremely primitive. The Indian is provided with a long gourd at the lower end of which is a horn. He places the small end, which is open, in the liquid and, applying his lips to an opening in the large end, sucks the sap up into the gourd. The sap is then emptied into a receptacle swung across his back which is made of a whole goat-skin or pig-skin with the hair on the inside. The *maguey* plant will yield six or more quarts of this "honey-water" in a day and the supply will continue from one to three months. It is then exhausted and withers and decays. However, a new shoot will spring up from the old roots without replanting.

This innocent looking and savoury sap is then taken to a building prepared for the purpose and there poured into vats made of cowhides stretched on a frame. In each vat a little sour liquor called "mother of *pulque*" has been poured. This causes quick fermentation and in a few hours the *pulque* of the Mexican is ready for the market. It is at its best after about twenty-four hours fermentation. It then has somewhat the appearance and taste of stale buttermilk and a rancid smell. After more fermentation it has the odour of putrid meat. The skins in which it is carried increase this disagreeable odour. The first taste of *pulque* to a stranger is repellant. However, it is said that, contrary to the general rule, familiarity breeds a liking. Great virtues are claimed for it in certain ailments and it is said to be wholesome. However this is not the reason why the peons drink *pulque* in such great quantities. Several special trainloads go in each day to the City of Mexico over one road, besides large amounts over other routes and it is a great revenue producer for the railroads. The daily expenditure for *pulque* in the City of Mexico alone is said to exceed twenty thousand dollars. Physicians say that the brain is softened, digestion ruined and nerves paralyzed by a too generous use of this liquor. Many employers of labour will not employ labourers from the *pulque* districts if they can possibly get them from other sources. *Tequila* and *Mescal* are two forms of ardent spirits distilled from a juice yielded by the leaves and root of the *maguey*. They are forms of brandy that it is best for the traveller to leave alone.

CHAPTER III
THE CAPITAL

The City of Mexico represents progressive Mexico. In it is concentrated the wealth, culture and refinement of the republic. It is the political, the educational, the social and the commercial centre of the whole country. It is to Mexico what Paris is to France. In fact it would be Mexico as Paris would be France. The same glare and glitter of a pleasure-loving metropolis are found here, and within the same boundaries may be seen the deepest poverty and most abject degradation.

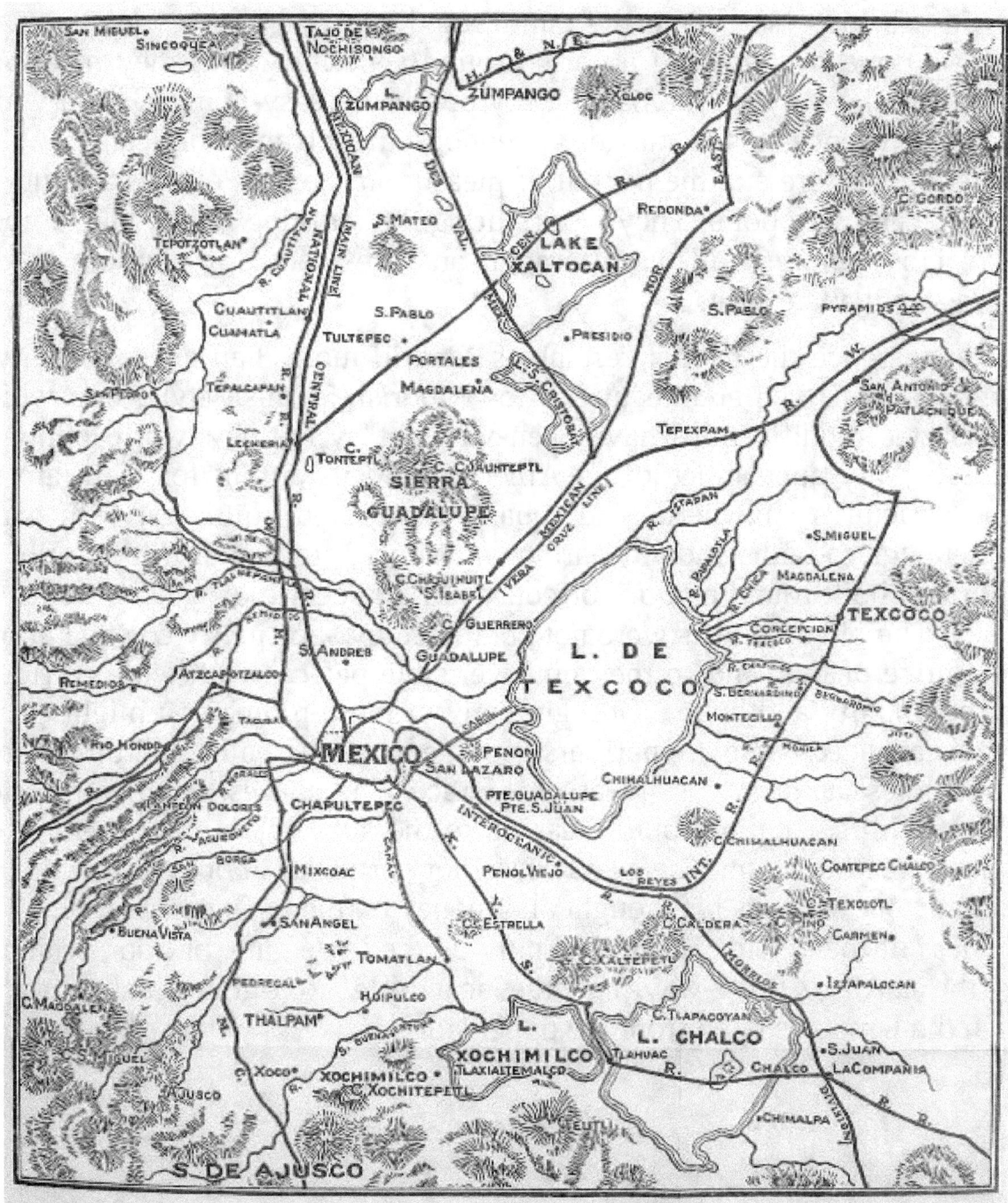

MAP OF THE VALLEY OF MEXICO

"Wait until you get to the City of Mexico," said an educated Mexican to me as we were crossing the sparsely-settled tablelands of northern Mexico, where the only inhabitants are Indians. The Mexicans are proud of their city and are pleased to have it likened to the gay French capital, for their ideals and tastes are fashioned after the Latin standard rather than the American.

The French, they say, have the culture and can embrace *a la Mexicana*, which is done by throwing an arm around a friend whom they meet and patting him heartily on the back. They prefer the easy-going, wait-a-while style of existence to the hurried, strenuous life of an American city. No people love leisure and the pursuit of pleasure more than our neighbours in the Mexican metropolis. They work during the morning hours, take a noon *siesta*, close up early in the afternoon and are ready for pleasure in the evening until a late hour.

In appearance the capital resembles Madrid more than any other city I have ever seen. The architecture is the Moorish-Spanish style, into which some Aztec modifications have been wrought by the new-world builders. The light, airy appearance of an American city is absent for there are no frame structures anywhere. The square, flat-roofed buildings, with walls thick enough to withstand any earthquake shock, are two or three stories in height and built round a *patio*, or courtyard, the centre of which is open to the sky. The old architects were not hampered by such paltry considerations as the price of lots, and so they built veritable palaces with wide corridors and rooms lofty and huge. Through many of these rooms you might easily drive a carriage. There are parlours as large as public halls, and throughout all one notes the *grandiose* ideas of the race. The houses, of stone or brick covered with stucco, are built clear up to the sidewalk so that there is no tinge of green in front. The Mexican is not particular about the exterior of his home, but expends his thought and money on the open court within. The plainness of the outside is relieved only by the large gate, or door, which is also the carriage drive-way, and the neat little, iron-grated balconies on which the windows open from the upper stories.

THE PATIO OF AN OLD RESIDENCE

These balconies afford a convenient place for the women of the household to see what is passing on the street, and also for the *señorita*, or young lady, to watch the restless pacing to and fro of the love-stricken youth who is "playing bear" in front of the house. The great doorway, which is carefully barred and bolted at night, and strictly guarded by the porter during the day, is the only entrance to the *patio*, which, in the better class of homes, is adorned with pretty gardens, statuary and fountains. Many of them contain an open plunge bath. Through the wide windows one catches glimpses of fascinating interiors, and through the broad doorways the passer-by on the street gets many a pretty view of the courtyards, and of these miniature gardens. One or two rows of living-apartments extend around and above the court, with broad corridors in front handsomely paved with tile, protected by balustrades and adorned with flowers and vines. Above, the red tiles of the roof add a little additional colour to the scene. There are no cellars nor chimneys. The latter were never introduced because of the mildness of the climate. In the courts protected from the winds, the people keep on the sunny side when it is cool and hide from the same orb when it is hot. Charcoal fires are used for cooking and heat when it becomes necessary. Cellars are made impossible because of the marshy nature of the soil.

It will be recalled that Tenochtitlan, the Aztec capital, has been called the New World Venice, whose streets were once canals. It must have been a gay and picturesque scene when the fair surface of its waters was resplendent with shining cities and flowering islets. The waters have since receded until Lake Texcoco, at its nearest point, is three miles distant. Mexico is now a more prosaic city of streets and cross-streets which extend from north to south and from east to west. Some of the principal thoroughfares are broad, paved with asphalt and well kept; but many are quite narrow, and especially is this true of the streets called lanes, though devoted to business. There is no exclusive residence section, except in the new additions, and many of the homes of the old families are found sandwiched in between stores. It is a difficult matter to become familiar with the names of the streets, for they are more than nine hundred in number, and a street generally has a different name for each block. If several blocks have the same name, as, for instance, Calle de San Francisco, one of the finest streets, and on or near which are some of the largest hotels, finest stores and richest private dwellings, then it is First San Francisco, Second San Francisco, etc.

A few years ago the streets were re-named. All the streets extending east and west were called *avenidas*, and the north and south streets *calles*, each continuous thoroughfare being given but one name. The people, however, in this land of legend and tradition, clung so tenaciously to the former designations that they have practically been restored. Some of the old names of streets commemorated historical events, as, for instance, the Street of the *Cinco de Mayo*, which is in remembrance of the victory of the Mexicans over the French at Puebla in 1862. Others are named in honour of men noted in the history of Mexico. Many religious terms appear, such as the street of Jesus, Sanctified Virgin, Holy Ghost, Sepulchres of the Holy Sabbath, and the like. Others owe their names to some incident or legend, which is both interesting and mysterious. Of the latter class may be mentioned the Street of the Sad Indian, Lane of Pass if You Can, Street of the Lost Child, Street of the Wood Owls, Lane of the Rat, Bridge of the Raven and Street of the Walking Priest. The Street of the Coffin Makers is now known as the Street of Death. It is a thoroughfare of one block, and is one of the few streets that still preserves its ancient caste, for it is devoted exclusively to the makers of coffins. All of the coffins are made by hand. It is a gloomy street and there are cleaner spots on the face of the earth.

Mexico is a very cosmopolitan city. Its three hundred and seventy-five thousand inhabitants include representatives from nearly every nation of the earth. The Indians are vastly in the majority, and they are the pure and original Mexicans. The Creoles, who are descendants of Europeans, generally Spanish, call themselves the Mexicans and rank second in number. They form the real aristocratic body from whom come the representative Mexicans. They are not all dark, but a blonde is a rare specimen. Most of them have an olive-brown colour, thus showing the mixture of Indian blood, for in early days it was not considered a *mesalliance* for even a Spanish officer of high rank to marry an Aztec maiden of the better class.

The old families cling tenaciously to the great estates, or *haciendas*, many of which have remained intact for centuries. Quite a number can even trace their estates back to the original grants from the king of Spain. Many of these *hacendados*, or landed proprietors, enjoy princely incomes from their lands, and nearly all of them own residences in the capital. They maintain elaborate establishments and keep four times as many servants as would be found in an American house.

The average Mexican does not care for business. Neither is he an inventor or originator, for he is content to live as his ancestors have lived. Nearly all lines of commerce and industry are in the hands of foreigners. The Germans monopolize the hardware trade; the French conduct nearly all the dry goods stores; the Spaniards are the country's grocers; and the Americans and English control the railroad, electric and mining industries. All these interests centre in the City of Mexico. Railroads are not very numerous until you approach the Valley of Mexico where they converge from all directions. The hum of industry is apparent here as nowhere else in the whole republic. The Mexicans boast of their capital, but they often forget the debt they owe to foreigners, for all the modern improvements have been installed by alien races and outside capital. It is another foreign invasion but with a pacific mission. The American colony alone in that city numbers more than six thousand persons, and the number is constantly increasing. Hatred of the American has almost disappeared, and the incomers are cordially welcomed. There are two flourishing clubs around which the social life of the expatriated Americans centre.

The society of the capital, and indeed of the whole country, is very diverse. What might be said of one class would not apply to another. The differences of dress and customs alone make known the heterogeneousness of the population. They all use the same language and all classes are brought together on a common level in their religion. No other nation has ever made such complete conquests as Spain. She not only subjugated the lands but forced her language, as well as religion, upon the conquered races. The English have succeeded in extending their sway over a large part of the world, but in no instance have they been able to accomplish these two results with the native population. The priests of Spain went hand in hand with the *conquistadores*, and, within a few generations after the conquest of Mexico by Cortez, the Spanish language was universally used and the Indians were at least nominal Catholics.

The climate of the City of Mexico is delightful. It is neither hot nor cold. It is too far south to be cold and the altitude, seven thousand, four hundred and thirty-four feet above the level of the sea, is too great to be hot. The temperature usually ranges from sixty-five to eighty-five, but sometimes goes as high as ninety, and as low as thirty-five, and frosts occasionally are experienced. The mornings and evenings are cool and at midday it is always hot. There is a great difference in the temperature between the sunny and shady side of the street. Only dogs and Americans take the sunny side, the Mexicans say. The rainy and dry seasons occur with great regularity, the former lasting from May to October. It is the best season in the year although most visitors go there in winter. The rains always occur in the afternoon and usually cease before dark. At this time, too, all nature takes on a beautiful shade of green which replaces the rather dull landscape of the dry season. There is also a brisk, electric condition of the atmosphere that is decidedly exhilarating and a good tonic.

This mildness of climate has greatly influenced the life of the capital. The streets, except during the noon *siesta*, are full of people at all times. To judge from the crowds, one might think the capital a city of a million people. In the morning the women go to mass garbed in black, generally wearing a black shawl over the head. Occasionally a black lace mantilla is seen half-concealing, half-exposing the olive-brown face, and bright, sparkling eyes of a *señorita*. Shoppers are out and business is active. The women of the wealthier classes sit in their carriages and have the goods brought out to them, or go to a private room where articles are exhibited by clerks. They think that it is unbecoming to stand at the counters, although the American plan of shopping is becoming quite popular in recent years.

About the middle of the afternoon the crowds again appear, and a little later the streets begin to fill with carriages. Nowhere, not even in Paris, have I observed so many carriages as can be seen here on any pleasant afternoon. They form one continuous, slow-moving line of many miles. The procession moves out San Francisco Street through the Alameda, along the Paseo de la Reforma, and then into the beautiful park surrounding the Castle of Chapultepec which is set with great cypresses, said to antedate the conquest. The cavalcade winds around through the various drives at the base of the rock, along the shores of the lake, past the castle and back to the city. The carriages go out on one side and return on the other, leaving the central portion for riders. It is a sight that never wearies for one to sit on a bench and watch the motley throng of people driving, riding on horseback and promenading. An oriental exclusiveness is observed by ladies of the upper class who always ride in closed carriages. All kinds of vehicles are to be seen, from fine equipages with liveried drivers and footmen, to the poorest cab in the city with its disreputable driver and broken-down horses, fit only for the bull-ring.

There are many horsemen and the Mexicans are always excellent riders. Their horses are Lilliputian in size but fast and enduring. The saddle, bridle and trappings are frequently gorgeous with their silver ornaments and immense stirrups fancifully worked and shaped. The rider is often a picture wonderful to behold from the heavy silver spurs which he wears, to the sombrero of brown or yellow felt with a brim ten to fifteen inches wide and a crown equally as high, the whole covered with heavy gilt cord formed into a sort of rope. Then there is the dude or fop, who is well named in Mexico. He is called a "*lajartija*" which means a "little lizard." He used to dress in such close-fitting and stiff costumes that he had not much more freedom of motion than the stiff little lizard. Now he is the dandy who is generally seen standing on a public corner, wearing a French cutaway suit, American patent leather shoes and an English stovepipe hat, with his fingers closed over the indispensable cigarette.

In the evening the populace attend the theatre or some social function. Sunday is the day of all others for recreation, and, with the average inhabitant of Mexico, is one continuous and eternal round of pleasure. After morning service the entire day is devoted to pleasure. Band concerts are always given by the military bands on the Plaza in the morning, in the Alameda early in the afternoon, and at Chapultepec about five o'clock. Then there is the bull-fight which occurs only on Sundays and holidays.

The average crowd in the City of Mexico is a good natured and peaceable one. The city Indian and his country cousin, the peon from the plantation, join the crowd on a feast day with their numerous progeny. They are not the pleasantest neighbours in the world for both have the odour of garlic and *pulque* and their baths are of the annual variety. That the little brown man is a peon is no fault of his. His uncleanliness is, in a measure, the result of centuries of neglect, and more particularly of a scarcity of water at his home. It is possible that if he had the water his condition would be just the same. Though he is poor and down-trodden, there is nothing of the anarchist about him. He is absolutely devoid of envy or malice; and withal his spirits are gay and he is as generous to his family or friends as his finances permit. The artificial refinements of modern civilization have not yet spoiled him, and there is a pleasant, even if malodorous, naturalness about him.

In no city do ancient and modern customs come into such intimate contrast as in the City of Mexico. Nowhere is a greater mixture of races to be seen than here. There are many tribes of Indians speaking scores of dialects, and there are *mestizos* of various degrees of mixture with African, American and European blood. Types of four centuries can be seen in any group on one of the plazas. The Plaza Mayor is a great, imposing, central square of fourteen acres in the centre of the city, and on its walks all the types can be seen at their best. Men and women come into the city through the streets lighted by electricity, bearing immense loads on their heads and backs rather than use a wagon. Peddlers carry around jars of water for sale just as in the olden times. Indians, who are almost pure Aztecs, pass along, taking the middle of the street in Indian file. Well dressed men in black broadcloth suits and wearing silk hats go by. The women of the middle class add colour to the scene with the red and blue *rebosas*, sometimes covering the head, or tied across the chest and holding an infant at the back.

Nearly all the passers-by show in their colour that they can claim kinship with the hosts of Montezuma. The general effect is kaleidoscopic but entertaining. The great cathedral on the north side of the Plaza is the one place where all are brought together and class distinction obliterated. Visit the cathedral any day and you may see an Indian with his pack on his back side by side with a young woman who may inherit a dozen titles. There are no select, high-priced, aristocratic pews for rent, but all meet by a common genuflection before the sacred altars. The poor Indian may not understand all the pomp and ceremony, the music of the vested choirs, or the solemn chanting by the priests, but it fills a deep want in his nature and he is satisfied.

At one side of the Plaza Mayor once stood the great Aztec *Teocalli*, the Temple of Sacrifice. This was a high imposing altar reached by a flight of more than a hundred steps. From the top was a magnificent view of the entire valley, and it was from this point that the envious eyes of Cortez looked out upon this beautiful scene. The altar was dedicated to the Aztec war god Huitzilopochtli, and here, to appease the wrath of this terrible god, human sacrifices were offered. The breast was cut open and the heart, still palpitating, plucked out and placed upon the altar. The bodies were cast down to the ground, whence they were taken and prepared for the banquet table.

THE CATHEDRAL

A part of the space once covered by this gruesome but majestic pile, is now occupied by the Monte de Piedad, or "mountain of mercy," one of the most unique charities in the world. It is nothing more or less than a gigantic pawn-shop, but it is one of the most beneficent institutions in the country. The Count of Regla, a noted personage in Mexico, founded this institution by a gift of three hundred thousand dollars. He did this in order that the poor and needy, and the impoverished members of families once genteel, might secure small sums upon personal property at low rates of interest, instead of becoming involved in the meshes of the blood-sucking vampires who prey upon this class of unfortunates. About three-fourths of the actual value of the property pledged as fixed by appraisers, will be loaned. If the interest is not paid, the property is kept for seven months, when it is offered for sale at a fixed price. If not disposed of in another five months it is sold at auction.

The truly remarkable feature of this establishment is, that if a greater sum is realized than the amount of the loan and interest, the excess is placed to the credit of the owner, or his heirs, and will be kept for one hundred years, after which time it reverts to the institution. Many old heirlooms of former grandees, Aztec curios, diamonds, gold ornaments and even family gods have passed through this organization of charity. For more than a century it has existed, having survived all the civil wars, revolutions and changes of government. The original capital has been more than doubled by the forfeitures, and many branches of this parent institution are operated in the capital and in several of the large cities of the republic. It is an example that might be suggested to some of our multi-millionaires who do not know what to do with their vast accumulations of wealth.

Even the funerals are conducted in a strange way. With the exception of funerals among the wealthy, the street cars are universally used. The enterprising owner of the street car system some years ago acting on the trust idea, bought up all the hearses and introduced funeral cars. After a short time the people became accustomed to the new plan, which seemed to give satisfaction. Now, trolley funeral cars of the first, second and third class are furnished at a price varying from five dollars for the cheapest class, to a hundred dollars or more for a first-class car. Some of the poor rent coffins which are returned after the burial. The very poor may be seen carrying their dead on their shoulders to the *Campo Santo*, or holy ground. Graves are usually sold only for a certain number of years, after which, unless the relatives pay the prescribed fee, the bones are taken up and the ground made ready for a new occupant. The dead are soon forgotten. A pile of bones in a corner of the cemetery represents all that is mortal of the generations who passed away not many years ago. There is an entire lack of reverence for the mortal remains of the departed, such as one is accustomed to find in our own country. One is reminded of the couplet

"Rattle his bones over the stones,
He's only a pauper, whom nobody owns."

The City of Mexico is not the healthiest city in the world. On the contrary the death rate is unusually high. The average duration of life is said to be only twenty-six years. This is due in a great measure to infant mortality. Typhoid and malarial fevers are prevalent because of the accumulated drainage of centuries, which lies just a few feet beneath the surface. Pneumonia is common and regarded as very dangerous because of the rarefied air, and patients suffering from this disease are immediately transported to lower altitudes for treatment. The entire lack of hygiene and sanitary conditions among the peon classes is in a great measure responsible for the unusual percentage of mortality. Few other cities in the world have such a high rate of deaths compared with the population.

Strange it is that the capital was ever built on this low, marshy soil when higher land was available and near at hand. It was one of the great blunders of Cortez, for Mexico might have been made a healthy city. No exigency of commerce dictated its selection, for it is far from the sea coast on either side and was difficult of access before the day of railroads. The new city was built on the site of the old, and the temples of the Christian religion were raised on the sites of the old pagan altars wherever possible. A plan of moving the city to higher ground was strongly agitated at one time but the vested interests succeeded in killing this project. It is hoped and believed that when the plans for sewerage are completed, the health conditions will be placed on a par with that of most cities. The authorities are making an honest and earnest effort to carry out these commendable projects.

> "Know ye not pulque,
> Liquor divine,
> The Angels in heaven
> Prefer it to wine."

Thus sings the lower class Mexican to whom this liquor has become a curse. To it is due much of his poverty and many of his crimes. For it he will neglect his family and steal from his employer. It does not contain a large percentage of alcohol, but, taken in large quantities, as is customary among these people, it puts them in a dopy condition which they sleep off. One railroad brings in a train-load each day, and, besides, large quantities are brought in by other lines. There are sixteen hundred pulque saloons in the capital, but they are all closed at six o'clock by a law which is strictly enforced. The pulque-shop betrays itself by its odour, as well as by the crowds of poorly dressed and even filthy men and women who surround its doors and press around the counter. It is a gaily decorated affair and is oftentimes adorned in flaring colours inside and out, with reds, blues, greens and yellows predominating, and frequently with a huge, rude painting on the outside walls. In some of the shops you will find a curious string knotted in a peculiar manner or strung with shells. This is a survival of the Aztec method of counting by means of beads, or shells, strung together.

As one writer says, "the pulque shop, notwithstanding its evil influence upon the life of the people, presents a very picturesque appearance to the tourist who has never seen anything like it before. The dress of the people, the curious, vivid colours of the walls of the building, the semi-barbaric appearance of the decorations within, the curious semi-symbolic pictures upon the walls, the unaccustomed groupings of the people, all combine to attract the attention of the stranger in Mexico."

A PICTURESQUE PULQUE SHOP

In the naming of the pulque-dens the imagination is allowed full play. I quote from a Mexican periodical the names of some of these resorts: A place in the suburbs of Mexico is termed the "Delight of Bacchus." One is called "The Seventh Heaven," another "The Food of the Gods," while still another bears the euphonious title of "The Land of the Lotus." "A Night of Delight" is another place near "The Heart's Desire." The above names are commonplace by the side of the following: "The Hang-out of John the Baptist," "The Retreat of the Holy Ghost," "The Delight of the Apostle,"

"The Retreat of the Holy Virgin," "The Mecca of Delight," and "The Fountain of the Angels." Nothing disrespectful is intended by these appellations but they sound very sacrilegious to us.

There is, however, a brighter side to the Indian life in the City of Mexico. In one corner of the Zocalo, and covering a part of the site formerly occupied by the great sacrificial altar, is the flower-market. This flower-market is always attractive and a never-ending source of interest to the tourist. Immense bouquets of the choicest flowers are sold so cheap that the price seems almost absurd. By judicious bargaining a few cents will purchase a large and varied supply of roses, violets and heliotrope, which only dollars could buy from a New York florist. No hot-houses are needed here at any season, for in this climate flowers bloom all the year round, and one crop succeeds another in a never-ending succession. The Mexican Indian is a lover of flowers. It is one of the redeeming traits of his character. He is not always particular as to his personal appearance; he may be unkempt and untidy to look upon; but he loves flowers, is prodigal in his use of them and shows good taste in their arrangement. This taste is innate, is no doubt inherited from his Aztec ancestors, and has survived the oppressions and exactions of the succeeding centuries. This love for flowers finds expression even in his worship, and it is no uncommon thing to find flowers before the image of the Virgin, and such an offering is one of the expressions of his good will. When we consider that our forefathers were taught to worship God with the first fruits of their husbandry, it is not surprising that this primitive and ignorant race should still find use in their worship for these beautiful products of a prodigal nature.

The gardens and parks of the City of Mexico attain a luxuriant growth that cannot be equalled in our northern cities. These breathing-places where one can sit amid scenes of tropical verdure, and admire the bright tints of the flowers while shielded from the hot sun by the broad-leafed foliage of the plants, are truly delightful spots for an American to visit. They contrast so strongly with the cheerless appearance of the streets. In the centre of the large Plaza Mayor lies the Zocalo, a little green oasis in the great paved waste. It is in the very heart of the city's throbbing life, and everything either has its beginning or ending on this imposing square.

On one side of the Plaza lies the Palacio Nacional which has stood there for more than two centuries. It covers the site of the ancient palace of

Montezuma, and has an imposing façade of nearly seven hundred feet. Over the main entrance hangs the Liberty Bell of Mexico which was rung by Hidalgo on the first call to independence at Dolores, where it had so often summoned the people to mass. The immense windows which look out upon the Plaza open into the various rooms where the official business of the executive department of the republic is transacted. Other parts of this immense structure, for it is almost a square building enclosing an open court, are occupied by the legislative chambers and barrack rooms for several regiments of soldiers.

A few blocks away from the Plaza lies the Alameda, which is the park of the better classes. Every city has an alameda, as the visitor soon learns, but this is *the* alameda of Mexico. It is a pretty place, and, with its beautiful trees, flowers and fountains, forms a resort for the fashionable people, who congregate here on Sundays and feast days to listen to the military bands. The visitor can almost lose himself in this part, for the view is circumscribed on every hand by the dense shrubbery.

It is on the subject of the Paseo de la Reforma that the Mexican becomes enthusiastic. This beautiful boulevard extends for a distance of two miles from a place near the Alameda to Chapultepec. It is a smooth thoroughfare averaging five hundred feet in width, with promenades on each side shaded by trees under which are stone seats, and with paved driveways in the centre. Here and there the Paseo widens into circles, called *glorietas*, in the centre of which are placed statues. Those already erected include statues to Charles IV of Spain, Columbus and Cuautemoc, the Aztec warrior and emperor. To Maximilian is due the credit for the Paseo, and a more beautiful boulevard cannot be found in Europe or America.

I have purposely described the old features of the city and the unique characteristics before touching upon the more modern innovations. The average visitor would follow that plan, for he would be more interested in the unusual than in that with which he is more or less familiar. Like all capitals and large cities affected by commercialism, the City of Mexico is fast becoming cosmopolitan. The traveller who visited it ten, or even five, years ago would be astonished at the changes wrought by improvements. The fine system of electric lights, the excellent electric traction lines with modern, cars, the asphalted streets and the attractive new suburbs of an entirely foreign architecture, link the old with the new, the sixteenth with the twentieth century. A city hindered by a racial conservatism, and obstructed at every turn by tradition, does not become entirely modern in a decade, but the trend is there and its progress has been really remarkable. It will never be a city of skyscrapers for a hard stratum is not encountered until a depth of a hundred and forty feet is reached.

A new and modern hotel is more needed than anything else. There are plenty of hotels of the Mexican kind, where it is almost impossible to find a room with an outside window. All the rooms simply have an opening on the *patio* which answers for both door and window. In cool weather which is sometimes experienced here, there is no means of heating these rooms except by an open pan of coals, which is not very satisfactory to one accustomed to modern steam-heated hotels or a good stove.

The national government controls the federal district within which is situated the City of Mexico, much the same as the District of Columbia, in our own land, and is assisted by a city council. Plans have been drawn for fifty million dollars' worth of public buildings, many of which are already under way. The fine new post-office which has been building for several years is now occupied by that department. It is a beautiful structure of the medieval Spanish style, and is a striking departure from the other public buildings. It is four stories high, equipped with every convenience and is finished within and without in elaborate style.

A new legislative palace is under construction, which is the most pretentious building yet planned. Its estimated cost is $20,000,000. Opposite the post-office a national theatre is being erected to cater to the amusement lovers, which is designed to be the finest theatre in the new world. An entire block is being razed to make room for the Panteon Nacional—a resting place for Mexico's illustrious dead. Within the marble walls of this unique memorial will rest all that is mortal of her heroes. An army and navy building, a museum of art and a department of public works are among the other improvements planned for the capital. These buildings are being scattered over the city instead of following the group plan as designed at Washington. The reason for this has been a desire to have every section of the city benefited and beautified by these public structures. The year 1910 marked the centennial of Mexican independence. The month of September was almost wholly given up to celebrations of this event in the capital. A number of public buildings were dedicated during the celebrations. Among these were a new insane asylum and several fine new public school buildings, which greatly added to the educational facilities of the city. A magnificent new monument to independence, recently erected on the Paseo, was dedicated with great ceremony. A number of gifts were made by foreign colonies and governments. Not the least of these was a monument to Washington, which was presented by the resident Americans. The ceremonies and functions of the centennial celebration were very elaborate, and the capital has been beautified in many ways as a result.

CHAPTER IV
THE VALLEY OF ANAHUAC

The dim traditional history of Mexico shows us shadowy tribes flitting across the stage, each acting its part like the different performers in a vaudeville show, and then making way for other actors. The Valley of Mexico, or Anahuac, meaning "near the water," seems to have been the centre of the civilization of these early tribes. It is a beautiful valley nearly sixty miles in length and thirty in breadth, and is enclosed by a wall of mountains which circumscribe the view in every direction. Six shallow lakes lie in this hollow: Texcoco, Xochimilco, San Cristobal, Xaltocan, Zumpango and Chalco, of which the first named is the nearest to the city and lies distant about three miles. It is easy to believe that the waters of these lakes at one time entirely surrounded the ancient city of Tenochtitlan, for within historic times their shores have greatly receded.

The history of these early races rests mostly upon tradition; yet a diversity of architectural ruins, and the few meagre records that remain, present certain general facts. These positive proofs leave no doubt that this valley was inhabited from a very early period by tribes or nations which made distinct advances in civilization. These tribes had developed certain of the useful arts and had evolved a social system that exhibited some refinement. The first of these races of whom we have reliable record are the Toltecs, who appeared in the Valley of Mexico in the seventh century at almost the same time that Mohammed was spreading his religion over Asia and Africa. Their sway lasted about five centuries, when they disappeared as silently and mysteriously as they came.

These peaceful and agricultural people were succeeded by the Chichimecs, a more barbarous race, who came from the north. They in turn were followed by the Nahuals. Lastly came the Aztecs, who entered the valley about 1196, and reached a higher state of civilization than any of their predecessors. War was their choicest profession, for they considered that warriors slain in battle were immediately transported to scenes of ineffable bliss. They offered human sacrifices to their gods. Prescott tells us of a procession of captives two miles long, and numbering seventy thousand persons who were sacrificed at one time. This is incredible, for at that rate the population would soon have been exhausted even in this prolific land. Furthermore we know that the Aztecs were not always successful in war, and may have furnished victims from their own numbers, for sacrifice to the gods of the other nations in the same land.

THE CALENDAR STONE

> CALENDARIO AZTECA O PIEDRA DEL SOL.
> EN EL MES DE DICIEMBRE DEL AÑO DE 1790
> AL PRACTICARSE LA NIVELACION PARA EL NUEVO
> EMPEDRADO DE LA PLAZA MAYOR DE ESTA CAPITAL
> FUE DESCUBIERTO ESTE MONOLITO Y COLOCADO
> DESPUES AL PIE DE LA TORRE OCCIDENTAL DE LA
> CATEDRAL POR EL LADO QUE VE AL PONIENTE
> DE CUYO LUGAR SE TRASLADO A ESTE MUSEO
> NACIONAL EN AGOSTO DE 1885

The Aztecs were clever workers in gold and silver, and were acquainted with a number of arts that are lost to-day. Their picture writings bear witness to a clever fancy and fertile invention of symbols. The numerous idols show their skill in carving and a true artistic instinct. Many antiquities have been exhumed from the swampy soil on which the capital city is built, in making excavations for improvements. The National Museum is a treasure house of these relics and it would take a volume to describe them. The huge Sacrificial Stone, which is generally supposed to have been placed on the top of the great altar, is preserved there. It also houses the horrible image of the god Huitzilopochtli, and a varied assortment of inferior gods, goddesses, and other objects of worship. But the most celebrated antiquity—the one showing the greatest advancement—is the Calendar Stone. This stone was buried for centuries, and when resurrected was placed in the west tower of the cathedral. From this place it was removed a few years ago and placed in the museum. It is a mighty stone, eleven feet and eight inches in diameter, and weighs more than twenty tons. The Aztecs divided the year into eighteen months of twenty days each, and then arbitrarily added five days to complete the year.

"Let us follow the cross, and if we have faith we will conquer," was the motto on the banner of Cortez. It was with this spirit that he led his little band over the mountains and into the heart of the empire of Montezuma, late in the fall of 1519. He was met by that sovereign, tradition says, on the site of the present Hospital of Jesus, with every manifestation of friendliness. For several months they were the honoured guests of the Aztec chief, but at length the aggressions of the Spaniards changed friendship to hate and the Aztecs, rising in their wrath, chased the invaders from the city. Driven before the infuriated natives like sheep, they fled over the present road to the suburban village of Tacuba, and many were those who fell. This rout of the Spaniards has been painted with wonderful vividness by Gen. Lew Wallace in "The Fair God."

It was an awful night of despair, that first day of July, 1520, and the Spaniards who escaped named it La Noche Triste, "the sorrowful night." The pursuit stopped at the little town of Popotla. In this village is a great cypress tree whose branches are blasted by the storms of centuries. For a moment the strong will of Cortez gave way and he sat down upon a stone under the spreading branches of this tree and wept. Whether he wept most for his fallen soldiers or disappointment over his ignominious defeat, we are not told by the chroniclers. This tree is now noted as *el arbol de la noche triste*, or "the tree of the sorrowful night." A high iron fence protects the ancient relic from the souvenir vandals.

The Spaniards retreated beyond the valley to their allies, the Tlaxcalans, at Cholula. Reinforcements and supplies arriving, they returned a few months later and began the memorable siege of Tenochtitlan, and made a triumphal entry into that city on the 13th of August, 1521. Then Guatemotzin, the last of the Aztec emperors, wept in his turn, because the sacred fires of the temple had for ever gone out, and his people would henceforth be slaves. "Take that dagger," he said, "and free this spirit." But, no, torture must come before death, for Cortez fain would learn where the gold was hidden that had so suddenly disappeared. To-day, in the City of Mexico, a statue stands in one of the circles of the famous Paseo, which commemorates this great warrior and his torture by the Spanish chieftain. This monument is greatly cherished by the Indians, who hold annual festivals in his honour and decorate it with a profusion of flowers and wreaths.

The great Valley of Mexico is without a natural outlet, and this fact has caused seven inundations of the capital during exceptionally rainy seasons. One of the lakes, Zumpango, is twenty-five feet higher than the city and drains into Texcoco, from which the waters spread over the city. When the first serious inundations came in 1553, 1580 and 1604, the project of removing the city to a higher level was strongly agitated. It was only the loss of millions of dollars of property that prevented this action. Then the idea of draining this valley was definitely adopted and the work was begun in 1607. A tunnel was decided upon and fifteen thousand Indians were set at work sinking shafts and driving the tunnel in both directions. Within a year a tunnel four miles long had been completed. This tunnel eventually caved in, so that very little good was realized from it and efforts were made to convert it into an open cut. But this undertaking was not finished until two centuries later. It is a great trench, however, with an average depth of from one hundred and fifty to two hundred feet, and from three hundred to seven hundred feet in width at the top. It is called the *Tajo de Nochistongo*, or Nochistongo cut, and its only use now is as an entrance for the Mexican Central railway. Even this waterway did not drain the valley, remarkable engineering feat as it was, but a new canal was constructed by American engineers a few years ago which successfully accomplishes the work of draining these shallow lakes and carrying off the sewerage of the city.

The first Aztecs who settled in this valley lived almost entirely in the marshes and lakes, we are told, because of the hostility of their fierce neighbours. They were thus obliged to depend almost wholly upon the products of these watered lands for their sustenance, and they acquired some strange and—we would say—depraved tastes. A reminder of those days is seen in the cakes made of the eggs of a curious marsh-fly, which are sold in the market of the City of Mexico to-day. The flies themselves are pounded into a paste and sold after being boiled, but the eggs are preferred. The Indians collect the eggs in a systematic manner. Bundles of a certain kind of sedge are planted in Lake Texcoco and the insects deposit their eggs thereon in great quantities. These bundles as soon as covered are shaken over pieces of cloth and replaced for another supply. The eggs thus collected are made into a paste and form a favourite article of food, especially during Lent.

It is interesting to learn what different races regard as toothsome dainties. In Southern Mexico I have seen bushels of common grasshoppers sold in the markets as a delicacy, reminding one of the locusts and wild honey used as food in Biblical times. In other parts of Mexico the honey-ant is greatly sought after for food. The natives of Central America are partial to the iguana, a large lizard sometimes reaching a length of three or four feet, and prefer it to beef. After all there is no accounting for tastes. A man who eats snails might criticize another who relishes oysters. And perhaps the man who want his cheese "ripe" should not criticize the poor Indian who has inherited a taste for the eggs of the fly.

SCENES ON THE VIGA CANAL

There are many places of interest round about the City of Mexico which are easily reached. One should not fail to visit the famous *jardines flotandos* or "floating gardens" where the beautiful flowers sold in the market are grown. These gardens, called by the Aztecs *chinampas*, are reached by the

Viga Canal. The inquirer is told to take a gondola and float down to them. The name gondola excites pleasant anticipations of a delightful trip. Entering a mule-car at the Plaza Mayor the canal is soon reached after traversing a number of narrow streets which would not especially delight the fastidious traveller. The gondoliers take the stranger almost by force and urge him into one of the flea-infested boats that abound at the landing, and which more resemble a collection of mud-scows than any other kind of floating fleet. Instead of using oars these queer gondoliers with the picture hats pole the boat through the muddy waters of La Viga, stirring up odours which cause the passenger to wish that he was not gifted with the sense of smell, or that he could temporarily dispense with breathing. However, there is life in the stream and on the banks that is typically Mexican, for boats are constantly passing up and down. Occasionally a load of Indians will float by playing native airs on guitars and other string instruments, with the light-heartedness and gaiety peculiar to this race. On the bank are scattered many native thatch huts around which idle natives group. Along the road pass men and women going to and from the city with loads on their heads or on their backs. The "floating gardens" are always just beyond. They are first at Santa Anita but, when this place is reached, they are at Mexicalcingo. Arrived there the visitor is sent to Ixtacalco, and then he is forwarded to Xochimilco, and so the real floating gardens are never reached. The fact is that they do not float and perhaps never did. This characteristic only exists in the imagination, for it sounds romantic to speak of gardens that can be moved around and anchored at will.

Disembarking at an unattractive mud and thatch village bearing the charming name of Santa Anita, self constituted guides are waiting to conduct you to the object of your visit, something which does not literally exist. Yet the "floating gardens" are all about you at this place. They are simply marsh lands with canals leading in and out and crossways by means of which the gardener can reach all parts in his boat. The earth may yield somewhat if you step upon it, but they do not float. It is possible, and historians so assert, that floating gardens did exist in reality during the Aztec invasion. These people were frequently driven to dire extremities to secure food. They may have adopted the plan of making floating gardens which could be moved about as necessity compelled. This was done by culling masses of vegetation with its thick entwined stems and pouring upon this mat the rich mud dredged from the bottom of the lake. Then, as the masses settled, more mud was put on until the whole anchored upon the bottom of the lake and became immovable. The gardens look beautiful, covered as they are with the many-coloured blossoms. By means of the canals the roots are kept thoroughly moist at all times, and the plants thrive luxuriantly.

This canal of La Viga was formerly a great trade route, for a large part of the natives came to the City of Mexico by this way. It leads back into regions where dwell full blooded Aztecs who speak a language that is said to be almost the pure ancient tongue. These natives can be distinguished from all others on the street and in the market by their features and peculiar dress. They are clannish and keep by themselves, except in the intercourse made necessary by barter and trade. They are proud of their lineage and rejoice in the fact that they have not mingled with the other native races.

Tacuba, distant only a few miles, is an interesting little village, and has many gardens and a fine old church. It is a good place to study the people and get snap-shots of quaint life. Its principal distinction is that it was a proud city when Tetlepanquetzaltzin was king once upon a time. Texcoco at the time of the conquest was the capital of the Tezcucans, who were a race in alliance with the Aztecs, but it is now principally in ruins, for its glory has passed away. El Desierto was once the home of the Carmelite monks and is frequently visited now in its decay. Coyoacan was the first capital of Mexico, for Cortez established the seat of government there for a time while the new city was being built.

Tacubaya is the home of the wealthy as well as the sporting element. It has beautiful gardens within the adobe walls surrounding the homes of the opulent. It is on higher ground and should have been the site of the capital city itself. It is also called the Monte Carlo of Mexico, for gamblers of all sorts and conditions congregate here in booths or under umbrellas, and you can lose any sum at games of chance as at that famous resort along the shores of the blue Mediterranean. Games, music, dancing, cock-fights, and bull-fights are a few of the attractions to amuse and entertain the visitor, and relieve him from the burden of carrying around the weighty silver pesos.

CASTLE OF CHAPULTEPEC

In all this beautiful and historic Valley of Mexico there is no more beautiful spot, or none around which so many memories cling, as Chapultepec, the Hill of the Grasshoppers. Historic and beautiful Chapultepec! A great grove of noble cypresses draped with masses of Spanish moss surrounds this rock, and between the trees and along the shores of a pretty little lake wind enchanting walks. One grand old cypress called Montezuma's tree rises to a height of one hundred and seventy feet. It is a magnificent breathing spot—with which no park that I have ever seen in America compares. Legend says that on the top of this rock was situated the palace of Montezuma, and it is probably only legend. No doubt that emperor often rested himself under the friendly shade of the great *ahuehuete*, and reflected on the glory of his empire before the disturbing foreigners came. The present Castle of Chapultepec dates from 1783 when it was begun by one of the viceroys. Later viceroys, presidents and an emperor added to the original building until now it is a palace indeed but not a beautiful structure. Ill-fated Maximilian made this his home and added greatly to the beauty of the grounds. It is now the White House of Mexico although occupied only a part of the year by the president.

Perhaps nowhere in the world does there exist a more beautiful scene than that which unfolds to the view from this rock. All around is the great sweep of plain with its wealth of cultivated fields; the distant mountain range with its ever varying outline; the snow-capped twin peaks, Popocatapetl (seventeen thousand, seven hundred and eighty-two feet) and Ixtaccihuatl (sixteen thousand and sixty feet), standing like silent sentinels and dominating the horizon; the silver line of the lakes; and beneath us the fair City of Mexico, the ancient Tenochtitlan. Legend says that Popocatepetl, "the smoking mountain," and Ixtaccihuatl, "the woman in white," were once living giants but that having displeased the Almighty they were changed to mountains. The woman died and the contour of her body covered with snow can be traced on the summit of the smaller peak. The man was doomed to live for ever and gaze on the sleeping form of his beloved. At times when his grief becomes uncontrollable he shakes with his great sobs and pours forth tears of fire.

As I stood on that historic rock I thought of the New World Venice described by Prescott, "with its shining cities and flowering islets rocking, as it were, at anchor on the fair bosom of the waters." Rising above all was the great sacrificial altar upon which the sacred fires were ever kept burning. Beneath this rock under the friendly branches of the giant cypress Montezuma has no doubt sheltered himself from the hot sun. Cortez here rested himself after his severe marches. French zouaves in their quaint uniforms have bivouacked in the grove. American blue-coats stacked their arms here after the victory of Molino-del-Ray. And Mexicans now take their siestas under the same friendly shade while other races are robbing them of their wealth.

Yes, historic scenes and tragedies have taken place on this plain. Nations have come and gone. Victors have themselves been led away captives, and taskmasters have in turn become slaves. How finite is man or his works in the presence of this great panorama of nature! Races have come and gone but the mountains endure. Human tragedies have been enacted here but the sky is just as blue and the sun just as bright, as when Cortez looked with envious eyes upon this beautiful valley. The mimic play of men, and women and races upon this amphitheatre has scarcely left its imprint. The only occasions when the calm serenity of nature has been disturbed were when the giant Popocatapetl, overcome with grief at the loss of his beloved, has shaken this whole valley with his sobs and poured forth plenteous tears of fire over its fair surface.

CHAPTER V
THE TROPICS

In no country in the world is it possible to move from one extreme of climate to the other in so short a time as in Mexico. Within less than twenty-four hours one can travel from the sun-baked sands of the Gulf coast to the snow-covered, conical peak of one of the great extinct volcanoes, thus traversing every zone of vegetable life from the dense tropical growth of the former to the stunted pines of the latter. By railway it is a journey of only a few hours from the plateaus, at an altitude of eight thousand feet, to the sea level, and a most interesting ride it is. The Mexican Railway, which is the oldest railway in the republic, runs from the capital to Vera Cruz and is the best route, for its wonderful engineering feats and beautiful scenery have drawn tourists from all parts of the world. Leaving the capital, the road skirts the bank of Lake Texcoco, through a pass in the mountains surrounding the Valley of Mexico, and across the Plains of Apam, the home of the maguey, for a hundred and fifty miles before the exciting part of the trip is reached.

The descent begins at Esperanza, which lies at the very foot of Mt. Orizaba. Esperanza means "hope" and it is well named for the traveller can "hope" for better things as the train approaches the coast. Noah's Ark rests near here, for I saw it with my own eyes labelled in plain letters, *Arc de Noe*, but it is now—sad to tell—devoted to the sale of pulque. Esperanza is eight thousand and forty-four feet above the sea and one hundred and twelve miles from Vera Cruz as the track runs, but much nearer as the crow would fly. There is a drop of four thousand, one hundred feet in the next twenty-nine miles and it is one of the grandest rides in the world. In places the road seems like a little shelf on the side of a towering mountain while a yawning chasm awaits the coach below. As soon as Boca del Monte (Mouth of the Mountain) is reached, only a few miles from Esperanza, the downward impetus is felt and all the energy of the curious double-ended English engines is devoted to holding back the heavy train with its human cargo.

Passing through a tunnel here, the scene bursts upon the traveller without any warning or prelude, in all its grandeur and magnificence. The engine accommodatingly stops for water so that the passengers have an opportunity to view this wonderful panorama. Maltrata nestles in the hollow, a dozen miles away by rail, yet the red tiles of the roofs, a red-domed church and the ever-present plaza gleam in the sunshine two thousand feet directly underneath. The valley is almost flat and is divided into squares by hedges and walls and, reflecting every shade of green, looks like a checker-board arrangement of nature. Beyond the valley, hill succeeds hill until they are lost in the purple haze of the horizon, or are overtopped by snow-capped Orizaba. Indians appear here with beautiful bouquets of roses, tulips and orchids, with their yellow, pink and red centres, for sale. The train passes on over a narrow bridge spanning a deep chasm and down the mountain until Maltrata is reached, where the same Indians will greet you with the same bouquets, for they have climbed down the two thousand feet in less time than it took the train to reach the same level.

Leaving Maltrata the road enters a cañon called *El Infernillo*, the Little Hell, goes through a tunnel and another beautiful valley, running through fertile fields and by wooded hills, until Orizaba, the border-land of the tropics, is reached.

This city at an altitude of four thousand feet is in the *tierra templada*, the temperate region. This zone is as near paradise in the matter of climate as any location on earth could well be. It retains most of the beauties and few of the annoying insects and tropical fevers of the hot zone. It has the moisture of the lowlands with the cool breezes of the uplands and is well named "temperate zone" because of its fine climate and equable temperature.

Orizaba is a town of thirty-five thousand people and a very beautiful and interesting place with its palm-shaded streets and low Moorish buildings. Its Alameda is a quaint, shady park with an abundance of flowers and blooming trees. Along the street the orange trees thrust their laden branches out into the highway over the low adobe walls. On the banks of the stream the washerwomen beat their clothes to a snowy white upon the smooth round stones. Life moves along in smooth, easy channels with these people. And it is not to be wondered at, for there is

> "A sense of rest
> To the tired breast
> In this beauteous Aztec town."

Between Orizaba and Cordoba, a distance of sixteen miles, is perhaps the best cultivated section in Mexico. The products of all the zones are mingled and corn and coffee grow side by side as well as peach trees and the banana. Cordoba is just on the border of the *tierra caliente*, or hot country proper, and is a much smaller city than Orizaba. It is a very old town and was founded as a place of refuge from the malarial fevers of the coast lands. This region is noted for its fine coffee, and there are numberless coffee plantations as well as many sugar *haciendas*. The Mexican of the tropics can be seen here dressed in immaculate white. Leaving Cordoba dense tropical forests of palm and palmetto begin to appear. These alternate with groves of coffee and bananas, gardens of mangoes, fields of pineapples and other tropical fruits. Nature begins to manifest herself in her grandest productions. Birds of brilliant plumage are seen. The towering trees, rocks and entire surface of the soil are covered with bright flowers such as orchids, oleanders and honeysuckles and luxuriant vines. These and the dense jungles are all reminders that the tropics have been reached at last. Soon the train enters Vera Cruz, the city without cabs, the landing-place of the great conquistador and his cohorts.

The principal port now, as it has always been since the landing of Cortez on the twenty-first day of April, 1519, is Vera Cruz, or, as he named it, *La Villa Rica de Vera Cruz*—the Rich City of the True Cross. Most Americans who pass through here leave by the very first train or boat for fear of pestilence. I met one fellow-countryman there who was almost beside himself because the boat he had expected to take was delayed a couple of days. This city is reputed to be the favourite loafing-place of the *stegomyia fasciata* whose bite results in the *vomito*, or yellow fever. If all the sensational reports sent out concerning this city were true then "Pandora's box was not a circumstance to the evils which Vera Cruz contains." I had read in Mr. Ober's excellent work on Mexico of an American consul who died here just thirteen days after reaching the port that his ambition had led him to; and of the terrible ravages of the scourge when deaths were averaging forty per day. I arrived there after night had set in. Eating a light supper and seeing that my name was duly posted on the big blackboard bulletin according to the custom prevailing there, I retired to my room, and only breathed freely after securely drawing the mosquito netting around my bed so that it would be impossible for a *stegomyia* to get through.

It was almost a surprise on the following morning to find able-bodied Americans and husky Englishmen pursuing their avocations in an unconcerned way as though such things as yellow fever or smallpox were not to be thought of. Then, again, I was alarmed at the numerous red flags hanging out, which I took to be quarantine flags, for everything is different here. Upon investigation this alarm was dispelled, for those places proved to be pulque-shops and the flag meant that a fresh supply of the "liquor divine" had just been received. It is probably true that Vera Cruz was a hot-bed for the *vomito* a few years ago, but Mexican statistics report only twelve deaths in 1904 and one hundred and twenty-two in 1905 from this disease, which is not bad for a city of thirty thousand people, where a large proportion of the population cannot be made to obey the ordinary laws of sanitation. I doubt whether the death rate is much greater than in our own cities on the Gulf coast. This change is due to the better situation that has been brought about by the authorities.

An adequate supply of pure water was the first important step in this move for improved conditions. This was secured by utilizing the water of the Jamapa River at a point about twelve miles distant and passing this water through several filtering beds before turning it into the mains which supply the city. A sewerage system has been constructed, by means of which the sewerage is carried out and discharged into deep water so that the harbour will not be contaminated. Disinfecting stations have been established and a plant for the disposition of garbage. Then in addition to the regular force of health officers, there is a large volunteer street cleaning brigade. These volunteer forces are not on the pay-roll and yet they do their work in a thorough manner even if their methods cannot be approved. Their only reward is the enforcement of a fine of five dollars for the protection of their lives. By the natives these street cleaners are called *zopilotes* but to an American they are plain, every-day buzzards. Hundreds of these birds can be seen perched on the roof-tops or waddling through the streets.

For centuries the port of Vera Cruz was the bane of vessel owners for there was no protection from the severe "Northers" so prevalent on the Gulf and it was one of the most inconvenient and dangerous harbours on that coast. It was for this reason that Cortez destroyed the vessels which had brought his forces over from Cuba. An excellent harbour has been constructed at great cost and ocean-going vessels can now anchor alongside of the main pier and unload. A large new union station will at once be erected by the four railways entering this city on a site adjoining the pier, which will further increase the facilities of this port.

BRIDGE AT ORIZABA

THE BUZZARDS OF VERA CRUZ

AVENUE OF PALMS, VERA CRUZ

The fortress of San Juan de Ulua, now a prison, and which is reached by a short sail through the shark-infested harbour, is an interesting structure and has seen many vicissitudes. Used as a fort for several centuries by the Spaniards, it has successively been occupied by the French, Americans, and again by the French and their allies in the war of the intervention. The buildings in Vera Cruz are nearly all low, one-storied structures of adobe, and the walls are tinted in red, yellow, blue and green, thus furnishing to the eye a pleasing variety and, with the bay, reminding one of Cadiz in old Spain. There is an attractive plaza and an imposing avenue of the cocoanut palm. Vera Cruz is the gateway to the capital and many millions of imports and exports pass through here each year, as much as at all the other ports of Mexico combined, leaving out Progreso, on the Yucatan coast, through which the henequen traffic is carried.

Tampico is the second Gulf port in importance and on the completion of a direct route to the capital will be a close rival to Vera Cruz. Coatzacoalcos is the Gulf port of the Tehuantepec railway and will become an important port. The Pacific coast affords better natural harbours. Acapulco is one of the finest natural land-locked harbours in the world. Though now of secondary importance because of the absence of railroad connections, at one time this picturesque harbour sheltered the old Spanish galleons engaged in the East India trade. Their freight was unloaded there and transported overland on the backs of burros and mules to Vera Cruz and re-shipped to Spain. Manzanillo is an important seaport on that coast and will soon be connected by rail with the capital, when its importance will be greatly increased. Other important ports on that coast are Mazatlan, Guayamas, San Blas and Salina Cruz, the Pacific port of the Tehuantepec route, where the great harbour is nearly completed.

The *tierra caliente* comprises a fringe of low plains which extend inland from the coast a distance varying from a few miles in width to a hundred or more. From thence it rises by a succession of terraces until the great inland plateaus are reached. The higher the altitude the lower the temperature, and it is estimated that there is a change of 1.8 degree Fahrenheit for each sixty feet of elevation in this region. This zone is characterized by the grandeur and variety of vegetable life, and it is an almost uninterrupted forest except where it has been cleared. A ride through the tropics is a revelation of what nature can do when aided by a never-ending succession of warm sunshine and abundant rain upon rich soil. Trees of great height and size are interspersed among plants which are generally of a tree-like nature, and are conspicuous for the development of their trunks and ramifications. The innumerable species of reeds and creeping plants that entwine themselves in a thousand different ways among the trees and plants make a passage almost impossible. It is for this reason that the natives always go around armed with the *machete*, a long blade very much like a corn-cutter, for it enables them to cut their way through the dense undergrowth, and is a protection, should any danger be encountered. The palms which are ever associated with the tropics are seen in great profusion and in countless varieties. Millions of ferns and broad-leaved plants which would be welcomed in the gardens and groves of northern homes are wasting their graceful beauty in these jungles and wildernesses. Trees are covered with beautiful orchids and vines coil about the trunks and limbs like great snakes, and then drop down to the earth and take root again in the damp soil.

To those who know them the tropics are not so terrible, treacherous though they may seem. Some enter this zone with a feeling of creepiness as though they were entering a darkened sick-room sheltering some malignant disease. They hesitate to breathe for fear that the very air is poisonous and they may take in the germs of some malady with an unpronounceable name. They shrink from nature as though she had ceased to be the kind mother to which they were accustomed in the colder climates. It is true that there is something horribly creepy and uncanny about this inevitable tropical growth, which is so frail and fragile outwardly but seems possessed of an unconquerable vitality. And yet in many of the so-called unhealthy places, there is scarcely more danger to health than elsewhere, if one but observes the same rules of right living. Continuous hard labour, such as the northern farmer is accustomed to devote to his little farm, is not possible. Exposure to the intense heat of the sun at midday and the heavy rains will bring on fevers and malaria just as surely as it produces the luxuriant vegetation. For this reason the tropics will probably never be suited for colonization by the small farmer who is fascinated with the possibilities offered by land capable of producing two or three crops in a single year.

In general, Mexico is poorly supplied with rivers. However, along the Atlantic coast they are very numerous and large, although not navigable for any great distance, or for vessels large enough to be of much aid to commerce. The size of the rivers is due to the great amount of rainfall, which varies from seventy to one hundred and eighty inches annually. When this is compared to an annual rainfall of twenty to forty inches in the northern states of the United States, the conditions in the tropics are better understood. This excessive rainfall washes down earth from the higher ground and this, together with the layers of vegetable mold, have formed soil from eight to fourteen feet in depth thus making it practically inexhaustible. The temperature varies from 70° to 100° Fahrenheit. The Pacific coast has a higher temperature and less rainfall than the Gulf coast. However, there is a stretch of land extending north of Acapulco along the coast and from eight to thirty miles wide that is unrivalled for tropical beauty and productiveness. There are many rivers and streams that traverse this land on the way from the great mountains to the Pacific.

There is a charm about the life in the hotlands that is missing in other parts of Mexico. Of all the inhabitants of that country, the life of the people in the hot country is the most interesting. This is probably due to the fact that these people have always had more freedom than the Indians on the plateaus who were practically slaves for a couple of centuries. The great estates there required sure help and the natives were reduced to serfs. In the mines they were worked with soldiers set over them as guards. In the hotlands it was easier to make a living, for a bountiful nature supplied nearly all their wants. And yet many employers of labour say that the peon from the hot country makes the most satisfactory workman. These Indians seem like a superior race. For one thing they are scrupulously clean which, in itself, is a pleasing contrast to the daily sights in Northern Mexico. Water is abundant everywhere; the extreme heat renders bathing a great comfort and their clothes are kept immaculate. They are fond of social life and almost every night groups can be seen gathered together in some kind of entertainment.

AN INDIAN HOME IN THE HOT COUNTRY

Their homes are different from those in the colder lands. The houses of the middle and lower classes are built of bamboo or other light material found in the tropical jungles, and thatched with palm leaves. The upright bamboo poles are often set an inch or more apart thus giving a free circulation of air. An Indian village generally consists of one long, winding, irregular street lined on each side by these picturesque huts, and bearing a strong resemblance to a village in the interior of Africa. Down these streets swarm in equal profusion half-naked babies and children long past the childhood stage dressed in the same simple way, and hungry looking dogs. The hot country is sparsely populated in comparison with the plateaus and there are no large cities, although archeologists tell us that the earliest civilization seems to have been located there. It could support a population many, many times larger with ease.

The most productive parts of the world are found in the *tierra caliente* which instead of being given up to impenetrable jungles, the homes of reptiles and breeding place of poisonous insects, should be made to produce those luxuries and necessaries which contribute to make civilized life tolerable. All over the world the fruits and other articles of the tropics are coming into greater demand each year. In the year 1906 the United States imported fruits and other food products of tropical countries, not including coffee, to the value of more than $150,000,000, or nearly two dollars for each man, woman and child in the country. Of the purely tropical products, sugar was by far the largest item on the list. Bananas to the amount of $11,500,000 were brought in, and were second on the list with cacao a close rival for this place.

As yet Mexico supplies but a small portion of these articles to the United States. Yet the possibilities of agriculture here are equal to those of any similar lands, and this, together with superior transportation facilities and a stable government, ought to greatly increase the trade. In addition to the above items, this soil is well adapted to the following fruits and useful products, all of which are native to the soil: oranges, lemons, limes, pineapples, grapefruit, vanilla bean, indigo, rubber, coffee, tobacco and many drug-producing plants. It is difficult for the small farmer to succeed, as he cannot do all his own labour in that climate and cannot get satisfactory help just when it is needed. He could not afford to hire a force of labourers by the year. Successful farming in the tropics can only be done on a large scale with a regular force of labourers maintained on the plantation. The title to the soil can be purchased cheaply but the first cost of the land is probably not more than one-third of the ultimate cost by the time it is cleared, planted, and the necessary improvements made. Furthermore many tropical plants such as coffee, rubber and cacao require several years of care before there is a profitable yield.

Coffee and banana culture go hand in hand, for the broad leaves of the banana provide the shade so necessary to the young coffee trees. The banana also furnishes a little revenue during the four or five years before the coffee trees have fully matured. The coffee region is very extensive, for it will grow at a height of from one to five thousand feet, and flourishes best at an altitude of two to three thousand feet. It requires plenty of warmth and moisture. The coffee, which is a tree and not a bush, is set out in rows several feet apart, and will grow twenty feet tall if permitted, but is not allowed to grow half that height. The tree is flowering and developing fruit all the time but the principal harvest is in the late fall. It is not allowed to ripen on the tree, for when the green berries have turned a bright red, they are gathered, dried in the sun, hulled and then marketed. The states of Vera Cruz and Chiapas produce the choicest coffee, but it is cultivated all over the republic where it is possible. Coffee was introduced into this country from Arabia by Spanish priests and was found to be adapted to the soil. The best grades are sent to Europe, for it is a common saying throughout Mexico and Central America that only the poor grades of coffee are sent to the United States. This is rather a slur on the tastes of the American people, but such is our reputation down there.

"Looking at it from my point of view—the lazy man's outlook—I can see nothing so inviting as coffee culture, unless it be a fat 'living' in an English country church," says a writer. For myself, the one thing that appealed to me above all others was the cultivation of the banana. The returns are quick, the income regular and the profits large. I travelled through the banana region of Honduras, where for thirty miles the railroad passed by one plantation after another of the broad-leaved banana plants growing as high as fifteen feet. Great fortunes have been made by the banana-growers of that country and Costa Rica. This fruit flourishes best in the lowlands. The preparation of the ground is very simple, for the young banana plants are set out among the piles of underbrush left after clearing and which soon decay in that climate. After nine months or a year the plants begin to bear, and each stalk will produce one bunch of bananas. The stalk is then cut down and a new one, or several, will spring up from the roots and will bear in the same length of time. Thus a banana plantation that is carefully looked after will produce a marketable crop each week in the year, so that there is a constant revenue coming in to the owner. The cultivation of this delicious fruit, for which there is an ever-increasing market, brings the quickest return of any tropical product.

RICE CULTURE

Sugar cane can be raised profitably as the stalks grow high with many joints and have a greater percentage of saccharine than in most countries where it is cultivated. Furthermore it does not require replanting so frequently. Cacao is another truly tropical product. It is from the cacao bean that chocolate is made. The trees are usually transplanted and bear in about four years and the beans are gathered three or four times a year. They are then removed from the pods and dried in the sun. The trees will bear for many years. Orange culture along modern scientific lines, such as are used in California and Florida, would be profitable, for the crop matures earlier and could be marketed long before the fruit has ripened in those states. The Mexicans are great rice eaters and there is a good field for its culture. The cocoanut palm offers good returns as there is a good market for its fruit. Rubber grows wild and many plantations have been set out in rubber trees. In the past year Mexico has shipped more than two million pounds of crude rubber, and the production is increasing. Vast tracts of mahogany are found down toward Guatemala in the states of Campeche and Tabasco. These great trees are cut down, hewn square and then hauled by mules to a waterway where they are formed into rafts and floated down to the ports. There is much waste in the present crude way of cutting and marketing this valuable wood. Logwood and other dyewoods are found in the same forests. The world's supply of chicle also comes from the same source.

What the Mexican tropics need is men of energy backed by capital sufficient to utilize large tracts of this rich soil. It is true that many plantations are now being cultivated and it is equally true that many have been abandoned as failures after unsuccessful attempts at cultivation. The fault has not been poor soil but poor management. Promotion and success are not synonymous terms, and much of the promotion has been done by unscrupulous persons whose only purpose was to dispose of stock to the gullible. Richer soil cannot be found anywhere, but it must be cultivated with intelligence and good judgment the same as in any other part of the world, or failure will result.

CHAPTER VI
A GLIMPSE OF THE ORIENTAL IN THE OCCIDENT

Some two hundred miles south of the City of Mexico lies Oaxaca (pronounced Wa-hâ-ka). The Valley of Oaxaca was looked upon by the Spanish conquerors as El Dorado, the traditional land of gold. The Aztecs told them that the gold of Montezuma came from the sands of the rivers in this and the connecting valleys, and that immeasurable treasure was to be found there. Believing these tales, Cortez secured large grants of land from the crown, and, with the consent and approval of his sovereign, assumed to himself the title of Marquis of the Valley of Oaxaca.

The cupidity of the Spaniards led them to employ every subterfuge to induce the natives to reveal the source of their plentiful supply of gold. The Indians, after considerable urging,—so we are told,—offered to conduct one man to this place, if he would submit to be blindfolded for the trip. This was agreed to and the party set out on their journey. Thinking that he would mark the way, the Spaniard dropped a grain of corn every few steps. After they had travelled a long distance, the Spaniard had the bandage removed from his eyes and he was allowed to look around, when he beheld such wealth as mortal vision never before had seen. His eyes glittered with the greed of his covetous nature, but his countenance soon changed when a dusky warrior stepped up and handed him a vessel which contained every grain of corn that he had dropped by the way. For this reason he was never able to retrace his steps to this wonderful region, and the wily Spaniards were again outwitted by the simple natives.

Oaxaca is reached by the Southern Railway which starts at Puebla. This road penetrates one of the richest sections of the republic, with abundance of timber and minerals, and unlimited beds of onyx and marble. Little of this wealth is seen from the railroad, as this line follows the narrow valleys, through one cañon into another, furnishing scenery as grandly picturesque as the great passes of Colorado. The mountains in places are lifted up thousands of feet with crags and peaks which the storms have cut into fantastic shapes and whose walls drop almost perpendicularly to the water's edge. Then again the cañon widens, and the panorama extends across the valley where gigantic rocks, stained in all colours by the oozings of the metals of the earth, form far-away pictures not unlike the battlements of an ancient fortress. The sun tinges each a different hue, with deeper tones in the near ones which fade as they approach the horizon, until all seem to blend into the intense blue of the sky.

As the train leaves the City of the Angels, just at daybreak, a wonderful panorama is opened up to view. Look in any direction, and the tiled domes of the churches rise above the plain, for each village and *hacienda* has its own. The forts erected on the surrounding hills which are emblematic of the force that subjugated this valley, are seen, and near them the pyramid of Cholula erected by those who were overcome. Over all tower those mighty monuments of nature, the white-capped peaks of Popocatapetl, Ixtaccihuatl, Orizaba and old Malintzi, with the morning sun reflected on their snowy heads. The road ascends and descends, and then ascends again before it takes a dip down into the *tierra caliente*. A number of native villages are passed but only one town of any size, Tehuacan, noted for its mineral springs. It is a pretty little city, and in the centre of a rich agricultural district. The road finally enters a wide, open country with rich valleys which extend to the hills beyond. At last, after a twelve hours' journey, our train rolls into this occidental Eden.

More than three centuries ago a Spanish writer described Oaxaca as "not very big, yet a fair and beautiful city to behold, which standeth three-score leagues from Mexico in a pleasant valley." It is located at the junction of three valleys and on the bank of a broad river, which meanders through a billowy sea of cornfields toward the Pacific. Whichever way the eye may turn the view is bounded by hills covered with forests. Viewed from one of these hills the city looks like a broad, flat-covered plain of stone buildings above which are seen many domes, and the whole scene has a truly oriental touch.

The people that the Spanish found in possession of these valleys were an industrious race. They had tilled the soil centuries before the Spaniards, in their lust for gold, despoiled these beautiful valleys. There is not a hollow, or knoll, where it is possible to scrape a little soil with a hoe, that has not at some time been cultivated. These early races had even constructed irrigation works which kept green their fields during the dry season. The rich basins filled with alluvium are now owned by the rich *hacendados*, or landowners, whose white buildings dot the landscape here and there and, with their trees, orchards and cultivated fields, lend life and colour to an otherwise dull prospect. The poor Indians are forced to work for these landlords who claim title to the land formerly owned by their ancestors, or retire to the hills where, well up toward the crests, they cultivate their little fields of corn and beans. There is one tribe of Indians that dwell in the mountains of Oaxaca who have never acknowledged either Spanish or Mexican sovereignty, and maintain their own tribal form of government. They can be seen at Oaxaca on market days.

We find Oaxaca to be a city of about thirty-three thousand people of whom three-fourths or more are Indians. It is laid out with narrow streets, down the centre of which runs a stream of water, from which rise at times odours not the most agreeable. The houses are low and one-storied, with grated windows after the style of architecture introduced by the Spaniards, and by them adopted from the Moors, who copied it from the Persians. The water supply is abundant, being brought in from the hills by an aqueduct. Fountains are located at numerous places, and a constant succession of Rebeccas with heads enveloped in their shawls, and carrying great earthen water-jars pass to and fro from them.

Oaxaca contains many fine churches of which one, Santo Domingo, has been both monastery and fortress, and has just been restored at a cost of $13,000,000 (silver) so it is claimed, making it the most costly church in Mexico, if not in North America. The gold on the walls was so heavy in former times, that the soldiers quartered here during revolutionary uprisings employed themselves in removing it. This city has been the scene of troublous times, and has been captured and re-captured by the combating forces. It has given to the country two great presidents, Juarez and Diaz, of whom it may well be proud. Of these two men, great in the annals of Mexico, the former was a full-blooded Indian, and the latter has a fair percentage of the same blood in his veins. A monument to Juarez has been erected, and some day—may it be far distant—when nature has claimed her own, this city will raise a memorial to her still greater son.

THE AQUEDUCT, OAXACA

A FOUNTAIN IN OAXACA

Oaxaca has a pleasant plaza, called the Plaza de Armas, adorned with various semi-tropical trees and shrubs, in the centre of which is the ever-present band-stand. The Cathedral and municipal palace face this square. My visit here was during a *fiesta* and this plaza was the favourite resort of the Indians as well as myself. The Indians living in the hills took undisturbed possession at night, and groups of tired *Indios* wrapped themselves in their *sarapes*, or shawls, and stretched their tired limbs out on the cold stones; or propped themselves against the walls of a building to rest. A number of catch-penny devices were running during the evening and the favourite seemed to be the phonograph. The Indian would pay his *centavo*, put the transmitter in his ears and listen without a sign of expression on his stolid face. Nevertheless, he enjoyed it, because he would repeat the operation until his stock of coppers was considerably diminished.

Saturday is market day in this city, and a visit to this popular place is worth a trip to Mexico. The atmosphere of the market is truly oriental, for these people have a genius for trading as the innumerable little stands where crude pottery, rough-made baskets, home-made *dulces*, etc., are sold, fully proves. The entrance takes one past the dealers in fried meats, where bits of pork and shreds of beef are dished out sizzling hot to the peons under the big *sombreros* by women cooks who crouch over earthenware dishes placed on small braziers containing a charcoal fire, and a three course meal can be obtained for a few cents. There is always a crowd around this department, for these people are ever ready to eat, and their capacity is only limited by their purse.

THE MARKET-WOMEN OF OAXACA

THE POTTERY-MARKET, OAXACA

Next is encountered the fruit and vegetable stands. The finest fruits and vegetables, and especially the latter, that I saw in Mexico, were right here in this market and this was in the month of December. Generally the vegetables in Mexico are not large, but here were fine potatoes, great red tomatoes, gigantic radishes and elephantine cabbages. Oranges, bananas, limes, plantains and pineapples were plentiful, as well as the less-known fruits such as *zapotes* (a kind of melon), *aguacates* (a pale green fruit and vegetable combined), granaditas, mangoes, granadas and pomegranates. The cocoanut of the hotlands is mingled with the *dunas*, the fruit of the prickly pear, of the higher lands. With these a great many drinks called *frescas*, or sherbets, are flavoured, the merits of which are announced by the dark-eyed, be-shawled vendors. The women merchants, many of them smoking cigarettes, sit around on the floor so thick in places that it is almost impossible to work your way through the mixed assortment of peppers and babies; corn, lean babies and peas; charcoal, beans and fat babies; naked babies, knives and murderous-looking *machetes*; hats, laughing babies, shawls and other useful articles; turkeys, crying babies, chickens, dirty babies, ducks, squawking parrots in cages, pigs and other live stock, including babies of all kinds and descriptions.

The pottery market presided over by the solemn-faced, oriental merchants is a never-ending place of interest, and these artistic vessels are carried over the mountains on the backs of the Indians. Crude baskets and mats made of the palm fibre are found in abundance as well as brooms which bear no union label.

No one could afford to miss the flower department where flowers are so cheap that it seems almost a sin not to buy them. Here are velvety sweet peas, purple pansies, tangled heaps of crimson and white roses, azure forget-me-nots, pyramids of heliotrope and scarlet geraniums. For a few cents one can buy almost a bushel of these, or, if preferred, can substitute marguerites, carnations, poppies, or violets. An American will probably have to pay twice as much as a native, even after the shrewdest bargaining.

Outside the market enclosure caravans of over-loaded donkeys jostle each other as a great solid-wheeled cart yoked to a couple of meek-eyed oxen creaks by, or a tram car drawn by galloping mules thunders noisily along to an accompaniment of loud cracks of the whip, and a constant repetition of "*mulas*" and "*arres*" the "rrs" being brought out with a long trill.

CROSSING THE RIVER ON MARKET-DAY

The Indian will travel for days on his way to market at Oaxaca. On the day before market I drove out the south road for a number of miles, and the entire distance was literally black,—or perhaps it would be better to say brown,—with the natives coming to town bearing the "brown man's burden," and travelling along in the middle of the road at a rapid pace. These Indians were coming from the "hot country" farther south and were bringing oranges, bananas, cocoanuts and other kinds of tropical fruits, besides chickens, eggs and other poultry. Most of them were on foot, though the more fortunate had donkeys to carry the load; but they themselves walked and drove the animal. The women bore large baskets on their heads, which they balanced gracefully, although sometimes the loads are exceedingly heavy. They will carry one hundred pounds or more in this manner. Frequently a baby is swung across the back as an additional burden. The little mites are good natured in this uncomfortable position, and do not make half as much trouble as American babies in their rubber-tired, easy-springed perambulators.

A small pot, a basket of tortillas, a few fagots and plenty of coffee complete the outfit of the man. Perhaps the value of his load is not over a dollar or two in gold, but his entertainment along the way costs little, for he sleeps out of doors, carries his food, makes his own coffee and needs to buy nothing except perhaps a little fruit and *aguardiente* (brandy). The entire family sometimes accompany him, for the wife is afraid to have her man go away alone for fear he may desert her.

On the opposite side of the city from the road just described is another main highway. I stood here for several hours by the river bank on the afternoon of a market-day, when the people were leaving for home. The sight never grew tiresome or monotonous, as there was a constant succession of pictures, which a moving-picture machine alone could adequately portray. Although there is a bridge across the stream, no one used it, for by making a short cut across the river bed a hundred yards or more was saved. The pedestrian would remove his sandals to wade through the shallow water, and then replace them on reaching the opposite bank. The Indians going this way had more burros, and, as their load was disposed of, the family rode. Frequently a poor, diminutive burro carried as many persons as could sit on his back, in addition to the large baskets. Many of the great carts drawn by one or two yoke of oxen passed this way. The cattle are all yoked by the horns, which seems a cruel way, for their heads are brought down almost to the ground, and it looks as though every jar must cause them suffering.

So this unique panorama continued all the afternoon. I could not think of anything but Palestine, as I gazed at this unceasing procession of donkeys, Egyptian carts, women with their shawls folded and worn on their heads in Eastern fashion; and in the background the white walls, red tiled roofs and domes of the churches of Oaxaca. For a moment I wondered if I were not mistaken, and had suddenly strayed into some corner of the Orient, and found myself involuntarily looking for the mosque, and listening for the cry of the muezzin calling the faithful to prayer.

A trip around about the valley near Oaxaca only served to strengthen the oriental cast of the picture. The types of buildings, and the signs of water and fertility in the midst of widespread aridity (for this was the dry season) are eastern. I saw many flocks of goats herded by the solitary shepherd in the truly old-fashioned way. Then, a slow-moving team of oxen followed by a peon guiding a one-handled, wooden plough deepens the picture. How powerful must have been the Moorish influence in Spain, for this is the plough of Egypt and Chaldea which was carried along the coast of Barbary into Spain, and left there as a heritage to the Spaniards who introduced it into the new world.

Yes, Oaxaca is an El Dorado, a land of treasure to the searcher after the picturesque. The real wealth lies in its delightful climate. The temperature is mild and does not vary more than twenty or thirty degrees during the year. The altitude is a little less than five thousand feet and the air is fresh and bracing. There is also an abundance of good, pure water. Some day this city will be known as a health resort for people from cold climates. They will find relief from the strenuous life in quiet, restful, oriental Oaxaca.

There is no more picturesque *hacienda* in all Mexico than that of Mitla a few miles away. Because of the bleak and rough nature of the country it has retained its early characteristics. The little store is a revelation of the simple and primitive life of these people. Evening is sure to find Don Felix, or his black-eyed son, behind the counter waiting on the groups of Indians who are constantly coming in to buy a couple of cents worth of *mescal*, or *tequila*, or cigarettes. One Indian woman came in to purchase a *centavo* (one-half cent) of vinegar, another of lard, and others an equal amount of honey, soap, sugar or matches. They would invariably buy only one article at a time, then pay for it and watch the copper disappear down a slot in the counter. Outside the door was an old Indian who had brought a load of wood down from the mountain, and the good housewives were noisily bargaining with him for a centavo's worth of wood, and trying to get an extra stick or two for that sum.

Bargaining is a part of the education of these people. A young Indian came in hatless and wanted a *sombrero* (hat). He was shown one with thirty cents worth of brim by the merchant. The Indian offered twenty-eight cents which was accepted and he went away happy over his bargain. An old Indian,—and an old Indian is but a child in worldly wisdom,—brought a large cassava root, which, after considerable haggling, the merchant purchased for five cents. He bought a package of sixteen cigarettes for three cents and told the young *hacendado* that he had another "*mas grande*" (larger), which he would sell for seven cents. He went away but returned in a few minutes with the other root, and looked around at the crowd with a grin. The merchant took it but told him it was "*mas chico*" (smaller), and he could only allow four cents. The Indian came down to six and the deal was closed at five cents, the same price as the first one was sold for. He bought a glass of *mescal* for two cents and vanished in the night air, with a smile of complete satisfaction on his face. It is a simple life that these people lead, and the same scenes may be witnessed any day in the year at this little *tienda* at the Hacienda of Mitla.

"When twilight falls, more near and clear,
The tender southern skies appear."

Twilight is very brief in this land. Scarcely has the sun dropped out of sight, when the moon appears on the opposite horizon, almost a counterpart of the former in its descending glory. Then the stars appear by hundreds, and myriads, and the night in all its magnificence is upon you, where, but a few minutes before, was the brightness of day. And the overhanging canopy of the heavens seems so much brighter, and clearer, and nearer than in our more northerly land.

As the hour grew late, I wandered forth from the little store and walked through the narrow, winding streets of the village. It was one of those brilliant tropical nights when the southern skies seemed ablaze with the light of innumerable stars, and the Queen of the Night was in her glory. It was such a night as would have appealed to the astronomers of old. The streets were silent except for the howling of some dogs near by. The porch of the *hacienda* was crowded with reclining figures wrapped in their *sarapes*. A belated traveller came up and with a sigh of relief deposited his load, and joined the sleeping crowd. A match illumed a dark face for a moment as he lit a cigarette. Finally, all voices ceased and quiet reigned supreme. It was a silence as deep and mysterious as that of the ruined city that lay but a few rods away.

CHAPTER VII
THE ISTHMUS OF TEHUANTEPEC

A trip from Vera Cruz to the Isthmus of Tehuantepec takes the traveller into the very centre of the tropics in Mexico. It is a most interesting ride. The entire journey is within the *tierra caliente* region and throughout the whole distance of two hundred and fifty miles there are only slight undulations that could hardly be truthfully called hills. It is not all jungle for there are plains that are sometimes several miles in width which furnish rich pasture for great herds of cattle. Here again is seen the picturesque Mexican cowboy riding his pony and carrying the ever-present lasso. The heavy saddles in this hot climate and especially the twisted bits which are universally used upon the horses in Mexico seem like a cruel imposition upon their faithful steeds. With this combination of rings and bars a rider could almost break the jaw of a horse. It is absolutely impossible for an animal to drink with this bit in his mouth.

This leads me to remark that the finer sensibilities with regard to the treatment of domesticated animals and fowls are generally absent among Mexicans. The poor burros which are obliged to travel day after day with great sores on their backs that are continually chafed by the loads they are carrying, and saddle mules with similar sores, excite no compassion from the average Mexican. No doubt many of these animals are obliged to work for months and possibly years, when every step under a load or the weight of a man must cause them suffering. They are seldom shod, and many an animal is obliged to travel over the rough trails until his hoofs are worn down to the sensitive part. Cruel spurs are jabbed into his sides until they are raw. I have already spoken of the bull-fight and cock-fighting. From a book "On the Mexican Highlands" I quote another form of cruelty:—"The stocky, swarthy Indian woman calmly broke the thigh bone of each leg and the chief bone of each wing, so that escape might be impossible, and proceeded right then and there to pick the chicken alive. She was evidently unconscious of any thought of cruelty. The legs and wings were broken in order that the bird might not run or fly away. The sentiment of pity and tenderness for dumb things had not yet dawned upon her mind, and the fowl destined for the pot received no consideration at her hands."

There are many villages along this route but no cities. Several broad rivers and innumerable small streams are crossed. The engines burn wood, and it is necessary to stop on several occasions and load up the tender with fuel. At Tierra Blanca are located the shops and division headquarters of the road. As the Isthmus is approached the tropical swamps become more frequent and the train passes through miles of territory where "still stands the forest primeval," a jungle of trees and shrubs intermingled with countless varieties of palms; impenetrable forests with creepers and parasites hanging from the boughs of trees, and replanting themselves in the moist earth. Within these jungles the "tigre" roams and beneath the heavy undergrowth, horrid, venomous snakes crawl. Overhead fly noisy parrots and paroquets in couples and flocks with all of the colours of the rainbow reflected from their gaudy feathers. Then in the waters of these streams live hundreds of repulsive alligators.

At certain seasons of the year the Indians live almost entirely upon the wild products of the forest. Nature furnishes fruits, and with the blow-gun or other weapon enough game can be killed to fill the larder. With a natural laziness and in an enervating climate the natives prefer existence of this kind to the more artificial one made necessary by labour.

The Vera Cruz and Pacific Railway connects with the Tehuantepec railway at Santa Lucrecia, a small village with a poor hotel. Here it was my lot to be obliged to spend Christmas Eve and the greater part of Christmas day. My companions were an Englishman and a Scotchman. The Englishman rummaged around in the little store and found a canned plum pudding, which rather cheered him and his compatriot and I was invited to share in their good fortune. However the heavens seemed to open up and let the water pour down in torrents and the mud was apparently bottomless so that our explorations were confined to the hotel porch. In spite of the plum pudding my spirits were rather low and I was reminded of Touchstone wandering in the Forest of Arden, when he says:—

"When I was at home I was in a better place,
But travellers must be content."

It was a real pleasure to step into a fine American coach drawn by an American engine and run by an American crew bound for the chief town of the Isthmus and the one that gave it its name.

THE MARKET, TEHUANTEPEC

Tehuantepec is a place where some twenty thousand souls are trying to solve the problem of existence under favourable skies. In this city of a hot midday sun and little rain the strenuous life has few disciples. It is situated on the Pacific slope of the Cordillera on both banks of a broad river and only a few miles from the ocean. It is composed of low, one-storied buildings, many of which show cracks that are the result of the earthquake shocks which sometimes visit here. The streets are narrow and the centre of the town is the market plaza. Until the opening of the railroad, which runs through the centre of the town, strangers were almost unknown and the quaint customs, costumes and habits still remain. The market and the river furnish the only life. The latter is always made lively and interesting to the stranger because of the crowds of bathers in the stream and washerwomen on the banks. It is an animated scene and has an air of naturalness devoid of any false ideas of modesty. These Indians belong to the Zapotec tribe and they are among the cleanest people in the world, as a race, as the long lines of bathers of both sexes from early dawn until nightfall attest. Woman's rights are recognized and undisputed among these people. The women run the place and do ninety per cent. of the business. The wife must vouch for the husband before he can obtain credit. In the market place where most of the bartering is done she reigns supreme.

The Isthmus of Tehuantepec is the narrowest neck of land in Mexico between the two great oceans and, with the exception of the Isthmus of Panama, is the narrowest point on the continent. The soil is extremely rich and the natural products and resources of the Isthmus are numerous and varied. All products indigenous to the tropics grow here. Different sections, according to elevation, are especially adapted to the cultivation of corn, cacao, tobacco, rice and sugar cane. Medicinal plants, spices, all tropical fruits, vanilla, indigo and cotton also will grow profitably in this climate. Cochineal dye has for a long time come from the Tehuantepec region, but this industry has been displaced by the more recent chemical dyes.

The forests abound in game and the rivers and lagoons in fish. The forests yield useful timbers, such as mahogany, also dyewoods and trees producing gums and balsams. Oil in paying quantities has been discovered in several places and the Tehuantepec National Railway, which crosses the isthmus, is one of the few roads in the world that uses oil for fuel. There are also profitable salt deposits. A great deal of American and European capital has been sunk in unsuccessful plantations along this route. This has been due to illogical and dishonest promotion. The fertile soil will produce immense crops of the things adapted for cultivation. With this fact in view it seems strange to see one abandoned plantation after another as you journey over the two hundred miles separating Coatzacoalcos and Salina Cruz, the two termini of the Isthmus of Tehuantepec trans-continental and inter-oceanic railroad route. In the matter of climate the Mexicans claim a great superiority for Tehuantepec over Panama, because of the strong winds that blow constantly from ocean to ocean.

For centuries this isthmus has attracted a great deal of attention from explorers and engineers in the effort to discover or provide the most convenient and economical route between the Atlantic and Pacific oceans. Cortez first realized the necessity of such a route and explored this whole section in the hope of finding a natural strait. It is even claimed that he conceived the idea of a canal across this narrow strip of land. Failing in these projects he planned a carriage road from coast to coast, which was finally constructed by the Spaniards. Many of the miners who flocked to California during the gold excitement went by this highway. Later civil engineers proposed and advocated a canal by this route even before the Panama route was seriously considered. The distance from ocean to ocean is only one hundred and twenty-five miles in a bee line. The land is comparatively level and the rise on the Atlantic side is very gradual culminating in the Chivela Pass at a height of seven hundred and thirty feet. From here to the Pacific the descent is more abrupt. A ship railway was at one time seriously considered and liberal concessions were granted by the Mexican government to the American engineer James B. Eads and his associates. This project although considered feasible by engineers has never been able to enlist capital for its construction.

The Panama Canal under French control was a colossal failure. A project which for a time seemed to promise a solution of the problem for a quick and economical route between the East and West ended in lamentable disgrace and for a long time remained in what one of our former presidents would have called, a condition of "innocuous desuetude." When the United States undertook this great enterprise, the completion of this desirable waterway was placed at ten years or even less. Now at the end of four years we are credibly informed that little has been done except the completion of plans, surveys, purchase of machinery and necessary sanitation. All of these preliminaries were essential and will greatly facilitate the real work when once started. All loyal Americans believe in the ultimate successful completion of this great undertaking. Yet, instead of ten years, we can see that fifteen years, or even twenty years would be a more accurate statement of the time necessary to complete the severing of the two continents. In the meantime, what?

While other countries have been planning, the Mexican government with the characteristic foresight shown by President Diaz has been quietly preparing to meet the problem of a short and economical route between the two oceans. This has been done without the blowing of horns and few people were aware until recently of what was being done and what had really been accomplished. The government of Mexico decided upon the plan of constructing a railway across the Isthmus from Coatzacoalcos, on the Gulf of Mexico, to Salina Cruz, on the Pacific Ocean, a distance of one hundred and ninety-four miles. Most railroads in tropical lands are narrow gauge but this line is constructed of standard width and was completed in 1895. When first opened to traffic the road was in a very imperfect condition. In 1899 a contract was entered into between the government and the English house of Pearson and Sons whereby the two parties became joint owners of the road for a period of fifty years and the net earnings should be shared on an equitable basis.

The construction was of a difficult character because the route passed through some cañons, rocky cuts and a great deal of swampy soil. The work has been well done and it is one of the best roads in Mexico to-day, with good equipment and traffic managed in an up-to-date and business-like manner. Already large orders for equipment have been placed and plans for double-tracking the entire road have been drawn. The headquarters and general offices are at Rincon Antonio, which is at the highest point and has the appearance of a typical new English town with its red brick terraces. This town receives the full benefit of the winds constantly blowing across the isthmus and enjoys a pleasant and salubrious climate. The shops and roundhouse for the railroad have been built at this place also and the employees are all comfortably housed. Some of the officers have built very commodious homes of their own, with every possible convenience. This town is in marked contrast with the old Mexican towns and villages along the route.

The general officers of the road and head men in the port works at both termini are all English and Americans. Formerly they were English, but in recent years the Americans have been replacing the English, as they have been found more satisfactory and better adapted for the work.

The government soon learned that the railway without good harbours was a poor proposition. The plans of the government were then made to include immense port works and safe, commodious harbours at Coatzacoalcos and Salina Cruz. At the former place the river forms a natural harbour of an average depth of fifty feet at low water. The only problem here was to remove a sand bar and construct piers. The work of removing the bar has been completed and several large steel wharves and warehouses have already been constructed and others are in course of construction. The total frontage of the wharves when completed will be over three thousand feet. It is intended to have a minimum depth of thirty-three feet alongside of the wharves which will be equipped with every modern contrivance for unloading cargo quickly and economically from ships, and transferring to the railroad and vice versa.

The work at Salina Cruz presented far greater problems. It has demanded the maximum of engineering skill and an immense sum of money. Here nature had aided in no way and everything had to be done by human effort. On account of severe wind storms it was deemed necessary to construct both an outer and an inner harbour in order to make a perfectly safe anchorage at all times and the work was begun in 1900. The outer harbour is being formed by thrusting two massive breakwaters like immense arms out into the bay with an entrance six hundred feet wide. The longest of these breakwaters will be three thousand feet, consisting of three sections, of different angles, with the convex sides toward the sea. The other is only one-half as extensive. The foundation for these breakwaters is started thirty feet below low water mark and in some places is two hundred feet in width. Upon a rubble foundation immense blocks of concrete and natural rock are placed at random. Then on top are placed regular rows of forty-ton concrete blocks. The amount of material already used and needed to complete this work is almost inconceivable. More than three-fourths of the largest breakwater is already completed. The inner basin will be wholly artificial and will occupy in part the site of the old town of Salina Cruz with an entrance ninety feet wide. Immense dredges are now at work on this basin which will be large enough to accommodate whole fleets of the largest vessels afloat. From two thousand to four thousand men have been and are still employed, the majority being natives.

Although the harbour at Salina Cruz is still incomplete, this route was formally opened on January 23rd, 1907. In the presence of a great throng of notables, including the representatives of twenty nations, President Diaz touched a lever which set in motion a steam winch that was used to carry the first load of cargo from a steamer to a freight car. After this car had been loaded it was transferred to Coatzacoalcos and the President touched another lever that set in motion the machinery for unloading the car and transferring the freight to a waiting steamer. In this manner was opened a route that is destined to take a prominent part in the handling of the world's commerce, and which has cost the Mexican government more than $25,000,000 in gold, and the end is not yet. After four hundred years the dream of Cortez has come true and the isthmian highway is open to the world.

What advantages are claimed for this route? The benefit to Mexico is self-evident. It will greatly facilitate the commerce between the two long coast lines of the republic. This great undertaking was not begun for the national trade alone. It is intended to compete for all that traffic which has heretofore gone around Cape Horn, through the Straits of Magellan, or across the Panama railroad. The Tehuantepec route is one thousand, two hundred and fifty miles shorter between New York and San Francisco than the Panama route. The average freight steamer would require from four to five days to cover this distance. The managers of the Tehuantepec National railroad propose to unload a cargo, carry it across the isthmus and reload it in two days. It will probably require one day for a vessel to pass through the Panama canal. This would make a net saving of from three to four days for the Tehuantepec route. The extra cost of loading and unloading would be made up by the saving of canal dues and expenses of the ship for that period. Thus there will be a net saving of three to four days in shipment, which might be quite a feature with many classes of freight. In cheapness of transportation, the continental railroads of the United States could not compete. Already contracts have been made with a line of steamers which have heretofore run between San Francisco, Hawaii and New York via Cape Horn to transfer their freight by this route. The government claims to have more freight in sight for 1907 than the Panama railroad has ever carried in a single year.

This route has been lost sight of in the enthusiasm over the Panama canal. It will be completed several years before the canal, and will during that interim, at least, have a great advantage over the present Panama railroad route. The same necessity of transhipment exists there, but without the fine, safe harbours, modern and commodious docks, and the quick loading and unloading machinery with which the Tehuantepec route is equipped.

NOTE TO REVISED EDITION. The success of the Tehuantepec National Railroad has greatly exceeded expectations, and it was found necessary to double track the entire length of the road. The improvements at Salina Cruz and Coatzacoalcos (now officially called Puerto Mexico) have been completed. Both cities have been made ports of call for all lines of steamers passing near. Through Pullman service is now maintained between the City of Mexico and Salina Cruz. Since writing the original edition of this book the writer has visited Panama and gone over the canal route with Colonel Goethals, the engineer in charge. It is a pleasure to record an appreciation of this great work, and to know that it will be ready for the world's fleets by 1915, and probably a year earlier. There will still be a wide field of usefulness, however, for the Tehuantepec National.

CHAPTER VIII
IN THE FOOTSTEPS OF THE ANCIENTS

"Builded on the ruins of dead thrones
Whose temple walls were old when Thebes was new;
On altars whose weird sacrificial stones
With ghastly offerings were crimsoned through;
Oblivion hides and holds thy secrets fast—
The dust of ages lies upon thy past,
        All wonderful, mysterious Mexico."[1]

Mexico is a land of ruins and the footprints of former races can be traced all over the southern half of the country. These ruins teach us that it must have taken many centuries to develop the land into the condition in which it was found by the Spaniards. It was not only the growth of a long time, but it was the product of the civilization developed by many different races and tribes. Otherwise Mexico would not be filled to-day with a hundred tribes speaking as many distinct dialects. There are many ruins of cities extending from the Valley of Mexico to the remotest corner of Yucatan, and many of them show evidences of wonderful structures that are the amazement of even the present generation. Not buried beneath volcanic lava, like Pompeii and Herculaneum, yet all are silent cities, for their inhabitants departed hundreds, perhaps, thousands of years ago. A few broken columns now remain where doubtless whole cities once stood.

Nothing is known of the history of these cities. The Spanish priests, with fanatical frenzy, destroyed all of the picture writings of the Aztecs that they could lay their hands upon. So many were destroyed, some chroniclers say, that great bonfires were made. What light these manuscripts might have cast upon the history of these early races cannot even be conjectured. As Prescott says, "it is impossible to contemplate these mysterious monuments of a lost civilization without a strong feeling of curiosity as to who were their architects and what is their probable age." They are undoubtedly very old, and some claim they are as old as the architecture of Egypt and Hindoostan. They have marked Eastern characteristics, as in the hieroglyphical writings at Palenque, in Yucatan, where are ruins of a palace and supposed holy city, with many sculptured figures of human and animal beings. The same is true of Uxmal, also in that same quaint and interesting corner of Mexico. These writings never have been and probably never will be deciphered. Then at Palenque can be traced the outline of the Roman cross which has greatly mystified antiquarians. We can only speculate on the origin of these monuments; whence came the people who constructed them; and in what period of the earth's history they were built; but speculation proves nothing and convinces nobody.

East of the City of Mexico about twenty-seven miles lies the village of San Juan Teotihuacan. Near this hamlet are traces of a great city covering more than four square miles, and remains of walls and fortifications, a part of the wall that still stands being more than two hundred feet thick and thirty-two feet high. The most marked features of these ruins are the numerous pyramids, great and small, which lie scattered over the plain. Teotihuacan means "City of the Gods," and doubtless these pyramidal structures were a necessary part of a holy city in the eyes of the race that constructed them, and were mounds of worship. Otherwise why would a race build such great structures at such an infinite cost of labour?

The largest of these numerous pyramids is called the "Pyramid of the Sun," which has a base seven hundred feet square, and a height of one hundred and eight-seven feet. The next largest is the "Pyramid of the Moon," which is one hundred and thirty-seven feet high, and has a base four hundred and fifty feet square. At a distance the pyramids seem rather insignificant, and their outlines resemble an ordinary steep-sided hill, but on nearer approach they are better appreciated. The comparison with the noted pyramids of Egypt would, at first glance, seem unfavourable, for the vegetation and vines that cover the sides rather hide the pyramidal outline. They were probably higher originally, but the destructive work of man and action of the elements have reduced the size. Recent investigation shows that these pyramids are built in layers of volcanic rock, cement, pottery and sun-dried brick. There are five layers—each layer being a complete pyramid in itself.

It is supposed that on the summit of each pyramid was a platform which supported great golden images of the sun and moon respectively, but no vestige of any such image has ever been discovered. If made of gold, and the Spaniards set their eyes on it, it would not have remained long. Authorities differ as to whether the Toltecs, or a race that preceded them, erected these mighty structures. The Mexican government has undertaken the work of restoring the two pyramids, and has appropriated a large sum of money to carry on the work. Several hundred labourers are now engaged in denuding them of the soil and growth of centuries that covers them.

Near Puebla, and situated in a rich and beautiful valley, of which mention has been made elsewhere, is the most noted pyramid in Mexico—that of Cholula. Legend says that it was built by a race of giants who intended to raise it to the very heavens themselves, but that the gods became displeased and destroyed them. It is very similar in nature to the Hebrew story of the Tower of Babel. Because of its great base, which is more than a thousand feet on each side, and covers twenty acres, and has a height of only one hundred and seventy-seven feet, it looks like a natural elevation that has been squared in places and levelled at the top rather than a pyramid. Like the other pyramids the sides are overgrown with trees and bushes. Examination shows that it has been constructed of sun-dried brick, clay and limestone. I quote the dimensions of two of the most famous Egyptian pyramids in order that the reader may better understand the comparative height and base of those and the Mexican structures:

	HEIGHT.	BASE ON EACH SIDE.
Cheops,	448 feet	728 feet
Mycerinus,	162 "	580 "
Cholula,	177 "	1,000 "
Sun	187 "	700 "
Moon	137 "	450 "

This valley was sacred in early times. Cortez says he counted four hundred towers in the city of Cholula (a much larger city then than now), and no temple had more than two towers. Above the city loomed the great pyramid, on the summit of which stood a sumptuous temple in which was the image of the mystic deity, Quetzalcoatl. He had "ebon features, wearing a mitre on his head waving with plumes of fire, with a resplendent collar of gold around his neck, pendants of mosaic turquoise on his ears, a jewelled sceptre in one hand, and a shield curiously painted, the emblem of his rule over the winds, in the other." This was the god who drew pilgrims and devotees by the thousands from the farthest corners of Anahuac.

This god was credited with power over rains, and was appealed to especially in time of drouth. Bandelier, who made an exhaustive study of this district, translates an early Spanish writer as follows: "To this god they prayed whenever they lacked water, and sacrificed to it children from six to ten years of age, whom they captured or bought for the purpose. When they sacrificed, they carried the children up the hill in procession, whither went some old men singing, and before the idol they cut the child open with a knife, taking out the heart, and they burnt incense to the idol and afterwards buried the baby there before the idol." Thus it is seen that the Nahuatl tribe, who occupied this valley, pursued the same bloody rites as the Aztecs.

The first act of Cortez was to destroy this temple and erect a Christian church on the spot, so that spires and crosses have replaced the pagan towers. All over the valley are many great churches so conspicuous in comparison with the humble homes of the natives. The view from the summit of this ancient structure is grand and imposing. John L. Stoddard is inspired by this scene and speaks as follows: "Whatever else of Mexico may be forgotten, I shall remember to my latest breath that wonderfully impressive vision from Cholula. Before me rose, against the darkening sky, a mighty cross, the sculptured proof that here Christianity had proved victorious; and as I lingered, my feet upon the Aztec pyramid, my hand upon the symbol of the conqueror's faith, my eyes turned towards that everlasting pinnacle of snow, I thought the lesson of Cholula to be this: that higher, grander, and far more enduring than all the different religions of humanity are the Eternal Power they imperfectly reveal; and that above the temples, pyramids, and crosses, which mark the blood-stained pathway of our race, rises a lofty mountain peak, whose glory falls alike upon the Aztec and the Spaniard, and in whose heaven-born radiance all races and all centuries may find their inspiration and their hope."

The Valley of Oaxaca seems to have been the favourite dwelling place of one or more of the early races of Mexico. All over the vales that centre at Oaxaca, and on the surrounding hills, are ruins of former cities and palaces that strongly resemble in outline and decoration the works of the Ptolemies and Pharaohs. Next to Mitla, the most noted ruins in this valley are those of

Monte Alban. The site of this ancient city is four miles from Oaxaca on the summit of a mountain, about eleven hundred feet above the valley. The ruins extend for a distance of more than a mile along the ridge, and enclose a great rectangular, depressed court nine hundred feet long, and three hundred feet in width. There are some well-preserved, sculptured stones with pictorial inscriptions, and images of gods. Because of its situation, which commands a complete view of these valleys in every direction, it is supposed that this place was intended for defence and a place of refuge in troublous times. The view from the summit is magnificent and well repays the traveller for a couple of hours' ride on the back of that sadly-wise, and much-maligned animal—the Mexican mule.

The village of Mitla is situated about twenty-five miles southeast of Oaxaca. It is best visited from that city by coach or mules. We hired a coach and driver, an unprepossessing looking outfit, and started on the journey.

"How long will it take?" I asked the driver.

"*A las doce*," he replied in idiomatic Spanish, meaning that we would arrive at twelve o'clock. As we had started at seven o'clock, that made it a five hours' journey.

About an hour's ride out of Oaxaca is the village of Tule, where, in the churchyard, and overshadowing the sacred structure, stands the famous Big Tree of Tule which deserves a passing notice. Although not a ruin, it is a relic of prehistoric days long gone by. This venerable giant is one of the largest trees in the world, exceeding in circumference the famous redwoods of California, and equalling the largest reported specimens of the gigantic baobab of Africa. This great tree is one hundred and fifty-four feet in circumference six feet above the ground. Twenty-eight people with their hands outstretched, and touching their finger tips, can just encircle its great girth. The height is one hundred and sixty feet, and the spread of the branches one hundred and forty feet. It is a species of the cypress called by the Aztecs *ahuehuete*. The great traveller, Humboldt, visited this tree about the middle of the last century and affixed a tablet containing his name and an inscription. As a proof that this old cypress is still growing, one sees that this tablet is now almost grown over with bark nearly a foot thick. Tule is a quaint village where the thatched huts are enclosed by fences of the prickly cactus, called *organo,* because of the resemblance of its branches to the pipes of an organ, and the lanes are shaded by trees. Underneath the higher trees grow the orange and lemon, while the oleander and other flowering bushes add their brightness to the scene.

After being held up for a road charge of seven cents by the officials of the village, which we paid, the driver is allowed to proceed. We pass through villages with the poetical names of Tlacolulu and Tlacochahuaya. As the coach bounces along the rough highway, over the road on a hillside are seen caves where human beings live who are literally cliff-dwellers. Then the valley opens up, and far ahead is seen San Pablo Mitla a typical Indian village built around the *hacienda* of Don Felix Quero, who is a sort of feudal lord over the neighbouring peons. Good entertainment is furnished for the traveller, and it is delightful to rest within the high walls of this hospitable stopping-place.

The first mention of the ruins at this village is by a Spanish writer nearly four centuries ago. His description would not be much amiss to-day. It is as follows: "We passed through a pueblo which is called Mictlan, signifying 'hell' in the native tongue, where were found some edifices more worth seeing than anything else in New Spain. Among them was a temple of the demon, and the dwelling of its attendants—very sightly, particularly one hall made of something like lattice work. The fabric was of stone, with many figures and shapes; it had many doorways, each one built of three great stones, two at the sides and one at the top, all very thick and wide. In these quarters there was another hall containing round pillars, each one of a single piece, and so thick that two men could barely embrace them; their height might be five fathoms."

To what purposes were these truly magnificent structures dedicated? Were they palaces, temples, tombs, fortresses, dwelling places, storehouses or places of refuge? Neither archeologists nor antiquarians have satisfactorily answered these questions. According to many of the leading archeologists they are the most interesting and best preserved ruins in North America. Here was a great city built by a race prior to the Aztecs, for that race could tell the Spanish conquerors nothing of its builders. The secrets guarded by the huge monoliths of stone, and the high mosaic-covered walls of Mitla are safe from prying eyes. Not one city alone stood here, for there are many remains of walls, columns and huge monoliths thrown down similar to these, scattered all over this valley. The best authority says that they were used for tombs but this could not have been the only use. They were probably also used for places of worship, public purposes, or cities of refuge, or perhaps for all those purposes.

ENTRANCE TO THE UNDERGROUND CHAMBER, MITLA

NORTH TEMPLE, MITLA

HALL OF THE MONOLITHS, MITLA

A close investigation shows that there are five distinct groups of the ruins, but some of them are in badly preserved condition. The village covers the site of a part of them. There is a similarity in the structure of all, as the outer walls are composed of oblong panels of mosaic forming arabesques and grecques. At first sight, or at a distance, it looks like sculptured designs on the walls. Closer inspection reveals the fact that this mosaic is formed of pieces of stone accurately cut and fitted into the face of the walls. These pieces are about seven inches in length, one inch in thickness, and two in breadth. The patterns cannot well be described as they are so complicated. All the ornamentation consists of geometrical figures, either rectangular or diagonal, and differs from all other ruins in Mexico, in that there are no human or animal figures.

There is an underground chamber beneath one of the temples, built in the shape of a cross with each arm about twelve feet long. The sides are worked into the same mosaic pattern as the rest of the walls. It is generally believed that these chambers were tombs, although some contend that they were the entrance to subterranean passages leading long distances away. If so, the passages were filled up long ago.

The northwestern group is in the best state of preservation. One of the buildings here covers nearly eight thousand square feet, and has all its massive walls intact with scarcely a stone thrown down. The characteristic entrance, consisting of three doors, side by side, is seen here also, fronting the interior of the court. The lintels are immense blocks of stone eighteen feet long, five feet wide and four feet high. How these immense stones were transported to this spot and raised without the aid of machinery, is as great a mystery as similar accomplishments by the Egyptians. Through these doors the famous Hall of Monoliths, or Columns, is reached. This is a wonderful relic of prehistoric architecture. The six monolithic columns, still standing in this room are each twelve feet in height and almost nine feet in circumference. They are plain stones having neither pedestal nor capital and are unique among the ruins of the world.

Torquemada, an old Spanish historian, writes of this hall in the following quaint style: "There was in those Edifices, or Square of the Temple, another Hall, all framed around Pillars of Stone; very high and so thick that scarce might two Men of good height embrace them so as to touch finger tips the one with the other. And these Pillars were all of one piece; and they say that all the Pillars and Columns, from top to bottom, was four Fathoms. The Pillars were very like to those of St. Mary, the Greater, of Rome, all very well and smoothly wrought." This hall is more than a hundred feet long, and twenty feet wide. These great stones may have supported a roof formerly but there is no evidence of it at the present time.

From the Hall of the Monoliths a dark, stone-covered passage leads into a room called the Audience Chamber. This is a splendid room with its walls in carved mosaics, or a setting of tiles, after the Grecian models. There are four long, narrow rooms, or corridors, on either side of this main chamber without other entrance except the one just mentioned. One of these, the West room, is most beautiful and is nearly perfect, as scarcely a tile is broken or missing from its exquisitely inlaid walls which at first inspection look like stucco work. The tiles are so accurately inlaid that no mortar was used, or needed, to hold them in place. This is the Corridor of the Mosaics. There are also traces of a lustrous, dark, red paint, used on a hard cement plaster. It is quite probable that all the buildings in the five groups were as carefully constructed and as exquisitely ornamented as this one, but they have been destroyed by succeeding races.

North of this group was another ruin on the walls of which a Christian church has been built. Most of the materials used in its construction came from this old temple or palace. The sacristy of this church is formed in part of a portion of the old building, and covered with a tile roof. This structure was the largest of all in size, extending over a space nearly three hundred feet long by one hundred feet wide, and with walls from five to six feet in thickness. One room is now used as a stable, and contains some strange hieroglyphics done in a lustrous red paint which have never been deciphered. These are the only semblance to anything like writing, or historical inscriptions, that appear anywhere in the ruins. In the centre of the main court is a hard cement pavement laid out in the form of a square with a cut stone border. This may have been intended for ornament or for human sacrifices. The latter conjecture might not be erroneous, knowing, as we do, the customs of those early Mexican races.

There are many other evidences of ruins near Mitla. Clay idols, or images, made of terracotta are found all over the neighbourhood. Children hunt for specimens and bring them to tourists for sale. It is also said that many stone wedges, and copper chisels and axes, have been discovered here but I did not see any of them.

A ZAPOTECO WOMAN

Who built these ruins? Bancroft, the historian of Mexico, says that they were built by the Zapotecs at an early period of their civilization. The Indians now inhabiting this valley are Zapotecs and they are a primitive, simple and harmless race. If these people, who now dwell in thatch hovels and caves, were the once proud race that erected these magnificent structures, then we must say, "How have the mighty fallen." What must these structures have been in the heyday of their prosperity that they are now so glorious in their mellow decay? The famous Palace of the Alhambra, glorious monument to the genius of the Moor, is scarcely more magnificent than these ruins lying here within the little Indian village of Mitla. The traveller can give his imagination full play for there is no written history to destroy the scenes he creates. He can in fancy re-create these beautiful structures; people these courts and halls with royalty, priests or warriors; make the air vocal with the chants of priests or shrieks of the victims of human sacrifice; and there is no one or no record to rebuke him.

CHAPTER IX
WOMAN AND HER SPHERE

The life and position of woman in Mexico varies much by reason of the heterogeneous character of the population. Because of the absence of a clearly defined middle class it is a fairly safe proposition to say that there are but two classes in Mexico, Creoles and Indians. Creoles include all those who are Europeans or in whom the European blood predominates. Domestic life among the Creole class savours of the East. The ideas with respect to women are Moorish rather than American. Although not obliged to appear on the street with face enshrouded in a shawl or veil, yet the young woman who has respect for her good name would not go abroad without the *duenna,* or some female companion. Another reminder of Oriental exclusiveness is seen in the life of the ladies of the wealthier classes who always drive in closed carriages even in this land of balmy air and splendid sunshine and, when shopping, do not deign to leave the carriage.

On account of the restrictions against the appearance of women in public, the custom grew up in Spain and Mexico of allowing them to use the windows and balconies for observation. In the cool of the evening the windows on the streets are opened and women, especially the young ladies, appear there to watch the carriages and passers-by and nod to their friends. The home life and social restrictions toward women are inherited from Spanish ancestors who were at one time the aristocracy and ruling class of Mexico. Nowhere is the sentiment of home stronger than among the Creoles. There may be no such word as home in his vocabulary but the *casa,* or house, of the Mexican is his castle and he protects it in every way from prying eyes. One writer has expressed his view as follows:—"The intense feeling of individuality which so strongly marks the Spanish character and which in the political world is so fatal an element of strife and obstruction, favours this peculiar domesticity. The Castillian is submissive to his king and his priest; haughty and inflexible with his equals. But his own house is a refuge from the contests of out of doors."

In the home the father is absolute lord and master and all bow to him. There never comes a time when the children are not subject more or less to parental authority. Yet, in general, the sway is so mild that it is readily yielded to and is scarcely felt. Grown-up sons and daughters do not forget the respect and obedience that was expected of them when they were children. The reverence for parents increases with the passing of the years. A man never grows too old to kiss the hand of his aged mother. The old lady dressed in sombre black and who looks like a poor relation may be the one whose wishes rule. Harmony does not exist in every family and the exceptions are striking ones. Where quarrels and family dissensions do occur, the pride and jealousy of the race renders them the bitterest and fiercest in the world. These vindictive feuds in families frequently led to duels and stabbing affrays to defend personal honour and dignity in former days. A man and wife will often live for years beneath the same roof without speaking. They cannot be divorced but neither will speak the first word and each rather admires the grit of the other.

The home life is jealously shielded from curious eyes. In no place in the world is the social circle more closely guarded than among the higher classes in the City of Mexico. The thick walls, the barred, prison-like windows and the massive, well-guarded doors prevent intrusion and perhaps serve to foster this inclination to lead exclusive lives. Cultured Americans, unless in the official set, who have lived there for years have found it impossible to break into these exclusive circles. Whether this action is due to jealousy, diffidence, a feeling of superiority, or aversion to aliens the fact remains that they are very loth to admit Americans into the privacy of their homes. The foreigner has few opportunities of judging intelligently of the women for they are immured so closely within the four walls of their dwellings. Social life in the semi-public, gregarious ways of American cities is unknown and would not suit these privacy-loving, domestic women.

In "The Awakening of a Nation" the author, Mr. C. F. Lummis, gives a very good description of the Creole woman: "Always and everywhere the Spanish-American female face is interesting; at least as often as in other bloods it is beautiful. Photographs tell but half the story, for complexion is beyond them. But a certain clearness of feature, the almost invariable beauty of the eyes and fine strength of the brows seem as much a Spanish birthright as the high-bred hand and foot. Not even the Parisian face is so flexible in expression, so fit for archness, so graphic to the mood. Yet there is a certain presence in it not to be unnoticed, not to be forgotten. To no woman on earth is religion a more vital, ever-present, all-pervading actuality; and that is why you meet the face of the Madonna almost literally at every corner in Spanish-America. And it is not a superficial thing. There is none to whom the wife-heart, the mother-heart is truer-womanly."

The Mexican men are passionate admirers of the fair sex. Perhaps it is because of the bewitchery of their black, sparkling eyes. Certainly it is not on account of the white paste which is plastered over their faces or the rouge on their lips. Nor have they added to their attractiveness by the substitution of the Parisian hat for the graceful lace mantilla which lent itself so well to the gentle art of coquetry. There are many handsome women among the Creoles but they are not all beautiful as some writers would lead the reader to infer. They are bright, vivacious and naturally clever. They have a quick understanding which only needs to be cultivated and perhaps this intelligence is quicker and more active than that of the men. They can weave and embroider with taste and skill. They know a little music and a little French but, in the American sense, they are not well educated. The real intellectual element is wanting and the understanding is uncultivated. The higher education for women has not received the stamp of approval in this land of "to-morrow" and the sex has not yet become an important factor in the business or professional world. "If only learned wives," says one, "are responsible for that poor, down-trodden, pitiable specimen of man called the henpecked husband, then a timid man would be safe in choosing a Mexican wife." The patriarchal element of society in which man is recognized as lord and master is still in force among these people. The question of woman's rights has never yet agitated the bosoms of these gentle women.

Domestic freedom in the sense understood by Americans is absent. The daughters are closely watched by their mothers who seldom permit them out of their sight unless accompanied by some older woman or faithful servant. Such a thing as permitting a daughter to have a young man call on her or accompany her to the theatre would never enter the mind of the Mexican mother. In her estimation the men do not deserve any confidence until they are married. The man, of course, thinks that these precautions are unnecessarily cruel. Nevertheless mammas think they are essential, pater familias approves and so the custom remains. Perhaps it is these restrictions that are responsible for the reputation the *señoritas*, or young women, have of being flirts or coquettes. They are overflowing with life and spirits and their black eyes look so full of mischief that sometimes they seem to be just spoiling for a flirtation. They are very animated in conversation and in talking keep time with hands, knees, shoulders, elbows and face. Their talk is full of the most extravagant and seemingly profane expressions.

"Oh, Jesus!" says one girl, "what a fetching hat."

"Mary Most Pure," replies her companion, "it must have cost five pesos."

They can stare an American out of countenance and look him straight in the eye but it is only a look of curiosity. The social pleasures resulting from the intermingling of the sexes that are so common with us are not enjoyed by them. At a dance the men retire to one side of the room after a number and the women take seats on the opposite side. Marriages among the wealthier classes are generally made by the parents without consultation with the principals in an affair supposed to be of the hearts. After the formal engagement the intended husband is allowed to call on his fiancée in the presence of the entire family and may take her out to the theatre when accompanied by the mother and all the female members of the household. Marriage is a formidable undertaking for the groom must furnish the entire bridal outfit, in addition to the house and its furnishings. Two ceremonies become necessary, too, if the couple wish to be married by the rites of the church. The civil ceremony is absolutely essential and cannot be dispensed with for under the law this is the only legal marriage. And yet with all these inconveniences to courtship and matrimony, bachelors are less numerous than they are where every facility is granted for love making.

Love and religion are practically the only two subjects with which a *señorita* is expected to concern herself. She is, probably, not intentionally or by nature a flirt and she might scorn to inveigle in her meshes the heart of an admirer, but she cannot refrain from using her irresistible eyes or entirely avoid the coquettish use of the indispensable fan with its wordless telegraphy. The Mexican lover pays extravagant homage to his sweetheart and a woman nowhere else is paid such delicate and elaborate compliments. The Spanish method of courtship in which the lady is pictured as sitting at a barred window or leaning from a balcony to listen to the honeyed phrases of her lover or the music of his guitar has reached its highest state of perfection in Mexico.

In the current language of that country a man who is courting a woman is "playing the bear." It is so named from the restless walking to and fro of the love-stricken youth in front of the window of his inamorata, in a manner not unlike a captive bear in a cage. The same method pursued in the United States would either result in a man being sent to the lunatic asylum as suffering from a "brain storm" or to the workhouse.

"PLAYING THE BEAR"

A young man who sees a young lady on the street whom he admires, begins by following her home although it may be days or weeks before he will venture to speak to her. Having reached her *casa* he will begin the *hacer el oso,* or "playing the bear," by walking back and forth in front of the house or standing on the street with his eyes fixed upon her windows or balconies for hours at a time, days and nights alike. The young lady, if interested at all, will remain back of the curtain and the slightest movement of the curtains or blinds is a sign that she is not entirely indifferent. After a day or two she may show her face or wave her hand as a further mark of encouragement, and after several days she may appear on the balcony for a few moments. If she goes to church the lover is probably not far behind and an occasional smile or glance from her eyes of midnight is given him as a reward for his faithfulness. Next come daily salutes and smiles when the lover appears. Flowers are sent by the aid of the water-carriers or charcoal-vendors in which notes are concealed. A system of wireless-telegraphy communication is established by means of a fan on one side and a cigarette on the other. This medium of communication has been developed until it has become an elaborate code. Letters become more and more endearing. When the courtship has so far advanced that the lovers will talk, the moonlight nights are all devoted to the love-making and several pairs of lovers can be seen on almost any street by the late home-comer—he on the sidewalk, she at the window. This courtship frequently extends over a period of years and the lover who makes himself so ridiculous sometimes loses the girl then. Jacob's seven-year probation has many counterparts among the Romeos of Mexico.

A young woman of my acquaintance and her sister recently visited a family in one of the large cities in Mexico. Like all young women they soon became interested in the subject of Mexican courtship and began to sigh for a "bear." Every time they returned from a trip down town a watch was kept from the window to see if a "bear" followed. At last one of these creatures appeared and began to pace in front of the house with his eyes bent upon the window opening out on the balcony. Contrary to all precedents and to the surprise of the neighbourhood, these women could not resist the temptation to go out on the balcony on this first occasion. This was such marked encouragement that the man came day after day to see *las Señoritas Americanas* and was still coming when their visit ended.

American women who have married Mexican husbands have found the ideas of the two races so radically opposed that the unions have not been harmonious. Their verdict is that a Mexican man makes an ideal lover because of his delicate attentions and consideration, but an unsatisfactory husband since he does not make his wife a companion and confidante such as an American woman considers her right and privilege.

The individuality of the woman is not so completely merged in that of her husband at marriage as in the United States. The woman retains her own name but adds that of her husband. Miss Mary Smith who marries Mr. John Jones becomes Mrs. Mary Smith de Jones, and she is not called so exclusively by her husband's name. However, when the Mexican woman is married she accommodates herself to the station in life provided by her husband. The wife usually accepts whatever condition fate has provided for her and bears it with patience and fortitude. They endure the petty ills of life with great cheerfulness. They do not go into society much as custom keeps them from attending mixed assemblages frequently. Their world is generally confined to their home, husband and children. An American woman would sigh for liberty if compelled to live this life. The Mexican woman in America shrinks from the freedom prevalent here and desires the seclusion of her native land. Families are usually large so that home duties require a great deal of attention. The respect and courtesy paid by children to their parents is truly delightful to witness and shows a real goodness of heart in them.

The mother cannot bear to see her family separated. She wants them all to stay close together so that each one can stop in and see her every day. The mothers are loving and tender and idolize their boys. It is regarded as a terrible thing, scarcely to be borne, for their sons to go out into the world as American youths do. To go to a distant city is like being transported to Australia. Even when they remain near home the mothers are very solicitous for fear they will work too hard. On each saint's day, which is religiously observed, presents are given and an old-fashioned dinner, to which all the cousins, aunts and uncles are invited, is served. In starting on a journey to a not-distant city, the youth must visit all his relatives in the neighbourhood and bid adieu.

It is interesting to notice these traits in an age of growing indifference; but not a little of the lack of progress in Mexico can be attributed to this unwillingness to sever home ties. Many of these young men could do better for themselves away from home but a mother's pleadings and a mother's tears keep them at home. Even after marriage they frequently continue to live under the same roof.

The religious element enters very largely into the life of women. Their very names are a constant reminder of their worship. Many of them are christened Mary with one of the attributes of the Virgin or some incident in the life of the Virgin added such as Conception, Annunciation, Sorrows or

Assumption. Or there are the attributes such as Mary of the Sorrows, of the Gifts, Miracles, Tears, etc. Religion is sustained by the women and you will seldom see men at the services unless it is some poor Indian. They are very pious in their way and attend to their religious duties with the same interest that they perform their toilet. The concrete symbols and observances of the church have a great influence over them. At mass these pious worshippers always dress in sombre black. They are very particular in training their children in the principles of the Church. Formerly great faith was placed in the healing power of certain shrines and relics but this is now dying out under the advance of modern physicians and their healing remedies. They are still great believers in signs, omens and other supernatural manifestations.

Above all these women are kind hearted and charitable. Though carefully guarding their homes, yet if a stranger is admitted into the family he is received with a generous welcome. Should he return after long absence, he is greeted almost as one of the family and without reservation. He is not only permitted but encouraged to call all the members by their given names and to use the pronoun *tu* or "thou" in his intercourse with them. This is an especial privilege among Spanish people who are very particular about familiarity in address. They will oftentimes deprive themselves for a friend. They have their faults too. Although smoking is not countenanced in public it is said that many of them smoke in their boudoirs and in the company of friends of their own sex. A great deal has been said of their lack of morality but this is a subject upon which only those very familiar with the facts should dare to speak, for it cannot be treated lightly, or solely with the intention of casting a slur on another race.

WASHING ON THE BANKS OF A STREAM

The lives of the Indian women of Mexico present a far different picture. Instead of living in great palaces, their homes are in little adobe cabins of one room, perhaps without the luxury of a window, or in bamboo huts covered with plantain leaves without chairs or table and only a mat of husks for a bed. There is no seclusion in their lives and the real duties of life begin at a very early age. I cannot call them serious duties for it is doubtful if these people regard any of the obligations of life as very serious. Their early experiences are with its hard realities. They can be seen on the streets and around their homes with baby brothers or sisters swung across their backs when they themselves are so small that the burden seems far too heavy for them. On the banks of the streams they can be seen doing the family washing with a great amount of rubbing and pounding and wringing. To the fountains and wells they come carrying earthen jars on their heads, which they fill with water and replace with a grace and charm that excites admiration.

Some of the Indian maids are handsome. Yet you can tell just what their future lives will be by observing those of the parents. They will live in the same squalor, the same poverty as their ancestors have dwelt for centuries.

They will go through life bareheaded and barefooted and empty-minded just as the generations which preceded have done. At twenty they have begun to fade and at thirty they retain scarcely a trace of their beauty. This is due to hard labour and deprivations. At fourteen few are unmarried or at least unmated. The marriage ceremony is frequently omitted because of the high charges of the priesthood, yet both parties are usually faithful. The number of children among this class is truly marvellous. More than one half of the younger women when seen on the street have infant children with them.

No people could be more poorly housed or more poorly equipped for domestic duties than these small brown women; and none use the little they have to better advantage or are more loyal to the man they call lord and master. They frequently live and sleep on the bare ground and possess no more clothing than they have on their bodies. They will pound away at the *metate*, or stone kneading-board, all day making the *tortillas* which are both bread and meat to the peon class. These comely Indian women will bend their lithe, active bodies for hours washing clothes on large round stones which serve as wash-boards.

Their clothes are simple and the latest fashion has no attraction. The *rebosa* is a universal garment and answers for a shawl, a carry-all for babies and bundles, and a covering for the owner at night. These black-eyed women with their half-concealed faces, sober, unemotional manners, high-coloured garments and curious Egyptian-shaped pottery might well be from the shores of the Red Sea. Their love of warm, bright colours is even seen in their love for flowers since the many-hued, brilliant-coloured blossoms are everywhere. Mignonettes and roses, flowering geraniums and scarlet poppies, gigantic oleanders and dainty pansies share attention with the brilliant-hued tropical birds in gayest colours which usually hang beside the open door in a home-made cage of dried rushes. They are faithful workers in fancy work and will follow the most intricate design and reproduce it with fidelity and ease. Their art needle work on handkerchiefs and other linen articles is extremely fine and their drawn work is praised everywhere. It is not the work of the dainty fingers of educated women but of very humble and ignorant peon women in floorless cabins of adobe and of hands accustomed to drudgery.

The women of Tehuantepec are remarkable for their beauty of face and form. They are easily the finest looking Indian women in America and in beauty of figure will compare with any race in the world. They are dark-skinned, almost a soft olive-brown, with sparkling dark eyes, masses of wavy hair, exquisite features and beautiful teeth, which are kept clean and white. Their carriage will attract attention, for they walk erect and with a peculiar stride probably due to the prevailing habit of carrying baskets and water jars always on the head, where they are carefully balanced. They are small in stature, with fine limbs, and seem born models for an artist.

The "Tehuanas" wear a quaint head-dress called "huepil," which is made of coarse white lace. It is arranged in three different ways according to the occasion. At a dance it is wound round the neck and stands out like a huge Elizabethan ruff. In church it is put on the head something like a Boulogne fish-wife's cap. For ordinary wear it is simply laid back on the hair and the folds hang down the back resembling somewhat the feather head-dress of a North American Indian chief. It is indeed curious but is quite befitting. They always dress becomingly, with the quaint little short jackets which expose a section of brown back above the skirt band and are cut low about the neck in a fashion that women the world over have found graceful, and with extremely short sleeves. On extraordinary occasions this short jacket, or waist, is of richer material embroidered in handsome designs of brilliant colours. Some of the designs show oriental characteristics. The skirt of the dress is of soft material, linen or cotton, to the knees and below the knees is of a heavy lace or embroidery starched very stiff. The material used is not the usual cheap and gaudy fabrics sold to the Mexican Indian, but is of good quality and specially made by a certain Manchester house for these people.

These belles of Tehuantepec have a great liking for American gold coins which are worn on necklaces. British sovereigns or French napoleons are usually not desired, but a big premium will be paid for the eagle, half eagle, or double eagles of Uncle Sam. Every centavo that a woman can save goes into her fund for purchasing gold pieces. The gorgeous necklace with the gold coins attached makes a showy and rather beautiful ornament. The fortune and standing of a "Tehuana" is indicated by the number of gold coins on her necklace. One Tehuantepec heiress has—it is said—a necklace which is valued at three thousand dollars. The most striking feature in the dress of these women is that not one will wear shoes. Dressed in all her finery, head-dress, starched skirt, polka-dot waist, necklace and smile, she will appear barefooted—a strange anomaly. Without shoes they will dance over a stone floor, or even a dirt, gravel-bestrewn surface, with a grace that violates all rules of art. These dusky princesses will be found as graceful as gazelles on all occasions.

A visit to Tehuantepec will long be remembered for it is an experience not easily forgotten. The quaint costumes, the striking dress, and the proud people combine to make a memory worth carrying away.

CHAPTER X
THE PEON

"And I have said, and I say it ever,
As the years go on and the world goes over,
'Twere better to be content and clever
In tending of cattle and tossing of clover,
In the grazing of cattle and growing of grain,
Than a strong man striving for fame or gain;

...

For these have the sun, and moon, and air,
And never a bit of the burthen of care;
And with all our caring what more have we?"

The distinction between the American and Mexican Indian is not one of colour alone. There is also a difference in nature. The American Indian has never been fully subdued, but the Aztecs were conquered by one overwhelming blow and their spirit crushed. The conquest wrought vast changes in the lives of these people who once roamed over large estates which they could call their own. The lands then tilled by their slaves, they themselves now cultivate for others. Yet they are a satisfied people, and no one ever hears them complain. Though poverty is their lot they are content, believing that some people are born rich and others poor, and that this contrast is in the very nature of things.

Centuries of neglect have not improved either the moral or physical condition of the peon, but it has not made a misanthrope of him. Neither has the fact that he bears no part in the government made him an anarchist or filled his pockets with bombs. So long as a beneficent providence provides present needs he is supremely content. The mania for the almighty dollar has not yet entered into his life so that envy of others does not exist. It is this envy that makes poverty a menace and element of danger in our own land. The peon neither feels shame for his own lowly condition nor desires pity from others in more prosperous circumstances.

A PEON AND HIS WIFE

Fully one-third of the population of Mexico are full-blooded Indians and another one-half are *mestizos*, those of mixed blood. Many of the latter and a number of pure-blooded Indians have reached high positions. A number of the presidents also, including Guerrero and the noble Juarez, were pure Indians, and more of them are representatives of the *mestizos*. This is proof that there is no prejudice against the Indians as a race such as the anti-negro sentiment in the Southern States. These illustrious examples are, however, the striking exceptions. Most of them are in about the same category as the southern negroes,—a race without ambition. Content to be the servants of another race they neither court nor welcome change.

These people make up the great peon class of Mexico who constitute the bulk of the population. They are the descendants of those who were enslaved by the early conquerors. The Aztecs were an industrious people as the great structures erected by them, the irrigating works still in use, and the evidences of judicious and careful cultivation of every foot of tillable soil bear mute witness. Poverty was almost unknown among them and rigid laws existed against begging. Among some of the early tribes of Mexico one-third of the land was divided equally among the able-bodied men in proportion to the families they had to sustain. Provision was made by the State for the sick and other classes of unfortunates. No doubt the enslaving of these people had a weakening effect upon their character.

A natural laziness, ignorance and a lack of interest will probably always keep down the peon's efficiency as a worker. The few and simple wants of his nature and his general contentment eliminate to a great extent the desire to improve his condition and accumulate property. Then, too, the evenness of the climate and the fact that at all times some crop is being harvested, thus making it unnecessary to lay up for an unproductive season, has had its influence. The labourer is usually given a certain task for his day's work. Nothing can induce him to do more than that task except the assurance that the excess, or over-time, will be credited to some future day so that he will get a longer holiday. These labourers are cheap and it requires many of them to accomplish much but there are millions to be had. They are happy-go-lucky and are unconcerned for the future. Yet the very fact that they do not possess self-control and are always willing to follow a leader who understands how to make an appeal to their prejudices or fanaticism, renders this class a serious obstacle to a progressive government and one that must be intelligently studied.

The little brown man in the tall, broad-brimmed hat which seems to give an unusual height to his sturdy frame is a picturesque figure and the landscape is not complete without him. In the presence of strangers his face is solemn, but among others of his own kind he is gay and light-hearted, his face easily bursting into smiles. He will wrap his tattered shawl about him with as much dignity as the Spanish cavalier his richly-embroidered *manta*.

The act of lighting a cigarette is a matter of studied ceremony. He will light a match, and first offer it to a friend with punctilious politeness. The recipient of the favour never fails to return *muchas gracias* (many thanks), señor. In fact, this elaborate politeness between these untidy, ill-clad Indians becomes a farce-comedy at times. He is polite and never fails to say *con permiso* (with your permission) if he is obliged to pass by another person, whether that person be in silks or rags. His own inferiority is admitted by calling a white man a *gente de razon* or "one who reasons," as distinguished from himself,—a peon.

The peon is indispensable in Mexico for he is not only the labourer, but the body servant as well. In the latter capacity, if he becomes attached to his employer, he will not think of his own wants until the master is provided for, and will be faithful unto death, if necessary. His wages are always small, but he is satisfied with the little he gets. Gambling is a natural trait and he loses or gains with a stoicism worthy of greater things. His money is likewise spent freely at the pulque shop so that his finances are never embarrassed by a surplus. A little money will make him very full of liquor, and a little liquor will sometimes make him a bad man to handle.

The tenacity with which these people cling to an environment is a most notable trait. The peon is a lover of locality. Seldom can these Indians be induced to go away from their accustomed habitations. It is this trait that has made peonage an easy system to maintain in Mexico. They do not apply much intelligence to their work. Scratching the surface of the soil with a crooked stick is the perfection of ploughing in their estimation. The peon does not know and does not care to learn any different way of doing his work than the one taught him by his fathers. The possibility of earning more money by the use of labour-saving devices does not possess the same attraction as for the American labouring man.

Peonage, which is a mild form of slavery, is in force in Mexico. Earning from eighteen to fifty cents (silver) wages per day and improvident by nature, it is only natural for the peon to want at some time a little more money than that earned. An unscrupulous employer can easily involve the poor, ignorant Indian in a net of debt. After a while a debt of $50 to $100 has accumulated and the worker is in bondage until this amount is paid. It is an impossible sum for him to save out of his small wages, for live he must and support a family, which is usually large. The price of freedom is the total amount of the debt. Until that is paid the law compels him to work for his creditor, but he is free to get some one else to advance this money and change masters. He cannot be separated from his family, nor compelled to leave the plantation on which the debt was incurred without his consent. The owner may, however, sell the plantation and transfer the debt to his successor, and the peon must serve the new master under the same conditions.

On the immense *haciendas* of the uplands the peons are almost as much of a fixture as the buildings themselves. It is a strange adaptation of the old feudal relation and the idea of changing their abode never occurs to them. They were born in debt, always remain in that condition, and transmit the same burden to their posterity. This condition is usually entered into voluntarily by the Indians, so that in the beginning he has only himself to blame. An Indian who desires work will apply to the manager of a plantation or ranch for a retainer which seldom exceeds thirty dollars. He then signs a contract which binds himself, his family and his posterity to work until this advance is liquidated. Only a small part of the weekly wages may be applied on the debt, and it is tacitly understood that the debt may be increased after a time. The employer is obliged to furnish medical assistance free in case of sickness, and to advance the necessary fees for marriage, baptisms, confirmations and burials. Furthermore, whenever overtaken by old age and no longer able to work, the peon must be taken care of and furnished the necessities of life.

Holidays, feast-days and saint-days are many, and the peon insists on celebrating them all. Whether he understands much of the ritual and doctrines of the Catholic Church or not, he understands full well the meaning of a feast-day or "*fiesta*" for on that day he rests from his labours. It would not be patriotic to work on a national holiday (and they are numerous) so he abstains from labour on these occasions. Sundays are rest days and it generally requires Monday to recuperate from the effects of the *pulque* or *tequila* imbibed on that day. Then as each person has a patron saint, he insists on celebrating the saint-days of the master, mistress and each one of their family, of his own family, his father, mother, his wife's father and mother, and, last, but not least, his own saint-day. Then each marriage, birth or death in the family gives occasion for another off-day. After this list is gone through with there remains only about two hundred working days for the average labourer. The peon is a philosopher. Knowing that it was a curse that man should earn his bread by the sweat of his brow, he tries to avoid as much of the curse as possible.

The system of peonage or contract labour in the tropics is revolting and often inhuman. The peon of the hot country is more independent, is fond of social life and is not so industrious as his brother in the uplands. Hence it becomes necessary to transport hundreds of labourers for work on tropical plantations. These are secured through contract agents who make this work a business. These agents pick them up over the country and deliver them in hundred lots to the plantation managers. The contractor advances from thirty to fifty dollars in silver to each labourer, and this amount together with his own fee, is then charged up against the peon who has contracted to work six months at perhaps fifty cents per day in the same white metal. The plantation manager binds himself to furnish rations, which usually consist of little more than *tortillas* (unleavened corn cakes), beans and rice and a little meat for Sunday, and a big palm hut will furnish accommodation for fifty or more men. But little space is allowed each worker, and here he spends all his time when not at work, for these contract men are, on many plantations, kept under guard night and day by armed overseers. Many of these poor fellows come from cities on the plateaus and soon fall a victim to tropical fevers. Many are men who have been convicted of petty offences and sign a labour contract in return for the payment of their fines by the contractor's agent and consequent release from confinement. All, however, are treated alike on the plantations and are worked under the lash if necessary. At the end of the six months, there are not many dollars due the poor peon after deducting the price of the drinks and cigarettes which he has purchased at the company's store. After drawing his money he is likely to make for the first town and drink or gamble it away. Then, not having funds enough to get home, he is again at the mercy of the contract agent or plantation owner.

The little brown man with back bent under a load has a countenance which is as full of rest and patient philosophy as a modern financier's face is of care and wrinkles of anxiety. It is almost unfair to the simple-minded, patient and docile peon of Mexico to speak of him as an Indian for he is at once confused with the bloodthirsty redskin of the north. He is a peaceful, if improvident, character, and is a child in nature. He represents cheap labour and is one of the great attractions that brings wealth to Mexico. After a day's work he is content to share his little adobe hut with the pigs and chickens, and can even find room for the chance wayfarer. A family of three or four generations, and numbering twenty people, will live in a hut that would not be considered a fit habitation for a donkey in the north. One American writer who was obliged to seek shelter in one of these huts gives an amusing account of his experience which shows the harmony and good-fellowship that exists in these households between the human and brute members. "I took an account of the stock before I turned in, and found there were three dogs, eleven cats, seven children, five men (not including five of us), three women and a dozen chickens, all sleeping, or trying to sleep, in the same room, under the one roof. And when I gave up sleeping, or trying to sleep, and wandered out into the night, I stepped on the pigs and startled three or four calves that had been sleeping under the porch." So it is not surprising that a village of fifty huts may contain a thousand souls.

A cigarette given in proper spirit every day will more effectually keep his friendship than a present of a new suit of clothes. The latter will not be remembered long while the former keeps the memory ever fresh. They have been called the best and the poorest servants in the world. A trusted servant is, however, usually an honest one. These wholly satisfied people with whom our essentials are non-essentials rather disprove the theory that modern civilization is necessary to true happiness. Will the peon in the future wearing shoes, eating prepared breakfast foods and sleeping in a bed, be any happier than he is now barefooted and sleeping on a rush mat spread on an earthen floor?

A constantly increasing number of the peon class are moving to the industrial centres. Slowly but surely the leaven is working, and the opportunity for better wages is withdrawing the labourers from the plantations. The railroads, the mines and the factories are paying much higher wages than formerly prevailed, and find it difficult to secure sufficient labourers. Only the selected men can fill these positions for the average peon has not sufficient intelligence. He has a great imitative faculty and can learn a task, but is not a success in an employment that needs the exercise of reason and judgment. In many lines of work more is accomplished at less expense by peons with the rudest methods than by the use of the latest labour-saving machinery operated by peon labourers.

Education will no doubt work great changes in the lives and habits of these people, but this will be a slow process in this land of "to-morrow." The present conditions are interesting to one who desires to see how the rest of the world lives, and it will be a long time before the peon class will change very materially.

There is one class of the Indian worker that deserves more extended mention. This is that time-honoured institution called the cargador. As you meet him at every place throughout Spanish North America it may be interesting to the reader to learn something of his history and his accomplishments. It is not necessary to institute a search for the cargador. At the station you will be besieged by a small army of them and the hotel entrance may be blocked by them. When travelling across the country there is a never-ending succession of these picturesque characters singly and in groups. Sometimes the entire family is along. In such cases the boys, even down to little tots, carry a small package on their backs and the wife and girls balance a basket on their heads. Perhaps all their earthly belongings are contained in these various bundles.

The cargador of Mexico and Central America claims an ancient and honourable lineage. His occupation may be a humble one, but he can trace his ancestry back to the followers of that haughty Aztec emperor, Montezuma, or even to the still older race of the Toltecs. Not many years ago almost everything in these countries was carried on the backs of cargadors. Even now in the City of Mexico the cargador is an indispensable factor in the carrying trade, though there are many express and transfer companies engaged in that business. In the smaller places of Mexico, in the mountain districts, and in Central America he holds his old-time prestige and, with the cargo mule, monopolizes the carrying business.

The strength of these little, brown-skinned cargadors is wonderful. Short in stature and with thin legs and arms they look very insignificant. They cannot lift a very heavy weight, but they can make their fairer-skinned brother cry out in astonishment at the load they will carry when it is once adjusted on their back. The average load for a cargo mule is one hundred and fifty pounds. A cargador will start on a journey of two hundred or more miles with such a load and will cover more miles in a day over a rough mountain trail than a mule. At the station you will see the little cargador pick up a heavy trunk that you can scarcely move and start off with it at a faster pace than you care to walk. They always move in a peculiar jog-trot, and can usually keep it up for a long time. Up and down hill they go at an even pace, and will average about six miles per hour. For short distances some cargadors will carry as great a load as five hundred pounds, a seemingly impossible burden for so slender a body.

The strength in the back is a matter of training extending over many centuries. The Aztecs had no beasts of burden and the baggage of their armies was always carried by cargadors. The Spanish conquerors were obliged to adopt the same methods. Now, although there are mules and burros in great numbers, the cargador is still the great burden bearer and takes the place of the fast freight in the commerce of those sections away from the railway lines. A traveller can take his mule and send his baggage by a cargador, and the latter will reach the same stopping place each night and sometimes ahead of the man on the mule. Many cargadors carry their loads in a frame, supported by a broad leather band across the forehead. When thus loaded they cannot turn their heads and they do not seem to hear well, so that I have feared many times they would be run over by the careless drivers. If there are several together they trot along in the middle of the road in Indian file. If going on a long journey they carry along enough tortillas for the entire trip, and must always be given enough time to make these preparations. Several times a day they will stop and make a fire, prepare their coffee, and eat their tortillas and fruit if it can be obtained. At night they will sleep out in the open air under a porch, if possible; if this shelter cannot be had, then they will lay themselves down to rest under the brilliant starlit canopy of this tropical clime.

A CARGADOR

Many of the Indians are very swift runners. An instance is told in Guatemala of a runner who carried a dispatch one hundred and five miles into the interior and returned with an answer in thirty-six hours, making the trip over mountains and a rough trail at an average speed of six miles an hour, including stops and delays. It is said that fish caught at Vera Cruz in the evening were served at the dinner table of Montezuma the following day at his capital near the site of the present City of Mexico, a distance of nearly three hundred miles by road. This was done by a system of relay runners stationed about a mile apart, and they made almost as fast time as the railway train to-day. Whether this is true or not it is well known that the Aztecs had a wonderful system of communication. The Spaniards were frequently astonished at the rapidity with which the news of their movements was spread. These runners were trained to great speed and endurance from their youth. Hundreds of them were in constant use, and the Aztec emperors were kept in communication with all parts of their empire. The Aztecs also used these runners as spies and they thus took the place of scouting parties in present-day campaigns.

So it is that these cargadors come and go. Each generation is like the last. They are happy in that they want but little and that little is easily supplied. They are contented because they live for to-day and worry not for the morrow. They are satisfied to go through life as the bearers of other people's burdens.

CHAPTER XI
CUSTOMS AND CHARACTERISTICS

"A land of lutes and witching tones,
Of silver, onyx, opal stones;
A lazy land, wherein all seems
Enchanted into endless dreams;
And never any need they know,
                    In Mexico,

"Of life's unquiet, swift advance,
But slipped into such gracious trance,
The restless world speeds on, unfelt,
Unheeded, as by those who dwelt
In golden ages, long ago,
                    In Mexico."

—Evaleen Stein.

It is always interesting to know how the rest of the world lives, but an experience with the customs and characteristics of a people impresses travellers in widely different ways. Mexico is a land of strange customs and strong characteristics which are deeply interesting to the sympathetic tourist. "Oh! the charm of the semi-tropical Spanish life!" says F. Hopkinson Smith. "The balconies above the patios trellised with flowers; the swinging hammocks, the slow plash of the fountains; the odour of jasmine wet with dew; the low thrum of guitar and the soft moonlight half-revealing the muffled figures in lace and cloak. It is the same old story, and yet it seems to me it is told in Spanish lands more delightfully and with more romance, colour and mystery than elsewhere on the globe." On the other hand many matter-of-fact, unsympathetic travellers see only the impractical ways, annoyances and inconvenient customs like the writer who describes Mexico as "A land of lace and lice and love, of flowers and fights and fleas; of babies and bull-fights where pillow slips are open at both ends and where passengers get off the front end of the street-cars; where keys often six inches in length are fitted in keyholes turned upside down and invariably turned backward; where the weather forgets to change from day to day and people sleep under the same bed cover the year around."

The Mexican has learned the secret of daily contentment. This is true generally of the creole class as well as of the peon. The fact that some seven thousand families practically own the entire landed estate of the country does not inspire envy in the bosoms of the other millions. It is a question whether the Anglo-Saxon and the Teuton can give these people more than mere mechanical contrivances. Home does not necessarily consist in an open fire, drawn curtains and frequent visits of curious neighbours. Here homes are found where privacy is respected, family affection is strong and there is respect for elders, love for parents and kindly relations between masters and servants. Such a country is not uncivilized and barbarous. There may be many odd and nonsensical customs but a reason can generally be found for them. When studying the natives it is enough to know that they are "an unselfish, patient, tender-hearted people; a people maintaining in their every-day life an etiquette phenomenal in a down-trodden race; offering instantly to the stranger and wayfarer on the very threshold of their adobe huts a hospitality so generous, accompanied by a courtesy so exquisite, that one stops at the next doorway to re-enjoy the luxury."

If one has absolutely nothing to do or suffers from the constitutional ailment of having been born tired, Mexico is the place for him to rest. Nor will he be lonesome in the occupation of loafing for on every bench is a wayfarer for company. There is no Mexicanism more pronounced than that of procrastination. Never do to-day what can be put off until to-morrow is the revised motto. Nothing is so important that it cannot wait until *mañana* (to-morrow). An American, whom I met in Mexico, and who had lived there a number of years characterized the country as the land of *mañana*, *esperase* and *poco tiempo*, or the land of "to-morrow" and "wait-a-while." Time is idled away. Nobody expects you to be punctual and you are not censured should you fail to keep an engagement. In fact, "you will probably be designated as a bore should you insist on scrupulously and punctually keeping all your appointments, for the man who always meets you on the dot is a nuisance in this southern land. If you have an appointment with a Mexican at noon, go at four o'clock in the afternoon and you will probably find him waiting for you. Had you gone on time, he might have been absent. Never be in a hurry, for constant hustle and bustle are the unpardonable sins. Respect the native customs and doze or read for a couple of hours after lunch and get busy as the sun nears the horizon." The Mexican pays a compliment to Anglo-Saxon push by adding *a la Inglesa* to an appointment which is intended to be kept punctually or "after the English fashion." It is impossible to educate the Mexican to American methods, so it behooves the foreigner who goes to Mexico to make up his mind to do business after the standards of that country. However lax or disappointing they may be he must remember that in Mexico his methods are the strange ones and not theirs, which are centuries old. In society calls lengthen to visits and last hours and the hurried five-minute calls are happily unknown. The longer the stay, the greater the compliment for it means that the visitor is enjoying herself.

In a country where, until recently, the purchase of a foreign draft was an all-day operation one cannot expect to do business in a very strenuous way. The people have breathed the somnolent atmosphere so long that they cannot be hurried. In fact, in some of the towns, the buzzards that encircle the town seem to be the only living creatures actually looking for something to do, for even the dogs would sneak down the alley to avoid trouble. And yet in the face of all this the Yankee drummer arrives in a town and scarcely takes time to brush the dust of travel from his clothes before he starts out to visit his prospective customers. He expects to round up his orders and take the train on the following morning for the next town. After running against a few *mañanas* from day to day without an opportunity to show his goods he feels about as disgusted as the enterprising American who, intending to revolutionize agriculture, took down a large stock of the latest American farming implements, but after a year's effort had made no sale. The salesman who will succeed is not the one who tries to introduce the hurry-up methods of his own land, but the one who adapts himself to the country and does not attempt to rush things. It will require days and perhaps weeks to work a large city.

I met an Englishman in one of these large Spanish-American towns who was a fair example of the successful European drummer. He had made this route for years and was thoroughly conversant with the language and understood the ways of the people. His methods were a good illustration of the reason why English and German houses have for many decades controlled trade in Spanish America. They keep their old men on the route as long as possible, for a new man will not do much on his first trip. We stopped at the same hotel and I had a good opportunity of observing his business methods. For several days after arriving in the town he did nothing but make social calls on his customers, take them to the theatre and entertain them in a general way. During the next few days he invited them to his rooms to inspect his stock which was large and varied. Then he began to take orders. This method seems like a waste of time but the orders secured were large and well repaid for the time taken. The American drummer could not have controlled his impatience to be on the move and would have made a failure. Many who drop into Mexico on a flying trip, jump to the conclusion that the Mexican merchant is not so shrewd a business man as the American. They are apt to mistake the deliberate methods of the Latin race for poor methods. He consumes more time in placing his order and there is less rush and bustle about his store, but an experienced man will tell you that in the end he drives a pretty hard bargain for he knows the market price of the goods and wants the best discounts and longest credit.

Even the legal customs are peculiar and have proven decidedly embarrassing to many Americans. A number of years ago, before railroads were so numerous, the local officers always arrested the engineer and conductor in the event that any one was killed, and they were thrust into jail "incommunicado." This means that you are to be incarcerated seventy-two hours in solitary confinement without bail, at the end of which time a judicial examination is given. An American whom I met there told me of his "incommunicado" experience. He was arrested because he had witnessed an affray and was held as witness, in solitary confinement, but was released by the official after the judicious use of thirty dollars. Their theory is that after a man has been kept in confinement for three days, with only his own thoughts for company, he is much more likely to tell the truth than if he had been in communication with his lawyers, friends and the reporters all that time. And who can deny the truth of their claim?

It is always best to keep out of the neighbourhood of trouble, or get out of it as quickly as you can if it comes your way, especially if in the remote districts, for offender and victim are both liable to arrest and imprisonment.

Most cases are put off from day to day until one party or the other is weary of the proceeding. An instance which illustrates this was related to me by a man who was arrested for misdemeanour. Knowing the custom prevalent in the courts he hired an attorney to appear each day for him. When the case was called the judge would ask "*Que quiere*" (what do you want). After the case was explained he would dispose of it with the simple word *mañana*. The other man appeared each day until disgusted with the procedure and then dropped the matter. Lawyers charge so much per word and are paid for each article as it is written. Mexican notaries are very important personages. They take the place to a great degree of the old-fashioned, family lawyer. They are regarded in much the same light as the family confessor and are told the family secrets. To their credit, be it said, that the notary is usually a man worthy of the confidence placed in him.

The ceremonial and punctilious politeness of the Mexican, be he Don or peon, is interesting and oftentimes amusing. The Spaniard on meeting a friend on the street will stop and inquire one by one after the health of his wife, each of his children and the various other members of his household and then in turn will submit to the same interrogations from his friend. After witnessing such a scene between two men in silk hats you can turn down a side street and see a meeting between a poor Indian in rags and an old withered woman selling lottery tickets. Removing his tattered *sombrero* he bows gravely, and, in the softest of Spanish, says, "*A los pies de usted, señora*" (at your feet, lady). This is done with a grace and ease of manner worthy of any station in life; and her answer "My hands are for your kisses, señor," is said in the same gracious way worthy of a duchess. Should you ask the man for his name he would be sure to add "*Su criado de usted*" (your servant).

The Mexicans are very proud and exclusive, and suspicious of the newcomer. Seldom indeed is it that an American gains the *entree* into their homes but, if he succeeds, they will be found among the most charming hosts in the world. This reserve is probably very natural. The Mexican has been educated in the strict Catholic schools and is a victim of custom old as his country, while the American coming to Mexico is a mercenary, ambitious person engaged in commercial strife and in the race for the almighty dollar. Then, the American is of a more matter-of-fact temperament and does not appreciate the impulsive nature of the Mexican.

Money does not appeal to him except for the pleasure of spending it, and no person is more lavish in the expenditure of money, if he has it, than a Mexican gentleman.

The Mexican is a home lover and yet there is no word in the Spanish language that corresponds to our word for home. *Casa*, or house, is the nearest to it and the Mexican always speaks of his house when he means his home. The exaggerated conventionalities are often carried to the verge of the absurd. Perhaps there may be as much truth in their expressions as in the polite but oftentimes meaningless civilities of our own land. An American, on being introduced to a stranger, will feel that he has satisfied the etiquette of the occasion by simply expressing his pleasure in the acquaintance. The Mexican goes a step further and presents the newly-made acquaintance with his house.

"*Su casa es numero* ——," he says with a graceful bow giving the street and number of his own house, which literally means "your house is number ——," and usually adds, "It is entirely at your disposal; make yourself at home." It is simply a polite way of saying "I am glad to meet you." Perhaps five minutes later the incident is forgotten by the giver. One writer has said that he met fourteen men at a club in Mexico and was presented with thirteen houses. The fourteenth man was unmarried and not a householder. Occasionally some one not familiar with the emptiness of the phrase has presumed on its literal interpretation and called at one of the houses presented to him but has been turned away without the least sign of recognition.

If one expresses admiration for some article worn by another, he is quickly informed that the article is "at his disposal." If you happen upon a Mexican at the dining hour, he will probably offer you his dinner. If you decline it, the occasion requires that you should do so with polite wishes for his digestion. These forms of hospitality are derived from Spanish ancestors and were by them probably copied from the Moors, after the open hand and open tent customs of the sons of the desert who meant these expressions literally. It has an empty meaning now, for nothing is left but the words. With all this seeming inconsistency and insincerity, the Mexicans are exceedingly kind hearted and will willingly do favours if approached in the right way; no service is too great towards those for whom they have formed an attachment. They will often accompany the departing guest for a long distance over hard roads as a mark of courtesy and friendship.

We are all victims of habit more or less. But, whereas the American welcomes innovations and adapts his habits to them, or forms new ones, the Mexican does not want any change from the customs of his ancestors. The expression *"no es costumbre,"* meaning it is not the custom, is a final and decisive answer that does not admit of argument. You might as well try to change the colour of the native as his habits. Americans who keep Mexican servants are for ever running contrary to the customs or prejudices of their help. For instance an American woman[2] who lived here a number of years relates the trouble she had to induce her servant to use a cook stove which she had imported from the United States. She refused because "it would give her disease of the liver." In all seriousness she believed that such would be the result and nothing could induce her to have anything to do with the new-fangled thing. A peripatetic merchant came around selling eggs at six for a real. He refused to sell two dozen for four reals because *"no es costumbre,"* as eggs are always sold at six for a real, an incontrovertible argument.

MAKING *TORTILLAS*

A household will have difficulty in getting along with only one servant for it is customary to employ three or four in a small family and from twenty to forty in a large house. Each servant will do his or her own particular work cheerfully and will move about so lightly and airily that you hardly know any one is around. However, ask the man *mozo* to scrub the floor, or the cook to make the beds, and you will see a regretful look of the eye and be met with the ready answer, *"no es costumbre."* Marketing is a right jealously guarded too, for *es costumbre* (it is the custom) and one of the perquisites of the man servant, since he receives a small fee from each person of whom purchases are made. The Indian servants are not accustomed to beds and want nothing but a mat to sleep upon. The traveller can see these in the halls at the hotel if he comes in a little late. Here these dusky natives sleep more soundly than do most Americans on the most luxurious of beds. An American lady in Oaxaca took pity on her girl servant and bought a comfortable iron bed for her to occupy. She then explained to her how the bed was used. Several days later she asked the servant how she liked her bed. The girl said it was fine—to lay her clothes on. The American woman finally gave up trying to change the habits of her maid. Servants become very devoted to their employers and their attachment is sometimes embarrassing. In case of a death in the family they immediately don black and mourn as though the lost one was a near relative of their own.

The economy of housekeeping and especially of the kitchen, even among the rich, is remarkable. The Indian or *Mestiza* women rule here and the customs of a thousand years ago are the customs of to-day. The *tortillas*, cakes made of maize, are the bread of the country. For centuries these dusky women of Mexico have ground the corn for their daily bread between two stones, the grains having first been soaked for several hours in a solution of lime water. This smoothed, dished-out stone is called a *metate*, an Aztec word, and the women work for hours in beating the softened grains to a fine paste. Small pieces of the dough are then worked between the hands, tossed and patted, and flattened out until very thin. After this they are thrown upon a flat, iron griddle over a charcoal fire. They are never allowed to brown and are without salt or seasoning of any kind. After becoming used to them they prove very palatable and many prefer them to the ordinary corn bread.

Frijoles, or beans, and generally black ones, are also invariably served and are eaten twice every day without intermission on the table of rich or poor. The *chili*, a pretty hot sort of pepper, is a favourite dish that had better be avoided by the Americans, for the ability to relish it can only be approached by degrees. *Tamales* are relished by the Mexican and can be found for sale in almost any of the markets. I never see *tamales* without thinking of the description given of them by a big Texan in his bread dialect, in answer to a question from me as the train was speeding across the mesquit prairies near San Antonio. "You take cawn meal, some hawt (heart), livah and a little peppah and you make a tamahle, suh."

The use of sacred names or names of great personages among these people is often astonishing. The names of Porfirio Diaz, Juarez and Hidalgo are as numerous as the George Washingtons among the negroes of the south. However, when the American stumbles upon a Pius Fifth, St. John the Evangelist or even Jesus, in a dirty-face brown man clothed in rags, it seems a strange incongruity. Talk with this humble bearer of a sacred name or offer him a gratuity, and, as you depart, he will say, *"Vaya usted con Dios"* (go, and God be with you), in such a simple and benign manner that you almost feel as though a benediction were following you.

We are told by the early writers that the Aztecs had few stores, but that nearly all the trading was done in the markets which were found in every city, or by the great merchant princes who traversed the country with their large army of burden-bearers and retainers, compelling trade as well as seeking it. It is interesting to note the description of the market in the capital in the time of Cortez written by Bernal Diaz, one of his followers, and the historian of his expedition. He expresses his astonishment at the great crowds of people, the regularity which prevailed and the vast quantities of merchandise on display. "The articles consisted of gold, silver, jewels, feathers, mantles, chocolate, skins dressed and undressed, sandals, and great numbers of male and female slaves, some of whom were fastened by the neck, in collars, to long poles. The meat market was stocked with fowls, game and dogs. Vegetables, fruits, articles of food ready dressed, salt, bread, honey and sweet pastry made in various ways, were also sold here. Other places in the square were appointed to the sale of earthen ware, wooden household furniture such as tables and benches, firewood, pipes, sweet canes filled with tobacco mixed with liquid amber, copper axes and working tools, and wooden vessels highly painted. Numbers of women sold fish and little loaves made of a certain mud which they find in the lakes, and which resembles cheese. The entire square was enclosed in piazzas under which great quantities of grain were stored and where were also shops for various kinds of goods."

A MEXICAN MARKET

This description would answer very well to-day except as to slaves and feathers. It is to be regretted that the beautiful feather work of that race is a lost art. The market of the capital is located but a short distance from the plaza and is an excellent place to study life. The outer portion is occupied by small shops covered with protecting piazzas but the central part is wholly occupied by the Indian merchants. During the morning hours it is so closely packed that it is almost impossible to force one's way through the dense throng of humanity. The native, squatted on the ground on a rush mat, with another mat suspended over him for protection from the fierce sun, and his stock in trade spread before him, is a picture worth studying. Many tribes are represented, as their dress indicates, as well as the products of many different zones from the cocoanut of the hot lands to the inferior pears of the cold zone. The pottery from Guadalajara can be distinguished from that of Guadalupe or Aguas Calientes by its colour and design. Each piece might tell a history of an art passed down from father to son for countless generations, for the son usually follows the occupation of his father. They never think of changing method of manufacture or design. It is quite probable that the pottery seen in the market to-day is the same as that viewed by Cortez. Many of the vessels are curious and fantastic in form but always ornamental in decoration. When one considers that much of this pottery is made with no tools but pieces of broken glass and a horsehair, the result is a marvel. With the hair they trim the top and with the glass smooth off the rough places. The pottery market is an important one, for articles used in the kitchen and on the tables of the poorer classes are exclusively of this ware. For a small sum an entire kitchen outfit can be purchased.

There are few Jewish merchants in Mexico for the Mexican is even more persuasive in his mode of selling and his prices are fully as elastic. In purchasing native articles on different occasions I tried several dealers in order to discover whether they had a uniform bottom price. They would invariably ask at least twice as much as they were willing to accept. I found that if one would only show surprise at the price asked, the question "What will you give" would immediately follow. They were perfectly willing to get as much from you as possible but the lowest price quoted by the various dealers was almost identical. Some persons have facetiously characterized Mexico as the land of *"no hay"* (pronounced eye) because it is such a common answer in marketing and means "there is none." In fact, the answer will always be *"no hay"* or *"si, hay"* (yes, I have).

CANDY BOY AND GIRL

There are many quaint and curious characters that one will find around the market place. The candy man, or, boy, moves around with noiseless tread crying his wares in a song which never varies any more than his stock, which is always the same and arranged in exactly the same way. His *dulces*, however, have merit and it is not necessary to change anything already good. The *evangelista*, or letter writer, is here with a jug of ink and pen on a little table ready to write a business letter, or a *billet doux* flaming with passion and extravagant phrases for the unlettered lover. On the corners of the street may be seen the cobblers ready to cut and fit sandals "while you wait." His whole stock in trade consists of a pile of scraps of sole leather and some leather thongs, while his only tool is a curved, sharp knife.

In and out of the crowd the faithful *aguador*, or water-carrier, winds his way bringing the refreshing water to thirsty mortals. He is not only a very necessary person in this land of little rain, but is a person of importance and knows the inner life of the household of his customers. His costume and water vessels vary in the different cities but he is the same honest character who ingeniously carries the love messages from the "bear" to his inamorata. After a morning of hard work his faithful wife brings his dinner of *tortillas* and *frijoles* to the fountain or well, and there he sits and eats his humble meal while she watches her lord and master until he has finished. Later in the day, tiring of his work or feeling the burden of prosperity as his stock of copper coins increases, he resorts to the pulque-shop and there shows his contempt for the beverage he has been distributing by imbibing large quantities of his favourite liquor.

Perhaps in no way is the general superstition and ignorance of the Indian shown to better advantage than in their ideas of disease and medicine. The *curandera*, usually a woman, admits having great knowledge of anatomy and chemistry, and has a pharmacopœia all her own. The accounts given here are vouched for by a writer in *Modern Mexico* who is a native of the country, understands these people and is entitled to belief. *Aire* (air), when introduced into the system through blows or unusually forcible sneezing, causes swellings, sore eyes and nervous tremblings. It is treated with plasters and bandages and lotions. When the alimentary canal is obstructed it is *empacho*, which means that undigested food has adhered to the stomach or the food has formed into balls and marbles that rattle around inside the stomach or intestines. This disease demands immediate and heroic treatment, and a drop of quicksilver swallowed at a gulp is prescribed and will generally dislodge it or kill the patient. *Tiricia* is indicated by homesickness, melancholia or insomnia, and is caused by a subtle vapour produced by the action of the moon on the dew and is absorbed through the pores. Change of climate, good company and tonics are a sensible prescription. *Mal de ojo*, or the evil eye, causes the sufferer to fade away or die of inanition, and is a common disease of children. Bright attractive objects are hung up to draw away the attention of the "evil eye." If a child is slow in talking, a diet of boiled swallows is prescribed. One writer positively asserts that blue and red beads ground fine and mixed in equal portions have been given to persons suffering with paralysis, and the sufferers survived the treatment. The *curandera* is also called upon to mix love potions and poisons that will cause delirium or even insanity and death.

Another instance is told in the same periodical of a woman who was very sick with a disease from the effects of which she was practically helpless. A *curandera* had told the husband to get a white turkey and tie it in the house and his wife would get well. When the turkey had failed to cure her an old man *curandero* was procured, who promised to make her well if supplied with plenty of *aguardiente* (brandy). Four dollars worth was supplied him, and four dollars will buy a great deal of poor brandy in Mexico. The old man laid himself down on the ground, after filling himself up with the firewater, pounded his head and kept repeating weird incantations which could be heard a long distance away. This was continued for several days until the supply of spirits gave out. In the meantime the patient had improved somewhat and could use her arms and body as far as the waist. The shrewd old man shrugged his shoulders and said, "I have cured her as far as I can. You will have to get a *curandera* to complete the cure." The poor woman soon died, because, as the husband declared, she had been bewitched.

CHAPTER XII
HOLIDAYS AND HOLY-DAYS

It is impossible to understand Mexico or the Mexicans without knowing something of their feasts and festivals which play such a large part in the life of these people. In fact there is very little of the social life in Mexico that is not the outgrowth of or intimately connected with the holy-days of the Church. The saint's day of each member, that is the day in the church calendar devoted to the saint after whom the person is named, takes the place of the birthday for gifts and family celebrations. The *fiestas*, or feast-days, of the church are very numerous and are pretty well observed, although business is not entirely suspended. The church holidays are either different from those in other Catholic countries or are observed in a truly national way in Mexico.

To one who enjoys mixing with the common people and learning their customs, habits and ways of thinking, in other words, endeavouring to get into their real, inner life, it is a perpetual delight to visit the cities and villages on the *fiesta* occasions and mingle with the people in their celebration. This association with a free-hearted, pleasure-loving people on their gala days unconsciously broadens the views of a traveller in a new country, and develops a sympathy which can be awakened in no other way. The crowds jostle each other good naturedly and will treat the stranger with respect. Too many visitors to this country try to judge everything from the American standard and find little to commend. They should remember that Mexico is Oriental rather than Anglo-Saxon, and that the Spanish-Moorish civilization is here blended with the Aztec. Such a civilization cannot be without merit and it must have some inherent good qualities. If one wants to understand a country rightly, he must first try to enter into the lives of the people and then look at life from their point of view.

It would be impossible within the limits prescribed to describe all the celebrations in honour of the hundreds of saints and the numerous secular holidays. A description of a few of these occasions, most generally observed, will give the reader a good idea of the nature of all.

Christmas celebrations in Mexico are very much different from those in the United States. There is no merry jingle of the sleigh bells in this land of Christmas sunshine and skies as blue as those of Naples; and there are no plans dependent upon whether the day may chance to be white or green. The few lofty volcanic peaks, on which alone snow is ever seen, would not tempt the most enthusiastic tobogganist. As there are no chimneys, the children need not sit up at night until sleep overtakes them, to see Santa Claus descend with his heavy pack filled with the things that boys and girls like. Even the time honoured custom of hanging up stockings is unknown to Mexican children. Perhaps they enjoy themselves quite as much after their own fashion as we do after ours. They have good things to eat, and the beautiful flowers are so cheap that no matter how humble the Mexican home may be, it affords a few sprays of the scarlet *Noche Bueno*, the beautiful Christmas plant. Their celebrations are long continued for they begin nine days before Christmas and last until the Feast of the Epiphany on the 6th of January; and this entire time is one long delightful jubilee.

These celebrations, which begin on the sixteenth of December and continue until the twenty-fifth, are called *posadas*. The word in Spanish means an "inn," or abiding place, and while the celebration, in its origin, was distinctly religious, it is now only semi-religious, and has become an extremely gay and sociable occasion. The *posadas* are limited to the cities but, in those places, the poorest as well as the richest families hold them and they are a celebration peculiar to this country.

The origin of the *posada* is in the gospel narrative of the Nativity. Because Cæsar had issued the decree that all the world should be taxed, Mary and Joseph came to Bethlehem to be enrolled. Mary made the journey mounted upon an ass which Joseph led. As the shadows of the night descended, they were obliged to ask for shelter, and it is no wonder that the request was not always granted readily and willingly, but was many times refused during the trip that is supposed to have taken nine days.

On the last day, having arrived at Bethlehem, and because the city was so full of people, they wandered about for a long time without finding admittance to either private house or inn. At last, being tired and weary, and because no room could be secured, they took refuge in a stable where Christ was born. Therefore, it is, that in order to celebrate this journey fully, the *posadas* begin with the journey at Nazareth. Each year a house is chosen in a family circle, or among a group of friends, and at that house for nine consecutive nights the festival is held. Or, sometimes, the celebration will be held at different houses during that period.

The journey from Nazareth to Bethlehem and the difficulties encountered on the way, are represented by the first part of the celebration. At the appointed hour the guests assemble at the house which has been chosen for the celebration on that particular night. Each person present, members of the family, guests and servants, is furnished with a lighted candle, and two and two, they march around the halls and through the corridors several times chanting the solemn "Litany of Loretto." As each invocation is ended the audience chant *"ora pro nobis"* ("pray for us"). At the head of the procession the figures of Joseph and Mary made of clay or wax, dressed in gay, incongruously-coloured satins are borne either in the hands or lying in a basket. Sometimes these figures are dressed in brilliant costumes of lace with tinselled borderings. At each door the procession pauses and knocks and begs admittance, but no answer or invitation to enter is given. When the litany is finished some of the party enter a room while the rest with the figures of Joseph and Mary remain outside and sing a chant something like the following:—

"In Heaven's Name,
I beg for shelter;
My wife to-night,
Can go no further."

The reply to this is:—

"No inn is this,
Begone from hence;
Ye may be thieves,
I trust ye not."

At last, however, the door is opened and all go in and Joseph and Mary have secured shelter for the night. The pilgrims are placed on an improvised altar and some prayers are recited, though the religious exercises are generally hurried through in the quickest manner possible. Sometimes, to make the scene more realistic, a burro is introduced in the procession to represent the faithful animal that carried the holy family in their wanderings. Frequently, on the last night, in a room, or on the roof, a kind of stable is arranged in which the figures of Joseph and Mary are placed with the utmost reverence. On this night a figure of the infant Jesus is also carried. After the litany the party proceed to have a general good time which is kept up until a late hour. Occasionally, in the homes of the wealthy, these entertainments are on a very elaborate scale and costly souvenirs are presented to each guest. Everywhere in the cities is heard the litany of the *posada*, for it is celebrated almost universally. It is sung in hundreds and thousands of homes and the processions wind in and out of the rooms and round the improvised shrines. The patios are hung with venetian lights, and fireworks blaze skyward in every direction. In the City of Mexico the *posadas* are most elaborate among the official and wealthy families, and the Zocalo plaza is a bewitching place with its many lights and the multitudes of children who gather here for celebration. The clergy are now censuring the "*posadas*" because of the irreverent spirit in which they are celebrated.

In Mexico the *piñate* takes the place of the Christmas tree. It is an oval shaped, earthen jar, handsomely decorated with tinsel and streamers of tissue paper, made up to represent curious figures. They represent clowns, ballet girls, monkeys, roosters, various grotesque animals, and even children almost life sized. The jars are crammed full of sweets, rattles, whistles and crackers. The breaking of the *piñate* follows the litany and is an exciting event, which generally occurs in the patio. It is suspended from the ceiling and then each person desiring to take part is blindfolded in turn, and, armed with a pole, proceeds to strike the swinging *piñate*. Three trials are permitted. Sometimes many are blindfolded before a successful blow brings the sweets and bon-bons rattling to the floor. Then there is a race and a scramble for the dainties. Thousands of these *piñates* are broken each Christmas season and the vendors of them perambulating the streets with a pole across the shoulders on which are suspended the grotesque figures, add life and zest to the season. Then to see a well dressed, sedate-looking, business man hurrying home with a grotesque tissue-paper creation of gorgeous hues with tinselled decorations and gay streamers under his arms is a curious but not uncommon sight.

BURNING AN EFFIGY OF JUDAS AT EASTER-TIME

Holy week, as the week preceding Easter is called, is celebrated in an elaborate and truly original way. The religious processions which formerly attended these celebrations are now prohibited by law. During these few days the bells, organs and choirs are silent, the stores are closed and there is a general holiday. As an evidence that vanity is not entirely absent, on Holy Thursday it is customary for men and women to turn out in good clothes and many of the ladies appear in handsome and elaborate gowns. Then on

Good Friday everything is changed and the whole country mourns. Sombre black takes the place of the more brilliant raiment of the preceding day; downcast eyes and solemn faces succeed the smiles and coquettish glances of yesterday.

On Saturday occurs the most grotesque and curious of all the festivals of the Church. It is the day on which final disposition is made of that arch-traitor Judas Iscariot, and the day is devoted to his humiliation and death. Effigies of the traitor are hung over the streets everywhere and all day long men parade the streets with figures of the betrayer of Christ upon poles. These effigies range in size from miniature figures to those of gigantic proportions. Each figure is made of *papier maché*, is filled with explosives and has a fuse which is generally the moustache. Hundreds of the images are sold to the children in each city who explode them with great glee. Judas is represented with folded hands, arms akimbo, with legs in running posture and in every conceivable attitude. Some of them bear suggestive mottoes such as "I am a scion of the Devil" and "Let me give up the Ghost." Each person must destroy a Judas.

At ten o'clock as the great bells of the cathedral in the City of Mexico sound and other bells follow, the fuses to these effigies are lighted. The great Judases strung across the streets or tied to balconies are exploded amid great rejoicing. Coins representing the thirty pieces of silver paid to Judas are sometimes thrown to the crowd from the windows of wealthy residents or clubs. Every one grows wild and the little folks become almost beside themselves with excitement. The bells in the towers ring out their rejoicings and a peculiar apparatus gives out a sound which represents the breaking of the bones of the thieves on the cross. The crowds also have innumerable rattles which make a hideous, grating sound intended to represent the same incident. The noise of the bells, the explosion of the firecrackers, and the shouts of the multitude form a strange, exciting, ludicrous scene never to be forgotten. When the last Judas has been demolished, the excitement subsides and a good-natured frolic follows.

The national holidays, of which there are many, are greatly overshadowed by those pertaining to the Church, and none of them are so universally observed. Not all the feasts and festivals of Mexico are of Romish origin. Some of them are founded upon the remains of Aztec idolatry, for the priests of the early days with a wise foresight adopted the same day for feast-days in many instances. Though these Indians probably could not tell why, yet they have a great reverence for the saints whom they worship after their own fashion. They are delighted to have more occasions for decorating themselves and their churches with flowers, marching in processions, dancing and letting off rockets.

The *Fiesta de las Flores*, or Feast of the Poppies, celebrated in April, is held on the Viga Canal and was originally a day devoted to the worship of the Aztec god Quetzalcoatl, the god of nature with them. On that day the bloody, sacrificial rites were suspended and all joined in this festival of flowers. This *fiesta* has lost all its religious significance but it is said to be celebrated much the same as in Aztec times. All day long the canal is filled with boats large and small manned by the dusky natives. Indian women and nut-brown maids with wreaths of poppies on their heads and garlands of the same around their necks, sing the songs of the people and dance as they move along. On the shore and in the boats the native bands play, and the broad highway along the banks of the Viga is crowded with long lines of carriages filled with the aristocracy of the Capital who have come out to witness this unique celebration.

Mexico, like each good Mexican Catholic, has a patron saint who presides over her destinies. This saint has not only been adopted by the government in times past, but has been proclaimed as the guardian of Mexico by the Holy See, and only a few years ago was duly crowned as the Virgin of Guadalupe in ceremonies made memorable by the large number of church dignitaries present. Her miraculous appearance came at an apropos time and greatly assisted in attracting the natives to the new worship.

The Aztecs had long worshipped a deity called Tonantzin, "Mother of Gods," who was supposed to reside on the Hill of Tepeyacac, now called Guadalupe. Tradition says that a devout Indian named Juan Diego, who resided in the village of Tolpetlac, and who recently had been converted to Christianity, was passing by this way on the morning of the 9th day of December, 1531, on his way to early mass. When at the base of this hill there suddenly burst upon his ears a melody of sweet music, as of a chorus of birds singing together in harmony. Surprised at this unusual music he looked up and lo, just above him, rested a cloud more brilliant than a rainbow and in the centre of the cloud stood a lady. Thoroughly frightened he fell to his knees, but was aroused by a voice which proceeded from the cloud and called "Juan." He looked up and the lady told him to go to the Bishop of Mexico, and tell him that she wanted a church built on this hill in her honour. He did so, but the Bishop was loth to believe this wonderful tale from a poor, ignorant Indian. A second and yet a third time did the same vision appear to the pious Juan and make the same request. On this last occasion Juan had passed on the opposite side of the hill to avoid the woman but to no avail. Upon the report of the third vision the Bishop told Juan to ask for some unmistakable sign. The lady appeared again on the following morning and Juan told her of the Bishop's request. She told him to go up the hill and gather flowers from the barren hillside where they had never been known to grow. As soon as he reached there many beautiful flowers appeared in a miraculous manner, which Juan gathered up in his tilma, or blanket, and took to the Bishop. When he had emptied his tilma the image of the Virgin was found on the blanket in most brilliant colours.

The Bishop reverently took the tilma and accepted it as an unmistakable token. He at once began the erection of a chapel where it had been commanded. As soon as the chapel was completed, he hung the tilma on the high altar where it has remained ever since except for a few short periods. It can now be seen under a glass upon the payment of a small fee. Some persons say that upon examination it proves to be only a cheap daub upon coarse, cotton material; others say that it was taken out a few years ago and examined and they could not find any trace of paint, but that the colours seemed to stay there in some miraculous way. Not being permitted to make a personal examination, I leave the reader to make his choice as inclination directs.

From the time of its origin this legend has had a wonderful and deep influence upon the Indians. It is even so to-day. Our Lady of Guadalupe is looked upon by them as their patron and protector. Coming so soon after the conquest and appearing on a hill already sacred to that race, it led thousands to the new religion. The main church is very large and imposing with a nave two hundred feet long and one hundred and twenty-two feet wide, and cost over two million dollars in gold. The altar is magnificent and it has a solid silver railing weighing several tons around the chancel. There is another chapel connected with the cathedral church. Back of these is the miraculous spring which burst forth from the very spot on which the Virgin stood at her last appearance. Half way up the hill are some stone sails erected by a grateful mariner, and on the top of the hill is another chapel. Back of this is a cemetery in which Santa Anna and other noted persons are buried. A beautiful view of the capital and the Valley of Mexico is obtained from the top of the hill which well repays for the exertion in climbing.

> "From Heaven she descended,
> Triumphant and glorious,
> To favour us—
> La-Guadalupana."

Thus sing the Indians on the 12th of December of each year. This is the day that has been appointed for the great *"fiesta"* in honour of the Virgin who appeared to Juan Diego. All others fade into insignificance and are completely overshadowed by the annual celebrations in honour of Our Lady of Guadalupe. Any one who happens to be in the City of Mexico on this date, or a few days prior thereto, should not fail to take the street car for Guadalupe, a suburban town about three miles to the eastward. The route follows an ancient Aztec causeway which was old when Cortez invaded this valley. To the merry hum of the trolley, which seems strangely out of place on this historic highway, the traveller is carried along. One does not need to be told that something out of the ordinary is about to take place. The streets of the capital and all the roads leading to Guadalupe are alive with people on their way to this most sacred shrine. It is said that many of these Indians tramp hundreds of miles to be present on these occasions, taking their food with them and sleeping out in the open air. Tens of thousands of Indians are present at each annual celebration and the number is said in some years to equal a hundred thousand souls and more.

CANDLE BOOTHS IN GUADALUPE

In Guadalupe the streets and plazas around the famous church are crowded with booths for the sale of native wares, candles, images of the Virgin and for the carrying-on of many kinds of gambling. There are many booths in which refreshments are served by women in native costumes. The viands include cold chicken, eggs, tamales, *frijoles* (beans), cakes and sweets. For beverages you can take your choice between beer and pulque. A motley assemblage is present. Indians from the hot lands mingle with the purer types of the Aztec from the mountains and table lands. The swarms of Indians fairly crowd the plaza and streets, some eating and drinking, some sleeping, some making love and some whiling away the time with cards or other gambling devices. All these people, of course, belong to the peon class. Mingled with the natives here and there are all types of Mexicans, and a number of Americans drawn here by curiosity add variety to the occasion. The lame, the blind and the halt are there too; for alms are plentiful and Our Lady possesses wondrous powers of healing. Many testimonials to this fact are seen in the little chapel which shelters the miraculous spring. Hundreds and thousands carry away with them a bottle of these healing waters.

A feeling of reverence pervades the sanctuary. The kneeling figures with bodies motionless and their eyes and faces fixed upon the high altar, crowd the floor until it is impossible to move. One can not help being impressed by this feeling of reverence pervading the church and chapels. Outside it is different; for here the throng moves around visiting the booths, eating, drinking and gambling. Indian minstrels play their weird airs. Beggars cry out to give them something *"por el amor del Dios"* ("for the love of God"). At night the plaza and streets are one indistinguishable mass of dark, reclining and slumbering figures wrapped in their blankets and shawls. The elements are kind in December for it is the dry season.

The next day after one of these celebrations I left the capital for Puebla. For many miles we kept passing Indians singly, in groups, and whole families together homeward bound. They followed well-worn paths which were plainly visible. The trails were narrow and all marched along single file in regular Indian fashion. They would stop and look at our train as it noisily passed by. Perhaps they were happy in their simple way in the thought that for one year more, at least, Our Lady of Guadalupe would watch over and protect them, her humble worshippers.

BEGGARS OF THE CITY OF MEXICO

CHAPTER XIII
A TRANSPLANTED SPORT

The bull-fight as an amusement is the exclusive property of the Spaniard. It originated in Spain and has never spread beyond the limits of Spanish conquest. Perhaps it is this very exclusiveness that causes them to cling to it so tenaciously, though legislatures and governments have made vigorous efforts to abolish the brutal spectacles. It is, according to a native writer, a proof of the superiority of the Spaniard, because "the Spanish men are as much more brave than other men, as the Spanish bull is more savage and valiant than all other bulls." Rather, it seems to me to be a survivor of the ancient gladiatorial contests, or fights between man and beast in the great amphitheatres of Rome.

I had never before, even when standing within the historic walls of the Colosseum, been able to picture in my own mind the scene of the arena crowded with combatants while the expectant multitude filled the seats in tier upon tier, until I found myself within the great bull-ring of Madrid. There was the arena, and round about were the eager throng, a crowd of fourteen thousand human beings who impatiently and anxiously awaited the sound of the bugle which would announce the opening of the spectacle of blood and brute torture. Then it was possible to understand how, in an earlier and more brutal age, the Roman populace gloated over the combats where the death of some of the participants was as much fore-doomed as the fate of the bull who enters the ring to-day with a defiant toss of his horns.

If popularity is to be judged by the amount of patronage, then the bull-fight is the most popular amusement in Mexico to-day. The national life is permeated with the sport. The Sunday bull-fight is the topic of conversation in the capital for the following week. Even the children indulge in imitations of this favourite game in their childish way. It is only on Sundays and feast days that the *corrida de toros* occurs. Six days shalt thou do nothing and on the seventh go to the bull-fight, runs an old Madrid saying. They probably go on the theory that a good entertainment is better on that day than any other. It is useless to argue with a Spaniard or Spanish-American about the brutality or inhumanity of these spectacles as they will immediately remind us of the prize-fights within our own borders which frequently result in death. This is a gentle hint that we should clean our own Augean stables before telling our neighbours what they should not do. Perhaps it is a rebuke that is not entirely out of place.

The Plaza de Toros is always a great, circular building of stone or wood with little pretence or ornament. It is built for the bull-fight and for no other purpose. The interior is an immense amphitheatre, with seats in tiers rising to the top where the private boxes are located. These alone have a roof, as all the rest of the structure is open to the sky. Half the seats are exposed to the bright sun and the other half are in shadow. The seats on the *sol*, or sunny side, generally cost only about half as much as those in the *sombra*, or shady part. The fights are usually advertised "if the time and weather permits." The ring itself is an arena about a hundred feet in diameter, encircled by a high board fence with a lower barrier on the inside, which serves as a means of escape for a *torero* who is too closely pursued by the irate bull. Sometimes a bull will leap over this first barrier and then an exciting race follows.

An American will not soon forget the first sight of the full amphitheatre. The scene is an exciting one and there is a tension of the nerves in anticipation of what is to come. The bands play and, if there is any delay, the thousands of impatient spectators will shout and yell themselves hoarse. There is usually a cheer when the president for the occasion and his companions take their seats. At length the gates opposite the president are opened and a gaily caparisoned horseman, called the *alguacil*, appears. He asks permission to kill the bulls. This being granted, the president tosses him the key to the bull-pen, which he catches in his hat. He is cheered if he does catch it and hissed if he fails. The gate opens again and the gay company of bull-fighters is announced by the blast of trumpets. These men arrayed in costumes of red, yellow, green and blue silks, satins and velvets, glittering with beads, jewels and gold braid, form a brilliant spectacle as they march across the arena to salute the president, after the manner of the gladiators of old. Every one taking part in this exhibition appears in this procession, from the *matador* to the men with wheelbarrows and shovels who clean up the arena after each performance. I said all, but the principal character himself is reserved until later. After saluting the president the company march around the ring to receive the plaudits of the people.

The bull-fight is a tragedy in three acts. After the company have withdrawn, the door through which the bull enters is unlocked and the first act begins with a flourish of trumpets. The bull rushes out from a dark stall into the dazzling light, furious with rage and trembling in every limb. This is an intense moment and all eyes are centred upon the newcomer. As he enters, a barbed steel hook covered with flowing ribbons is placed in his shoulder. The ribbons indicate the ranch or *hacienda* from whence he came. Even the street urchins can recognize the colours of a *hacienda* which has the reputation of producing animals that are noted for their belligerent qualities.

Startled by the intense light and enraged by the stinging of the steel hook, the bull stands for an instant recovering his senses. Sometimes he will paw the earth, toss the dust over his back and bellow his defiance. Around him in the ring are the *capeadores*, men on foot carrying red capes, and *picadores*, men on horses armed with lances. These latter sit motionless as statues upon their steeds that are blindfolded ready for the sacrifice.

After a moment of uncertainty, the bull dashes either at a *capeador* or *picador*. The former quickly runs to the barrier and nimbly leaps over, leaving the bull more infuriated than ever. The horse attracts his attention next and there is no way of escape for this poor, old, broken down servant of man. The *picador* makes no effort to save his steed, which is blindfolded so that he may not see his danger, but simply plants his blunt spear-point in the shoulder of the brute. Sometimes this will save the horse, but it does not please the audience for a certain number of horses must be sacrificed. More frequently the bull will, with a single toss of the horns, overthrow both horse and rider in a heap. The *capeadores* then hover around with their cloaks and distract the attention of the bull from the prostrate rider who is helpless because of his iron armour. Once I saw a rider fall on the back of the bull much to the surprise of both. It is seldom that a *picador* is killed, for the bull will nearly always leave him and chase a red cloak.

Fortunate, indeed, is the horse that is instantly killed. If able to walk, he is ridden around in the ring again with blood streaming from his wounds and trampling upon his own bowels. Or the poor brute may be sewed up in a crude, surgical way in order to enable him to canter around the ring a few more times. Once, only, in an experience covering several bull-fights in several countries, have I seen a horse drop dead from the first blow. The fight is not complete without the shedding of the blood of horses, and sometimes the crowd will clamour for more horses before this act is closed. There must be enough, for economy in this feature will place the people in a bad mood. The audience must be catered to, for if disappointed they are likely to demolish the ring and tear up the seats as a method of showing their displeasure. This, in itself, is sufficient to prove the debasing and brutalizing influence of this sport.

In the second act the *banderilleros*, men who plant the *banderillas* in the neck of the bull, appear in the arena. This is the most artistic and most interesting act in the entire performance, for great skill is displayed and little blood spilled. These men come in the ring without cape or any means of defence and depend entirely upon their skill and agility for safety. They are finely dressed and are usually superbly built fellows with lithe and muscular bodies. The *banderillero* takes with him a pair of barbed darts about two feet long and covered with fancy coloured paper with ribbon streamers. He shakes these at the bull, thus provoking an assault. Then, just when he seems to be on the bull's horns and the novice turns his face away to avoid the scene, he plants the darts in the gory neck of the bull and steps lightly aside. These darts re-enrage the bull, who has been getting rather tired of the whole affair. He attacks whatever engages his attention. It may be only a dead horse which he will then tear open, being aroused to fury by the smell of the blood.

PLANTING THE *BANDERILLAS*

There are usually two of these men and each plants four darts in the bull's neck. They must be placed in front of the shoulder and so firmly inserted that they will not be shaken out. If successful in these particulars, then the *banderillero* who is a favourite will receive prolonged applause and a perfect volley of complimentary comments. Even the *matador* himself ofttimes deigns to take part in this act. If so, he performs the act in some daring and novel way. They will sometimes sit in a chair and thus plant the darts, or take a pole and vault over the bull after placing them. Occasionally a bull is cowardly and will not fight. Then "fire" is called for and darts filled with powder which explodes in the flesh are used. This will cause the bull to dance and skip around in his agony, which is very pleasing to the audience and furnishes variety to an otherwise monotonous exhibition.

The trumpet sounds the last act. This is the duel,—the death. Everything has been done with reference to this act. The first two acts have been intended to madden the animal and tire him by the violent exercise and loss of blood. He is panting, his sides heave as though they would burst, his neck is one mass of blood over which, as if in mockery, hang the many-hued darts. The man with the sword would not stand much show with a fresh and unwearied animal. This actor is the *matador*, or *espada*, and, if known as one who kills his bulls with a single stroke of the sword, he will receive great applause on entering. He steps forward to the president's box and makes a little speech, offering to kill the bull to the honour of Mexico. Throwing his hat to some one in the seats, (for it is considered an honour to hold any of his apparel) the hero advances sword in hand toward the bull, who, during this by-play, has been entertained by the cape-bearers again. He bears in his left hand a staff, called the *muleta*, over which is a red flag, and in the right a keen-edged sword. The flag serves both as a lure to the beast and a protection to the man. He is usually pale and always alert, and studies the animal for a moment to ascertain his disposition. This can not be prolonged for the audience will not brook delay. The tension of nerves is too great. As the bull makes a rush for the red flag, with head lowered, the *matador* plunges the keen blade into the bull's shoulders up to the hilt. The bull staggers and dies.

It is wonderful to see how excited and enthusiastic the crowd becomes when the *matador* has made a skilful killing. They rise and cheer and wave their handkerchiefs. As he passes around the ring to receive their applause, a perfect volley of hats, coats, handkerchiefs, and cigars are thrown toward him. These are tossed back except the cigars or any money that may have been included. If the killing has been poorly made, or in a bungling manner, hisses replace cheers and boards or chairs may be thrown instead of hats and cigars. At a fight in Guatemala City I saw one *matador* chased out of the ring, and he did not return again during that performance. This was done after he had made three unsuccessful attempts to kill the bull and had plunged two swords into the poor, tortured animal without striking a vital spot.

Then comes the finale. Teams of gaily-decked mules are brought in to drag out the dead bull and horses. The bloody places are covered over with sawdust in order to prevent slipping. Even before the dead animals are removed, the two or three *picadores* appear on other sorry-looking steeds, even worse than the first ones if such a thing were possible. The trumpet sounds, the door flies open and another bull comes rushing in to meet the same fate as the first. The play begins again with the same variety of sickening incidents. Others follow in regular order until the usual number of six bulls have been dispatched. The management is usually very careful not to promise more than will be performed, for they know the temper of the audience too well. At a bull-fight in Madrid, which I attended, the management had promised ten bulls in its posters but the tickets only called for eight. After the eighth bull had been dispatched the end was announced, but the crowd refused to leave. All over the vast amphitheatre rang the cry "*otro toro*" (another bull), repeated over and over again in one swelling cadence with ever-increasing volume. The management was obdurate and the multitudes left muttering their maledictions.

Formerly gentlemen of the court mounted on the finest horses in the kingdom entered the arena and fought the bull like the knights of old. Now the sport has degenerated and is performed by professionals hired for the purpose. I once had the opportunity of witnessing a bull-fight by the Portuguese method. This is the bull-fight deprived of its disgusting details. It is even more exciting and dispenses with the killing of both bull and horses. The men with the red cloaks are employed just the same but the men who place the *banderillas* are mounted on horses. They are not broken-down hacks, but magnificent, well-trained animals and good care is taken that the bull does not make sausage meat of them. As a further protection, the points of the bull's horns are covered with balls to prevent injury to the horses. Their sport consists in riding past the bull, and placing the darts without permitting the bull to touch the horse. It is a feat that requires great skill and a steady nerve. After the bull is thoroughly tired out, a number of oxen are driven in the ring, the exhausted bull is taken out and another one brought in to continue the sport. In any form bull-fighting is bad enough, but if a line can be drawn between degrees of evil, the method of the Portuguese is the least to be condemned.

Tauromachy has many devotees who follow the fights in all their features as the base ball fan watches the sporting page of the American newspaper. In some places the spectacles are reported in all their most minute details, even down to the number of minutes it took the bull to die after receiving the fatal stroke. The killing of bulls is a science and there are many different schools which have been founded by great masters. A renowned *matador* receives as much attention as the champion prize-fighter in English speaking countries. They receive great sums of money but are almost invariably improvident and save little. The fights are not unattended by danger, for deaths are not infrequent and serious injuries are a common occurrence.

Ladies attend these spectacles and seem to derive as much pleasure as those who are supposed to be made of sterner stuff. Their black eyes sparkle with excitement and they shower their appreciation upon the successful one without reserve. It is the place for dress as the opera is in other lands. All the gallantry in the Spanish nature comes to the front on the way to and at the bull-fight. The enthusiasm, the manners, the expressions—all are distinctly national.

In Mexico the light on the horizon seems to be growing brighter, and the beginning of the end of this brutal and un-American sport is apparently in sight. It is not in favour with the present officials in the national capital and in many of the state capitals. Three of the most important states absolutely forbid the bull-fights, and heavy penalties are provided for any violations of the law. Statutes to prohibit them have been enacted in the federal district on more than one occasion, but they have been as often repealed so great was the popular demand for them. The best people do not now attend the performances in the City of Mexico but this fact has made little diminution in the crowd. Their places are taken by foreigners resident there, many of whom are among the most ardent supporters of the sport. I predict that within the next decade there will be few states in the Republic of Mexico that will permit the bull-fight within their borders. Such action may curtail a profitable industry and remove a good market for worn-out horses, but these material losses will be more than compensated in the development of those elements of character which can not be measured by the low standard of mere dollars and cents.

CHAPTER XIV
EDUCATION AND THE ARTS

Any one who is acquainted with the conditions existing in Spain or any part of Spanish America would naturally surmise that education in New Spain is at a low ebb. What education does exist is confined to a few. When you know that districts can be found in Spain to-day where scarcely ten per cent. of the inhabitants have mastered the art of reading or writing, it is not surprising to learn that after three centuries of the rule of Spanish governors and viceroys, ninety-five per cent. of the population of Mexico still remained in profound ignorance. Learning for the masses was regarded as prejudicial by those representatives and misrepresentatives of the home government. One viceroy voiced this sentiment by saying that only the catechism should be taught in America. Students are not likely to go beyond the learning of their teachers, and these were obliged to pass examination in only the most elementary branches. As a natural result, instruction soon fell into the hands of the incompetent. Teaching did not attract the bright minds. Those who cared for scholastic attainments prepared for the church or law. Others became soldiers or adventurers.

The first viceroy, Mendoza, was a broad-minded man and interested in his new empire. At his death he left a sum of money with which to establish a university to be open to all classes. This institution was actually established as early as 1551.

Very few of the aborigines attained much culture, although a few of the Aztec nobles were notable exceptions. Education was in general left to the church but was neglected by that institution. The Jesuits, whatever their faults may have been, were interested in education, and at the time of their expulsion in 1767 conducted a large number of colleges and seminaries.

In the seventeenth century the City of Mexico was looked upon as a great seat of learning and a literary centre. Even before the Shakesperian era of English writers, literature had its beginnings in that city. Bishop Zumarraga, the first "Bishop of the Great City of Tenuchtitlan," encouraged writers as well as miraculous visitations such as the Virgin of Guadalupe. Through his efforts, the first printing press of the new world had been set up in this seat of ancient Aztec civilization, in 1535, about a hundred years before one was in use in the British colonies. A dozen books had been printed in the City of Mexico before 1550, and almost a hundred before the close of the sixteenth century. Some of these were printed in the Indian languages including the Mixtec, Zapotec, Nahuatl, Huaxtec, Tarascan and others.

The very first book printed on this first press bore the following impressive and "elevating" title: *Escala Espiritual para llegar al Cielo, Traducido del Latin en Castellano por el Venerable Padre Fr Ivan de la Madalena, Religioso Dominico, 1536.* Translated into English it means the Spiritual Ladder for reaching Heaven, Translated from Latin into Spanish by Father Ivan, Dominican. This book was written especially for students preparing for the priesthood, and no copies of it are in existence so far as is known. The second book was a Christian Doctrine, printed in 1539 "to the honour and glory of Our Lord Jesus Christ and of the Most Sacred Virgin, His Mother." It was published in the native language also "for the benefit of the native Indians and the salvation of their souls." A few of the books departed from a strictly religious character, but all of them drew deep religious truths from every event. One of the early books was an account of a great earthquake in the City of Guatemala which, as the title page suggests, should be an example that "we amend our sins and be prepared whenever God shall be pleased to call us." Nearly all of these early books were written by Spanish priests and members of the religious orders. The first music of the new world was printed here also in the old illuminated style, as well as the first wood-engraving.

The first newspaper in Mexico was the *Mercurio Volante,* or The Flying Mercury, established in 1693. From that time until the present day, newspapers have existed, but they were so hampered and restricted in their utterances that their influence and circulation was small until long after independence had been proclaimed. Now there are a great many newspapers and periodicals of all kinds and descriptions published in the capital. However, no American would class them with our own newspapers, for the reason that they do not seem to have the "nose for news" of the American journalist. A Mexican reporter would not think of invading the sanctity of the home even for a "scoop" over his competitors. Likewise the family skeleton is generally safe, which is certainly a commendable feature.

Not one of the many newspapers published could be classed as sensational or of the "yellow" stripe. Mexico's reading public is comparatively small even to this day because of the still large illiterate class. *El Imparcial*, the leading daily and official organ of the government, does not have a circulation exceeding seventy-five thousand, scattered all over the republic. Its editor is an influential member of congress. It publishes an afternoon edition called *El Mundo* (the world). The *Popular* is second in circulation. *Tiempo* (times) is the leading Catholic daily. Other papers are *Pais* (country), *Patria* and *Sucesos* (events). There are two English newspapers published in the capital of which *The Mexican Herald* is the leading one and is the best newspaper in the country. It is widely read by both foreigners and official and influential Mexicans. There is an illustrated weekly, *El Mundo Illustrado*, an agricultural paper, *The Heraldo Agricola* and many other periodicals of various kinds. *Modern Mexico* is an excellent illustrated monthly magazine edited in the City of Mexico and published in New York. It is printed in both Spanish and English and is devoted to Mexican interests in general. Many of the cities have daily newspapers, but they are generally inferior and uninfluential publications. The best paper published in Vera Cruz could not compare with an American newspaper published in a little hamlet.

Mexico has produced many writers and some of them have been very prolific in their productions. It can not be said that there was much originality to the early writers when they departed from historical lines, but there is a sprightliness and rhythm in their epics that holds the attention of the reader. The bright spots in the history of literature for the first generation after the conquest are made by a group of Indian writers, bearing the unpronounceable names of Ixtlilxochitli, Tezozomoc and Nitzahualcoyotl. These men recorded the glory of their ancestors in prose and poetry. Although their Spanish is faulty, their genius is clear. Bernal Diaz, the early companion of Cortez and afterwards governor of Guatemala, wrote from the latter place his "True History of the Events of the Conquest of New Spain." It is a very readable work and a fascinating account of an interesting country and a primitive race. The writings of Las Casas have been much criticised but they deserve mention. Other chroniclers are Bustamente, Alvarez and Iglesias.

Poetry has always had a leading place in the literature of Mexico for the Spanish language is well suited to verse and their love poems have the highest rank. Some of the modern writers are better known in Europe than on this continent. The two leading poets are Juan de Dios Pesa, called the Mexican Longfellow, and José Peon y Contreras. The latter is foremost in the ranks of living poets.

Literary talent is much encouraged by the government and any one showing marked literary ability is almost sure to be offered some government position. An instance of this is seen in the career of Vicente Riva Palacio, a well known novelist and dramatist who has been governor, cabinet member and Justice of the Supreme Court. Another example was the poet Prieto who served in the cabinet of several presidents and died a few years ago. The Minister of Fomento (encouragement) can issue deserving books from the government press, if he so desires, and a number of works, especially historical treatises, have been issued in this way. The reason is, I suppose, because the reading public is not yet very large and a meritorious book would possibly have only a limited sale. These conditions are fast passing away. The drama and the tragic have ever filled a large place in the life of the Mexican people. A number of their dramatic books have become well known in Spanish-speaking countries but have not been translated into English.

After the struggle for independence, nothing was done in the way of education until almost the middle of the last century. The colleges and schools already established had begun to languish. Even after that date little was done, because the church was so occupied in retaining its own foothold, and each successive government inherited only a burden of debt from its predecessors. Juarez had the desire to establish schools but not the means. Maximilian would no doubt have promoted education but his throne was never secure.

The development of the school system is so recent that it may safely be said to date from the first inauguration of President Diaz in 1876. Listen to what this so-called republican despot says upon this subject, which expresses the attitude of the present government: "Education is our foremost interest. We regard it as the foundation of our prosperity and the basis of our very existence. For this reason we are doing all that we can do to strengthen its activity and increase its power. I have created a public school for boys and another for girls in every community in the republic. Education is such a national interest that we have established a Ministry of Public Instruction to watch over it. We have learned from Japan, what we indeed knew before, but did not realize quite clearly, that education is the one thing needful to a people; if they but possess it, all other distinctions are added unto them."

The educational system has been revolutionized, it might be said created, within a little more than a quarter of a century under the guidance of one man except for a period of four years. The schools are non-sectarian and the teaching of religion is absolutely prohibited. "That" says Diaz, "is for the family to do, for the state should teach only scholarship, industry and patriotism." The schools in the Federal District, which includes the City of Mexico and suburbs, and the territories of Tepic and Lower California, are under the direct control of the executive. The Federal District alone has nearly four hundred schools, and a number of fine new school buildings have been erected in the past four years after American models. The idea of a school building without a play ground is strange to an American, yet in Mexico none, except the new ones, have any recreation ground whatever, and they are housed mostly in the old church properties that reverted to the government after the disestablishment. Another strange idea to the American mind is the separation of the sexes which is almost universal. The girls' schools contain fewer pupils, for the parents, if possible, send them to private institutions or employ private teachers. Within the past year several million dollars was appropriated by congress for the erection and equipment of new buildings in the Federal District. Commissioners have been sent to the United States to study school systems, and we find their schools divided very much as our own.

AN AZTEC SCHOOLGIRL

The schools in the various states are under their own control, and the number and condition varies accordingly.[3] In most of them primary instruction is compulsory. There are not many hamlets except in remote mountain regions where primary schools have not been established, although in many places greatly inadequate, if all those of school age should attend. In the cities, schools for the higher education corresponding to our own high schools are maintained at public expense. The English language is a compulsory study in certain grades, and one can almost see the time in the future when there will be two idioms in Mexico. Free night schools are maintained in some places for the benefit of those who can not attend during the day. The duties of citizenship are particularly impressed upon boys, and some feminine work is taught to the girls even in the primary schools. In addition to the government schools, the churches and private associations support many schools for pupils of all ages.

Perhaps nowhere are the results of the campaign for education seen to better advantage than in the soldiers' barracks and penal institutions. The soldiers are mostly recruited from the Indians and are without education. The same is true of those who fill up the jails and penitentiaries. However much they may deserve their punishment, humane methods prevail. Attendance upon classes is compulsory upon both soldiers and convicts, and instruction is given in practical morals, civil government, arithmetic, natural science, history of Mexico, geometry, drawing and singing. If the prisoner is studious and obeys the rules of the institution, he is graduated and given his freedom. This little insight into a better life has made a good citizen out of many a former convict, and a better one out of a soldier who has completed the term of his enlistment. The native Mexicans are bright and intelligent, but self-culture is not common because of natural indolence. The Indians, and especially the *Mestizos*, are promising and quick to learn. Although there are no accurate statistics, it is estimated that nearly one-half of the adult population can at least read and most of that number can also write.

The first college established in North America was founded in Mexico in 1540 and is now located at Morelia. The federal government supports normal schools for the preparation of teachers, and schools of music, agriculture, dentistry, medicine, law, mining, fine arts and trades for both sexes. There are also schools for the blind and mutes, and reform schools for incorrigibles. The medical college has had a greater reputation than any of the other institutions of higher learning. This college now occupies the old home of the inquisition. The staffs of these schools are generally finely educated men, and will compare favourably with the staffs of similar institutions in other countries.

The Biblioteca Nacional, or National Library, occupies a magnificent building that was formerly a noted monastery. It contains several hundred thousand volumes, and is a storehouse of ancient documents and volumes of the colonial periods. When the monastic orders were suppressed, more than one hundred thousand volumes were added to the national library from these institutions. Although most of their books and pamphlets were religious works, yet many of them are extremely valuable and almost priceless. There are a few books here that date back before the discovery of America by Columbus, and many rare old documents on vellum and parchment. A few of the picture writings of the Aztecs are also preserved in this interesting library. The National Museum is a vast storehouse of the antiquities of the country. One can wander around through the rooms and corridors for hours and days and continually find some new object of interest in the vast collection of relics of the prehistorical races.

Like all Catholic countries Mexico has the traditional reverence for religious art. This love has caused a careful preservation of all the paintings that have been brought to the country, and the names of the donors as well. Nearly every church is adorned with some cherished painting, most of which are copies of works by the noted masters held in the great collections of Europe. However, here and there will be found a Michael Angelo, a Velasquez, a Guido, a Murillo or a Rubens. Perhaps the most cherished canvas in the entire country is a Titian at the village of Tzintzuntzan on the shores of Lake Patzcuaro. It is a large canvas on the walls of a little dilapidated church and represents the entombing of Christ. The room that contains it has but one outside opening and that an unglazed window.

Mexico herself has developed some expert copyists but few talented artists. One of the most noted was Cabrera, a Zapotec Indian, who has been called the Rafael of Mexico. He was architect, sculptor and painter, and has done some fine work in each line. Politics has in times past absorbed too much of the time of the young men of Mexico so that the arts have been neglected.

The Escuela National de Bellas Artes, or National School of Fine Arts, in the City of Mexico is an excellent institution and is liberally supported by the government.

Charles Dudley Warner says: "It was a marvellous time of original and beautiful work that covered Mexico with churches, and set up in all the remote and almost inaccessible villages towers and domes that match the best work of Italy and recall the triumphs of Moorish art."

No one with even the slightest love of architecture can help but be impressed with the great variety of design and grandeur of construction of the churches of Mexico. Though designed by Spanish architects and retaining the Moorish characteristics of that period, they are the work of native workmen and have received some Aztec touches. On the façades, towers and portals are designs and figures made by these workmen which are doubtless Indian legends or traditions of a prehistoric age. They resemble strongly those strange symbols of the ancient Egyptians and Persians. Some of the churches which the traveller encounters in villages consisting of low adobe huts fairly overwhelm one with their splendour. In places a great church will loom up in the horizon with scarcely a sign of human habitation near it. Only in the tropics are these great houses of worship wanting. The danger of earthquakes precluded the building of lofty structures there, and the priests of the conquering age, which was the great era of construction, rather avoided the hot lands for the cooler plateaus.

The beauty and originality in the churches is principally in the exterior. This is the reverse of the architecture in the homes, for there the outside walls are plain, and skill and ornamentation are devoted to the decoration of the patio. The interior is generally quite commonplace, and a church in one city is very much like a church in another. The ornamentation of the exterior is very elaborate and of the rococo or, as some would call it, the over-done style. However when looking upon the extreme richness of detail, one can see and appreciate the beauty and merits of the style, even if there is a certain floridness and flamboyancy present. The towers resemble the towers which are a part of the mosques in Moslem countries from which the call to prayers is made by the priests. As Mr. Warner says: "There is a touch of decay nearly everywhere, a crumbling and defacement of colours, which add somewhat of pathos to the old structures; but in nearly every one there is some unexpected fancy—a belfry oddly placed, a figure that surprises with its quaintness of its position, or a rich bit of deep stone carving; and in the humblest and plainest façade, there is a note of individual yielding to a whim of expression that is very fascinating. The architects escaped from the commonplace and the conventional; they understood proportion without regularity, and the result is not, perhaps, explainable to those who are only accustomed to our church architecture."

CHAPTER XV
MINES AND MINING

Humboldt speaks of Mexico as the treasure house of the world. It is one of the most richly mineralized regions ever discovered, and has produced one-third of the world's supply of the white metal. Mexico, together with Peru, furnished the wealth that enabled Spain to build up her great empire. And many a real castle in Spain was built with the gold and silver taken out of these rugged mountains of New Spain. The thirst for gold became a disease among Spanish adventurers. The mind of Columbus was distracted by the sight of natives along the coast of Honduras, who were wearing pure gold suspended around their necks by cotton cords, and he temporarily gave up his voyage of discovery to search for the source of this great wealth.

No country can compare with Mexico in the amount of silver of pure quality that has been produced. The largest lump of silver ever found, weighing two thousand seven hundred and fifty pounds, was discovered by a poor Indian in the State of Sonora. Because of a dispute as to the ownership, the crown solved the question by appropriating the entire amount. In fact the crown at first claimed two-thirds of all the precious metals mined which was afterwards reduced to one-fifth. Some authorities estimate the amount of silver that has been produced in Mexico at the enormous sum of $6,000,000,000, but two-thirds of that sum is probably in excess of the real value. The Taxco, Tzumepanco and Temezcaltepec mines date from 1539 but the greatest number of the "bonanzas" were discovered between 1550 and 1700. Many of them were located by priests, who, urged on by a fanatical zeal to convert the natives, pushed forth into unknown regions, and literally stumbled upon the rich ore-bearing quartz. The Spanish viceregal government kept an accurate account of the silver mined in their red-tape method, for the royal one-fifth was carefully and jealously looked after. Mine owners were compelled to make their reports regularly and correctly. A reference to these reports shows a record of almost untold wealth when it is remembered that this was long before the depreciation of silver.

The story of the bonanza kings makes interesting reading. They made money so fast that it was almost impossible to spend it except over the gaming table, in those days before the invention of modern surplus-reducing luxuries. One man, Zambrano, discovered a mine that made him extremely wealthy. Although he lived in the various capitals of Europe as extravagantly as the age permitted, yet he left a comfortable little fortune of $60,000,000 for his heirs to fight over. He even proposed to lay a sidewalk of silver bars in front of his house, but the authorities objected. He took out fifty-five million ounces of silver from one mine in twelve years as is shown by the government records.

Many of those who accumulated great fortunes were made grandees of Spain and some of the present titled families in that country are descendants of the famous bonanza kings of Mexico. Juan de Oñata who colonized New Mexico at his own expense, founding Santa Fe, and became its first governor about 1598, was a son of one of the mining kings, and the wealth dug out of the earth in old Mexico by his father furnished the means for founding that state.

Joseph de la Borda was one of the romantic characters of this age. He was a wandering Frenchman who came from Canada in the first half of the eighteenth century and no one ever learned anything further about him. He made three fortunes and lost two of them because of his lavish gifts, most of which went to the church. He built several large churches in what is now the state of Hidalgo. After losing his second fortune, the Archbishop of Mexico gave him permission to sell a magnificent diamond-studded ornament that he had given to the church in Tasco. From this he realized $100,000, and after a great deal of prospecting, finally discovered another rich mine which yielded him many more millions.

Pedro Romero de Terreros, from a humble shopkeeper, became Count of Regla, after acquiring great wealth from his mine, La Viscayne. He built two large ships, one of one hundred and twelve guns, and presented them to his sovereign. He also loaned the crown $1,000,000 as freely as a man gives a friend a dollar, which sum the king never found it convenient to repay. In later life he founded the national pawn-shop, which he called the Mount of Piety and which has grown to be such a great humanitarian institution in the capital and other cities.

The Conde de Valenciana who discovered the famous Valenciana mine of Guanajuato is reported to have made and spent $100,000,000 in a few years. One man discovered a rich mine on his ranch near Durango that rendered him immensely wealthy. He sent a present of $2,000,000 to the king of Spain and asked permission to build galleries and *portales* of silver around his fine new home. This was refused on the ground that such display was the privilege of royalty only.

A Guanajuato miner paved the street with silver ingots for a distance of sixty yards for the procession to pass over on their way to the church on the occasion of the christening of his son. Another story is told of a mining king who, on a similar occasion, paved the main aisle of the church with bars of silver for the baptismal party to walk upon. After the ceremony he wanted to remove the silver bars, but the wily priest told him that it would be an act of impiety which the Almighty would surely punish. It was not done and the occasion proved to be an expensive christening for the crœsus. Godfathers became so reckless in throwing away money that one viceroy issued a proclamation forbidding them to fling handfuls of money in the street as had been their custom, because such acts encouraged improvidence.

I have seen the statement that there is one man at Mazatlan to-day who owns a mine whose entrance is protected by massive walls and gates. Whenever he wants a hundred thousand or so of lucre, he simply takes in a few miners and digs out the ore and then gambles it away.

There is one noted mining king of to-day, Pedro Alvaredo, a full-blooded Indian, who is known as the peon millionaire. A few years ago a mine that he owned "bonanzad," as they call it, and he became immensely wealthy. However, he and his wife still dress in the peon clothes to which they were accustomed. He has built a mansion and furnished it with every kind of musical instrument to be obtained, including many makes of pianos. A few years ago he announced that he would pay off the national debt, but he found it a little too large.

The Spaniards worked only the very richest of the mines. They would not touch ore that did not yield nearly a hundred ounces to the ton. Their early methods were of the very crudest sort until the *"patio"* process was discovered and came into general use. If difficulties were met with in mining, these men simply worked around them and left great amounts of rich quartz untouched. The ore was so plentiful that they did not attempt to do their operations in a thorough manner. However they protected the entrance by building great fortifications around the shafts, that look like the walled cities of old and were patrolled by armed guards. Vast shafts were constructed down which run ladders. The poor peon toils up these ladders which sometimes aggregate more than a thousand rounds carrying a rawhide sack on his back containing two hundred and fifty pounds of ore without a rest, and will make several trips a day. In early times the natives were compelled to work in these mines to all intents and purposes as slaves, and were beaten and flogged even to death if they refused to obey their taskmasters. At night each peon was searched for fear he might conceal some of the precious metal. However as their costume was exceedingly simple the search was a very easy matter. The mines were cleared of water in the same way by the peons carrying it up these long ladders in rawhide buckets. Many mines were abandoned on account of water in those days long before their wealth was exhausted. Transportation was slow and expensive, and the mountain trails were kept dusty by the long trains of pack mules transporting treasures and supplies.

PEON MINERS AT LUNCH

Until within the last few years since American capital has undertaken to develop many of the Mexican mines, only the most primitive methods were in use. Even to-day many are operated in the same old way, although modern machinery is being rapidly introduced. The expense of fuel has been a great drawback in the less productive mines, and the shafts many hundreds of feet deep are worked with a windlass and mule power. Coal costs as high as $15 (gold) per ton at the mine and is then cheaper than wood at $14 (silver) per cord. At these prices steam power becomes very expensive. In those early days only those ores could be mined at a profit that could be treated at the mine, because of the great expense of transporting the ore-laden rock on the backs of mules.

The patio process of amalgamating silver is still generally used. This first came into use in 1557, being discovered by Bartolome de Medina, a miner. The ore is first crushed into a powder by an immense rolling stone that is revolved by teams of mules. This powder is then carried into a patio, or paved court, by a stream of water until the mass is about two feet deep. Quicksilver, salt and blue vitriol are then thrown into it and several teams of mules are driven around and around until the mass is thoroughly mixed, which requires several weeks. This is then thrown into troughs of water, where the amalgam of silver and quicksilver will sink to the bottom. By a process of distillation the silver is then separated from the quicksilver. Within five years after the discovery of this process Zacatecas alone had thirty-five of these reduction works in operation. It is claimed that not over ten per cent. is lost by this simple method. The poor mules eventually become horrible looking sights from the action of the vitriol on their legs. This patio mud has been used in the construction of the huts of the peons. A company was formed to tear down a whole row of these huts in Guanajuato just to extract the little metal that was left in them. The crown retained a monopoly on the quicksilver, and realized great profits upon this necessary metal in treating the silver ore.

The first bonanza mines were discovered at Zacatecas in 1546 by Juan de Tolosa. So rich were they and so great was the influx of miners, that the place was made a city forty years later. For two hundred and fifty years fabulous sums of silver were taken from the hills surrounding this quaint city. Some of the richest mines of the country have been located near

Pachuca. More than three hundred silver mines are found there and in the near-by districts of Regla and Real del Monte. One mine, The Trinidad, is said to have yielded $50,000,000 in ten years. There was very little stock speculation with the mines in the early days. There was at least one exception where an English company bought an old producing mine and the $500 shares rose to $80,000 but in the end the mine proved to be a failure. Catorce is also a rich mining town, and the mines have produced many millions of silver ore. The State of Oaxaca is likewise rich in gold and silver bearing quartz. None of the great bonanzas were found there, but a steady stream of gold and silver has been produced by the Oaxaca mines. I heard an interesting story of a young prospector who had spent several years and all his money in the search for wealth near Ejutla in that state. Having only a few dollars left he invested his all in dynamite and placed it in the lode with a prayer for luck. The blast revealed a rich "lead" which he sold for $600,000 a few days later.

The richest mineralized section in the whole republic is probably that in and around Guanajuato, the "hill of the frogs." This district was discovered by two mule drivers in 1548 who were on their way from Zacatecas to the City of Mexico, and from that date until the present time a billion and a half dollars' worth of silver has been produced. A hundred years ago Guanajuato was one of the largest cities and it is admitted by all travellers to be one of the most picturesque cities in the New World. Its wealthy mine owners lived like princes and spent their money like drunken sailors. Fortunes were made and lost. About a hundred years ago two mines there were producing four million ounces of silver annually. These mines were worked by the Aztecs long before the Spaniards came. This is called the La Luz district.

To-day Guanajuato is a much smaller city than it was a half century ago because of the decrease in mining activity. The Theatre Juarez is a beautiful building and was built and is owned by the state, which seems strange to an American. The state or municipal ownership of theatres in Spanish-American countries is quite common. The Republic of Guatemala takes more pride in its national theatre, the Teatre Colon (Columbus), than in any other public building. A curious sight in this city of Guanajuato is the panteon, or crypt, where bodies are buried for five years. If burial fees are not paid again at the end of that time, the bones are thrown in a heap.

However, many of the bodies are found mummified and these are placed against the wall making a horrible, gruesome sight,—one that will not be soon forgotten by the traveller. It is like the crypt underneath the Capuchin Church in Rome.

The Spanish conquerors mentioned nothing of silver among the Aztecs, but all their ornaments were of gold. The value of the presents of gold ornaments given to Cortez by Montezuma is estimated by Prescott at more than $7,000,000. The source of this great gold supply has never been discovered, for, although gold in small quantities is found in many places intermingled with silver, yet the amount mined was very small in comparison with the value of the silver. In more recent years owing to improved methods of separating the precious metals from the quartz, the proportion of gold produced has been increasing. From 1810 to 1884 mining reached a very low ebb because of the unstable form of government and constant revolutionary movements. The crude methods formerly in use became unprofitable, and foreign capitalists were afraid to invest money for fear that a change in the government might occur over night and wipe out everything. The old mines had been worked to such a depth that they were flooded and could not be kept in workable condition by the bucket brigade. The disturbed political conditions had developed large and bold bands of robbers; and as all traffic had to be carried over lonely mountain trails, mining became very insecure and consequently unprofitable.

Since the extension of the railway systems and the establishment of a stable government, mining is again attracting a great deal of attention. The government encourages foreign investments in the mines. Many of the old bonanzas have been taken over by new companies with both good and bad results for the investors. The introduction of modern machinery has so reduced the cost of mining that lower grade ores can be profitably worked. Even the dumps that have been accumulating for centuries are being worked over at a fair profit. Smelters and mills for the cyanide process are springing up in all of the mining regions. Modern pumps are taking the place of the mule and windlass in keeping the mines free from water. The fame of the old bonanzas has no doubt aided in fleecing the gullible through fake companies organized by unscrupulous and even criminal promoters. American miners and prospectors are met with all over Mexico in the mining districts. It is safe to say that the majority of them have either met with disappointment or are living in hope of a "strike." These conditions are the same in every mining district the world over.

The mining laws are simple and practical. Boards are established in every mining community who look after the mining interests. Any one discovering a claim can "denounce" it before this board and he is protected. Foreigners have the same rights as citizens in "denouncing" a claim. A mining claim is called a *"pertenencia"* and is one hundred metres square thus consisting of ten thousand square metres. The surface ground must be settled for with the owner. A tax of ten dollars must be paid annually to protect the claim from forfeiture. More than twelve thousand claims are now on record as shown by government statistics. The government only claims a one-twenty-fifth instead of the royal one-fifth exacted by Spain.

The number of men employed in the mines at the present time is about two hundred thousand. Wages are low and average about fifty cents for common labour and one dollar for native miners in Mexican money. However, in recent years wages at the mines have had a tendency to rise. Mexico's annual production of silver amounts to from $30,000,000 to $35,000,000 in gold value and gives it first place. As the price of silver is advancing, the production will no doubt be further stimulated. It now occupies fifth place in the production of gold, being exceeded only by the Transvaal, Australia, United States and Russia. The production of Mexico in 1906 reached a value of $15,000,000.

Many other minerals are found in Mexico. Perhaps the most valuable, next after gold and silver, is copper of which there are a number of rich deposits. In 1906, one hundred and thirty-five million pounds of copper were mined. When this is compared with a production of nine hundred and fifteen million pounds in the United States for the same period it is not a bad showing for Mexico. Iron is not generally distributed but there is a mountain of nearly ninety per cent. pure iron ore at Durango. Tradition says that the Indians first led the Spaniards to Durango by tales of a mountain of gold where the yellow metal sparkled on the surface. When they arrived at this mountain, now called Cerro del Mercado, they pointed to the outcroppings of pyrites which the ignorant natives thought—or pretended to think—were of the same metal that these strange white men had come across the unknown seas in search of. A little coal has been found but not in quantities sufficient for local consumption, so that considerable coal and coke are imported each year from England and the United States. Lead is found in large quantities, and most of the graphite used in the United States is imported from Mexico. The greatest development in recent years has been in the production of petroleum. Some of the most remarkable flowing wells in the world have been struck near Tampico. Great rivalry has resulted between the English and American interests, and the Mexicans have profited by it. Another profitable field has been found on the Isthmus of Tehuantepec. The total production for the year 1910 exceeded four million barrels. Several of the railways have already adopted this fuel.

Wonderful progress is being made in developing the mineral resources of this country, and it is possible that greater discoveries will yet be made. The wealth of Mexico to-day is not being squandered after the manner of many of the bonanza kings; but it is being spent along legitimate lines, and is one of the greatest aids in building up a strong republic and developing a nation of intelligent and liberty-loving citizens.

CHAPTER XVI
RAILWAYS AND THEIR INFLUENCE

A work upon Mexico would be incomplete without a description of the railways and the present progressive railway movement. Nothing has contributed in such a degree to the great progress that has been made in the last quarter of a century in Mexico, as the rapidly increasing railway lines. This is true not only of the influence these advance agents of progressiveness have had upon commerce, but they have enlarged the intercourse with other nations, especially with the United States. Through this means the dormant energies and ambitions of the Mexican people have been awakened, and a new era has dawned in our Latin neighbour.

The centres of population in Mexico have always been situated in the great central plateaus in the interior. Only a very small proportion of the population live on, or near the coast. Communication with the ports was over long, narrow and rough trails. The transportation of commerce was slow and expensive, and required great droves of slow-moving pack mules and patient burros, and whole armies of cargadors. Furthermore, the very isolation of the people and difficulty of communication kept them aloof from modern progress, and left them content with things as they were, with no ambition for anything more advanced or better than had been enjoyed by their forefathers. It also prevented the development of a real, national spirit, because one community was, in a true sense, not familiar with the neighbouring cities, and took a special pride in its local interests rather than in the idea of a homogeneous, strongly-centred whole.

So jealous were those employed in the business of transportation in the old crude way, that, in order to placate them, some of the earlier roads were obliged to commence construction at the point furthermost from the port, in order to give employment to these people in transporting the material from the port to the place of beginning. Those who are familiar with the great development of the west, since the construction of our own trans-continental lines, will better appreciate the change that railroad construction has wrought in Mexico. There is this difference, however, that the people were in Mexico before the railroads were built, and, instead of a newly-developed country it is a rejuvenated old country.

Prior to the beginning of the railway movement, Mexico was noted chiefly for its minerals. Now, although only a small portion of the mineral wealth has been dug out of the earth, mining has become of secondary importance. The increase in commerce and manufacturing, and the stimulus to agriculture brought about by these avenues of communication, have swelled the general wealth of the country far more than the millions of white metal extracted from old mother earth each year. Manufacturing plants have sprung up on every hand, and the products of the mills are increasing in volume and variety each year. Mexico could, probably, after a fashion, supply all the wants of her people without any imports from the outside world. The factories include almost every line of trade from the making of articles to adorn the outward man to the solid and liquid goods which cheer and sustain the inward man.

The railroads have tended to enlarge the wants of the people by throwing them into contact with other civilizations and have raised the general standard of wages so that the people have more money to expend for material needs and luxuries. The abolishment of the *alcabales*, or local customs, was the logical result of the development of railways and was almost revolutionary. From the time of the Spanish conquest each city had collected a local tariff on all goods brought into the town for sale, and had raised a great part of its revenues in this way. Changes come slow in this country, but are nevertheless sure. It may be that at some time in the future the brown back of the burden-bearing cargador will be relieved of its load. It is a question, however, whether this change would be welcomed by the dusky descendants of Montezuma.

The encouragement given to railroad construction has been done with a lavish but well-directed hand. It is estimated that more than one hundred and fifty million dollars have been spent by the Mexican government in subsidizing railroads and in developing harbours, and the end is not in sight yet. Perhaps the motive has not been altogether unselfish for no one influence has assisted so much in centralizing the power in the hands of the Diaz government or been such a potent force in tranquillizing a naturally turbulent people, as the railways and the telegraph lines which always accompany them. Instant notice would be sent of any embryonic revolutionary movement and troops could be hurried to the affected district at once. There were at the close of 1906, according to government report, twenty-one thousand six hundred and eleven kilometers of railway track in Mexico, or about thirteen thousand five hundred miles, and this is increasing at the rate of several hundred miles each year. The subsidies on the principal lines have averaged from $10,000 to $15,000 per English mile, with the provision in most instances that after a certain period (generally ninety-nine years) the roads shall revert to the government at a certain fixed valuation. Construction is either of such a difficult character, or over such long stretches of semi-desert territory with poor and scattered population, that most of these roads would never have been built except for government assistance.

After the manner of the Romans and with equal truthfulness, the Mexicans say that all roads lead to the City of Mexico. This saying is almost literally true. The Valley of Mexico is traversed from every direction with the *ferro carriles*, or roads of iron, converging toward the capital. It now has direct communication by rail with almost every part of the republic except Yucatan and the Pacific slope, and can reach this coast at one point by a roundabout way to Salina Cruz.

The back-bone of the extensive railway system is formed by the two great trunk lines which reach out to the north from the City of Mexico, gradually diverging until at the places where they cross the muddy Rio Grande they are several hundred miles apart. These railways traverse the broad central plateau of which Humboldt, the great traveller, wrote, "so regular is the great plateau and so gentle are the slopes where depressions occur, that the journey from Mexico to Santa Fe, New Mexico, might be made in a four-wheeled vehicle." There are hundreds of miles where construction work was exceedingly easy, as it consisted simply of shovelling up a slightly raised bed and laying the ties and rail. Rough mountain construction in other places, and especially in entering the Valley of Mexico, required the work of the very best engineers. By whichever route the traveller enters Mexico it would be well if he could sleep over the first two hundred miles while the train is passing over the semi-desert plains of Northern Mexico where the dust filters through the car windows in clouds.

The government of Mexico has entered the railway field for economic reasons. It is simply another indication of the intention on the part of President Diaz to control the railway situation in behalf of the people by preventing excessive rates through the pooling of interests. The spectre of railway consolidation similar to the merging of the great systems in the United States influenced the officials more than anything else, and the government did not want the railway situation in Mexico controlled by any of the large American companies. The project was begun only a few years ago by actual purchase in the open market of a controlling interest in the National railroad. This purchase was made by a select firm of New York brokers, and the real buyer was not revealed until sufficient stock had been secured to insure control of the properties. These lines are now known as the National Lines of Mexico and have a mileage of about eight thousand miles. They will be held by a corporation with a capital of $250,000,000, organized under the laws of Mexico, the control of which will be vested in the Mexican government, although there will be a minority board in New York. They include one hundred and sixty miles of track in the United States from Laredo to Corpus Christi, Texas.

The main line of the system is the former National Railroad extending from Laredo to the capital, a distance of eight hundred and thirty-nine miles, several hundred miles shorter than the Central. It passes through the important cities of Monterey, Saltillo, San Luis Potosi and Celaya. Originally constructed as a narrow gauge line, it has been changed to standard width throughout its entire length. The Mexican International Railroad, which enters Mexico at Eagle Pass and runs through Torreon to Durango with a branch to Monterey, has been added. The Interoceanic Railway, whose main line connects the capital with Vera Cruz, passing through Puebla, the third largest city in Mexico, is also now a part of this system. At the present time this line is narrow gauge, but preparations are now being made to widen it to standard gauge. Quite recently the government purchased the Hidalgo Railroad, which extends from the City of Mexico to Pachuca, State of Hidalgo. It is the intention of the government to extend this line immediately to Tampico, thus making a short and direct route to this port.

In December, 1906, the government announced the purchase of the Mexican Central Railway, its only large competitor, and this road will be added to the system known as the National Lines. The reasons for this purchase were stated by Minister of Finance Limantour to be "the aggressive attitude assumed by certain great railway systems in the United States." It was feared that the great railways of the United States would step in and absorb this important line, and saddle upon the people the trust evil. The Mexican Central is the largest railway system within the republic and owns more than three thousand five hundred miles of track. The main line extends from El Paso, Texas, to the capital in a southeasterly direction a distance of one thousand two hundred and twenty-four miles. This was the first road constructed to the United States border and received the largest subsidy of any line, amounting to $15,200 per mile. Construction work was begun in 1880 at both terminal points and rushed to completion so that through trains were running less than four years later. This made an average of nearly one mile for each working day. It traverses sections rich in agriculture and mineral resources and passes through many of the important cities. Among these are Chihuahua, Torreon, Zacatecas, Aguas Calientes, Leon, Irapuato, Celaya and Querétero. It reaches a population of several millions on the table lands.

Two important branches of the main line run to the gulf port of Tampico, which is second only in importance to Vera Cruz. One of these lines branches off at Aguas Calientes passing through San Luis Potosi, and the other at Torreon, passing through Monterey. At Irapuato a branch line runs west to Guadalajara, the second largest city in Mexico, and is being extended through to Manzanillo, a good harbour on the Pacific coast. It is expected that this road will be completed January, 1908, and will give the capital what has long been needed—a direct route to the Pacific. The difficulty and great cost of construction in reaching this coast has delayed the various projected lines, for the drop from the high plateaus to the sea level is very abrupt. It is estimated that the last hundred miles of this extension will cost $5,000,000 in gold. Another branch of this system extends south from the capital through ancient Cuernevaca to the Balsas River, with an ultimate destination of Acapulco, the finest harbour on the Pacific Coast of either North or South America. There are also numerous smaller and less important feeders.

The Mexican Railway which connects the port of Vera Cruz with the City of Mexico is the oldest railroad in the republic. It was first incorporated under the empire in 1864 as the Imperial Mexican Railway and exceedingly favourable concessions were granted. Owing to the political disturbances it was not completed until 1873. It was built with English capital and cost a fabulous sum. The monopoly which it held for years enabled it to pay big returns to its owners for a long period and even now its earnings compare favourably with our own western lines. This road is noted as one of the most picturesque railways in the world, for in a few hours one is transported from the high plateaus to the sea level.

ALONG THE MEXICAN SOUTHERN RAILWAY

The Mexican Southern Railway is another English road extending from Puebla south to Oaxaca, which was opened for traffic in 1893, a distance of 227 miles. This road received a bonus of about $10,000,000 in government bonds, and well it needed such an inducement, for the traveller wonders in passing over the line where the profit can come from, as there are only a very few places of any size between the two terminal points. It opens up a rich agricultural and mineral section in the Valley of Oaxaca, and will probably develop into a profitable property in the future. As the line runs through narrow ravines a great part of the way, following streams, the traveller does not see the best part of the country traversed.

The Southern Pacific has a branch which runs from Benson, Arizona, to Guaymas, the chief port on the Gulf of California, passing through Hermosillo, the capital of the State of Sonora, the home of the Yaqui Indians. It passes through an intensely interesting country, possessing a wealth of scenery and natural resources. This line is being extended farther south, with an ultimate destination of Guadalajara or possibly the capital city.

Another important link in the system of railroads in Mexico, and one which is practically owned by the government is the Vera Cruz and Pacific Railway. This road extends from Vera Cruz to Santa Lucrecia, a station on the Tehuantepec National Railway which is described in another chapter. A branch line also extends to Cordoba, there connecting with the Mexican Railway, and forms what is at present the only all-rail route from the capital to a Pacific port. This road runs through the heart of the tropics and alternately passes over prairie and through tropical jungle.

A trip over this road is a revelation to the traveller who has never visited a tropical land. No one except those who assisted in the work fully appreciates the enormous difficulties that had to be overcome. I doubt if even mountains present more perplexing problems in railroad construction than these level prairies and swamps, where there is no solid rock or gravel and the country is deluged with an annual rainfall of from twelve to sixteen feet. The surface is a soft clay unfit for roadbed or ballast. After heavy rains the ties and often the rails would sink into it until completely covered. For a few years the road was practically abandoned for several weeks during the heaviest rainfall. The track would sometimes slip sideways, or in a cut the banks would slide in and cover it. In the two hundred and forty-two miles of the main line, the road crosses six large rivers, whose size is due to the amount of rainfall rather than the extent of territory drained. These rivers and many smaller streams require an average of more than one bridge for each mile of track. The uncertainty and inefficiency of native help and difficulty of getting skilled American labour to go there because of the fear of tropical fevers, rendered the work of the contractor no easy task. Even an American workman could not accomplish more than about half as much as in a colder climate.

I made this trip when it required twenty-six hours to cover the two hundred miles from Vera Cruz to Santa Lucrecia. No one asked the engineer to go faster, and we considered ourselves in luck not to run off the rails, which in many places resembled the track made by a wobbly wheel after we had passed over it. It has now been placed in better condition, and the run is made in much quicker time. No one must expect quick time on Mexican railroads, for twenty-five miles an hour is fast travelling and the average is nearer fifteen miles. The section traversed by this road must inevitably be the richest part of Mexico in the near future, now that it has an outlet. It passes through the region best adapted for tropical plantations where the soil is inexhaustible.

One of the dreams of the late James G. Blaine was a Pan-American railroad or all-rail route from the United States to the southernmost republics of South America. President Arthur appointed a commission in 1884 which was sent to the republics of Central and South America along the proposed route. At the first Pan-American conference held in Washington, this projected railway was discussed at considerable length. All the representatives were in favour of it and a survey was decided upon. Several parties of surveyors were set to work at different points along the proposed route, and a complete survey was made from Oaxaca, Mexico, to the northernmost point reached by the railways of the Argentine Republic. The proposition excited a great deal of interest and discussion at the time, but little has been heard of it in recent years. There is one man in Mexico, however, who has not lost sight of the great project, and that man is J. M. Neeland. He organized a company to build the Pan-American Railroad from San Geronimo, a station on the Tehuantepec National Railroad to the boundary of Guatemala, a distance of about three hundred miles. The Mexican government promised a subsidy of $10,000 gold, per mile. He has followed the base of the mountain range in order to lessen the expense of construction, and render it easy to connect with the ports by means of branch lines. It follows as nearly as possible an old military road constructed by the Spaniards.

Quietly and unostentatiously this line has been pushed forward until it has been completed to Pijijiapam, only one hundred and twenty-six miles from the Guatemala boundary, and a contract has been let for its completion by the close of the year 1907. The importance of this line to Mexico can hardly be overestimated, for it connects the seat of government by an all-rail line with the most remote corner of the republic. It also opens up the rich coffee lands in the State of Chiapas, the best coffee territory in Mexico. The ports along this coast are all open roadsteads without piers, and freight is carried to and from the steamers in lighters. At one time a steamer on which I was a passenger lay at San Benito, the most southerly Pacific port of Mexico and on the line of this railway, three days in order to load a few thousand bags of coffee. This part of the country has been so isolated heretofore that it has never been developed to any extent. The completion of this Pan-American railroad will greatly increase the influence of Mexico in the little Republic of Guatemala, and will have a tendency to render that country less turbulent. The promoters aim to continue this road through all the republics of Central America, clear to the Isthmus of Panama. They have already secured a concession with the promise of a good subsidy from Guatemala, and will utilize a portion of a railroad now in operation in that country. A remarkable fact in connection with this road is that it is already meeting its operating expenses and fixed charges, which is an unusual showing for a newly-built Mexican railroad.

The government is now endeavouring to have a railroad constructed from some point on the Pan-American Railroad to connect with the railways of Yucatan. This road and the other lines already under construction will connect all parts of the republic with the bands of steel, with the single exception of Lower California. It will not be many years before this great plan of a great president will be a reality. Step by step progress has been made but the improvement has been permanent. In some places the innovation was not welcomed at first, because of extreme conservatism. Now everyone reaps some benefit from it. Before the days of railroads each community lived by itself, and the poor natives were at the mercy of the rich plantation owners in the dry years which sometimes occurred. Now, transportation is cheap and quick, and everyone can have food at a reasonable cost. The paternal character of the government in this respect was shown a few years ago, when the corn crop was a partial failure and a "corner" was attempted by the dealers. The government immediately removed the tariff, imported great quantities of grain, and sold it to the people at cost. This could not have been done except for the facilities afforded by the railway lines. The traffic does not seem large, and there is only one train per day each way on most of the lines, and on the branches this is frequently a mixed passenger and freight train. The tonnage is increasing each year as the wants of the people increase, and money to purchase things heretofore regarded as luxuries becomes more abundant.

NOTE TO REVISED EDITION. In 1911 the railway mileage of Mexico exceeded 15,000 miles. The Pan-American Railroad is now completed to Mariscal, on the Guatemala border. Work on the connecting link with the lines of that republic, only about thirty miles, is progressing, and it is estimated that within a year it will be possible to travel by rail from New York to Guatemala City. The Pan-American and the Vera Cruz and Pacific Railroads are now a part of the National Lines. The name of the latter has been changed to the Vera Cruz and Isthmus Railroad. The Manzanillo branch was completed almost on time. The extension of the Southern Pacific as far as the city of Tepic, and the Kansas City, Mexico and Orient Railway are described in a succeeding chapter.

CHAPTER XVII
RELIGIOUS FORCES

The Aztecs, who originally believed in one supreme invisible creator, Taotl, adopted the gods of conquered races, like the Romans of old, and became polytheists. The Toltecs, one of the vanquished people, were nature worshippers, and made offerings of fruits and flowers to their deities. After their defeat, the peaceful gods of the Toltecs, who took pleasure in the offerings of the fruits of the soil, soon took a place by the side of the terrible god of war of the Aztecs, Huitzilopoxtli, and shared with him the offerings of human sacrifices. This repulsive deity is portrayed as a hideous idol with broad face, wide mouth and terrible eyes, but was covered with jewels of gold and pearls and girt with golden serpents. At the altars hung censers of incense and braziers filled with the hearts of the victims offered in sacrifice. It is said that this god was ministered to by more than five thousand priests.

When the Spanish conquerors came, the policy of Cortez left the Mexicans no alternative but the adoption of the Christian religion. "Conversion" and "Baptism" became interchangeable terms and the baptized pagan was immediately considered a good Christian even though the conversion only followed the judicious use of the fire and rack. One of the priests boasted that his "ordinary day's work was from ten to twenty thousand souls." Within a few years after the conquest baptism had been administered to more than four million Indians. Dreams of avarice swayed the minds of the conquering legions, for it was believed that from the unknown, western world was to come the gold that was to make every man a Crœsus. But first these ungodly people must be converted to Romanism. As the unlettered Indians could not understand the real spirit and meaning of this new religion, visible symbols and pictures were substituted for the former idols. Humboldt, the traveller so often quoted because of his careful research, says: "The introduction of the Romish religion had no other effect upon the Mexicans than to substitute new ceremonies and symbols for the rites of a sanguinary worship. Dogma has not succeeded dogma, but only ceremony to ceremony. I have seen them marked and adorned with tinkling bells, perform savage dances around the altar while a monk of St. Francis elevated the Host." It soon became a religious duty for the Spaniard returning from Europe to bring paintings and statues of saints to adorn the newly-erected churches, and holy relics of the saints to place therein. In this way these cruel invaders no doubt sought to satisfy their consciences for their outrages upon a mild and unresisting people. It is little wonder that the Indians could not fully appreciate the humanity of the lowly Nazarene when represented by such ferocious invaders.

A few of the Aztec gods blossomed out as Christian saints soon after the Conquest, through the ingenious schemes of the early priests who adopted this method to make the new religion accepted. They brought with them into the Roman Church the particular characteristics and powers which they were credited with as gods. As for example, the goddess of the rains who was much worshipped in the regions of little rain can be recognized in Our Lady of the Mists, or Our Lady of the Rains of the Mexican church. These saints are appealed to for the much-needed rain and are believed to have the same power to bring it which they, as Aztec or Toltec gods, were supposed to have had. In many places there are shrines erected to these saints of the Church who are supposed to have power over the rain. It has been proven that, in most instances, in Aztec times, a temple existed on the same spot dedicated to the goddess of the rains or mists, as the case might be.

These schemes of miraculous appearances upon scenes already sacred made the transition from the native ceremonies to the ritual of the Catholic Church easy to a people who were accustomed to outward show and symbolism. The striking ceremonies of the Catholic Church, as practised in Mexico, and its impressive services in an unknown tongue, seemed in harmony with the rites of the Aztecs, and it was not hard for Cortez to force his religion upon the simple and superstitious mind of the poor, conquered Indian, who was more interested in form than sentiment. The religion of the Roman Church in Mexico is not free from pagan features even to this day. As one writer expresses it "paganism was baptized, Christianity paganized." Outward display means more than spirituality and piety with the ignorant who constitute a very large proportion of the population.

One can still recognize in the rites of the Catholic Church, as practised to-day in Mexico, a tinge of the Aztec worship. A noted French Catholic prelate, Abbe Domenech, in 1867 wrote of that church as follows: "Mexican faith is a dead faith. The abuse of external ceremonies, the facility of reconciling the devil with God, the absence of internal exercise of piety, have killed the faith in Mexico. The idolatrous character of Mexican Catholicism is a fact well known to all travellers. The worship of saints and madonnas so absorbs the devotion of the people that little time is left to think about God. The Indians go to hear mass with their poultry and vegetables, which they are carrying to market. The gobble of the turkeys, the crowing of the cocks, the mewing of the cats, the chirping of the birds in their nests in the ceiling, and the flea-bites rendered meditation impossible to me, unaccustomed to live in such a menagerie."

WAYSIDE SHRINE WITH AN OFFERING OF FLOWERS

In remote caves of mountain regions it is claimed, and, I believe, truthfully, that the ancient deities are still worshipped. It is no infrequent occurrence to see a bouquet of flowers before the image of the virgin in the churches or wayside shrines. Sometimes even offerings of wheat or fruits are found, the gift of some poor peon in whose mind the conception of the Saviour and his mission on earth is very vague. Several writers assert that they have personally seen Indians on their way to the mountains to sacrifice lambs, chickens and flowers to their gods, thus proving that the grosser forms of paganism have not been stamped out entirely. The priests, of course, do not approve of this, and try in every way to stop these practices, but without success.

The Catholic Church used to be all-powerful in Mexico. It held the wealth and the learning, and the priests preyed upon the people as well as prayed for them. They were taxed to the utmost, and "Pay or pray" was the motto affixed to the cross by the priests. Rich men gave freely of their substance. Poor peons—and they are vastly in the majority—went clothed in rags that the Church might be benefited. The favourite method was by the sale of indulgences. General Thompson, United States Minister to Mexico in 1845, wrote as follows: "As a means of raising money, I would not give the single institution of the Catholic religion (in Mexico) of masses and indulgences for the benefit of the souls of the dead for the power of taxation possessed by any government. I remember that my washerwoman once asked me to lend her two dollars. I asked her what she wanted with it. She told me that there was a particular mass to be said on that day which relieved the souls in purgatory from ten thousand years' torture and that she wished to secure the benefit for her mother." It is like the harangue that so aroused Martin Luther: "The very moment the money clicks on the bottom of this chest the soul escapes from purgatory and flies to Heaven! Bring your money, bring money, bring money!"

Shrines and chapels were so numerous that the true believer passed through the streets with head uncovered and hat in hand, for fear that he might pass one unobserved and not remove his head covering as piety demanded. During the latter years of Spanish rule in Mexico, the Church became so enormously rich that it was reported to have in its possession one-third of all the wealth in Mexico. In addition to the power the Church naturally held, this immense wealth gave its leaders great prestige in governmental affairs, for wealth everywhere commands power and respect among those in authority. At one time the clergy held property to the value of about $180,000,000, yielding an annual income of $12,000,000, according to reliable authorities. Some have estimated the wealth at more than $600,000,000.

It had secured control not only of the wealth, but also much of the best agricultural land within the republic, owning eight hundred *haciendas* and more than twenty-two thousand city lots. All this was tied up and became useless and non-productive. The Church used its great influence to oppose all progress. The opposition finally broke forth, and the immense wealth of convents, shrines and monasteries was poured forth with lavish hand in what the Church considered a holy war against heretical ideas and persons. Reformers set envious eyes upon this property, and numerous attempts were made to dispossess the Church of it. An edict aimed at the power of the Church was issued by Commonfort in 1857, but the Indian reformer and president, Juarez, was the first to actually accomplish the separation of church and state several years later. The establishment of the empire with Maximilian as Emperor was simply a reaction, and an attempt to establish a government in which the interests of the Church would again be paramount. It is not much wonder that the native population yielded so readily to the overthrow of the priestly power. In accomplishing the complete overthrow of church and state, Mexico only did what Italy did a few years later, and what France is endeavouring to do at the present time. Even in Spain, the handwriting on the walls seems to point to the same ultimate result. And yet it is strange to see a nation so rigidly and even unmercifully regulating a church to which ninety-five per cent. of the people belong.

The reactionary movement on the part of the Church under the guise of French intervention failed. The reform anti-clerical movement prevailed once more, even though opposed by the enormous wealth of the Church. The greater portion of the property once owned by the Church has been lost. The country abounds in ruined churches and convents. The law went so far as to prohibit the Church from holding the title to property, and if it wished to own property, it must be in the names of individuals. Priests were forbidden, under penalty of fine and imprisonment, to appear in the streets in their clerical dress. Religious processions outside the walls of the church, or churchyard, were prohibited. Civil ceremonies were made obligatory to render a marriage valid. Sisters of Charity and the Jesuits were sent out of the country, and even the ringing of bells was regulated by law. It has now lost not only its property but its prestige as well.

The property was confiscated, or "denounced," and sold for beggarly sums in numerous instances. Many hotels are now located in former churches or convents, and schools and barracks innumerable occupy former homes of nuns. Even the famous prison of Belem in the City of Mexico, where more than three thousand offenders (most of them justly no doubt) have been incarcerated at times, was the old convent of that name; and the military prison, Santiago de Tlalteloco, was one of the oldest churches in Mexico, having been founded by the first viceroy. Protestant services are held in a number of places that were former Catholic churches, the buildings having been purchased by these organizations, or the use of them granted by the authorities. The rich silver plate and the altar rails were looted from the sacred edifices, or were sold for small sums by the officers.

For many years Mexico has thus gone along the line of reform. The ambition of the Church has been held in check but not killed. They are regaining some of their former power, and recovering much of their former property, so it is claimed by good authority.[4] The average Mexican is superstitious. He is boastful and bold in times of peace, but craven when the time of trial comes. Consequently, when sick and about to die, he will send for the priest, no matter how he may have fought the Church when in health. The priests, or some of them at least, claiming that the Catholic Church, as the chosen of the Lord, has a lien on all earthly goods, refuse to administer the sacrament without some restitution. If the dying man owns a confiscated church property, he must restore its value before he can get a clear title to a home in Heaven. With the persistence characteristic of the Mexican Catholic priests, they are ferreting out their former property and again accumulating wealth for their beloved Church. Their fees are utterly out of proportion to the earning capacity of the people. Marriage costs $14.00, baptism $2.25 and plain mass $6.00. Many of the poor peons are obliged to forego the services of the Church because of these high charges, for all services must be paid in advance.

They are also openly disregarding the established laws in some of the restrictions imposed. I travelled for two days on the railroad with the Bishop of Tehuantepec who wore his purple robes of office all the time. At nearly every station priests met him, and he was given a continuous ovation. A few months ago, according to a Mexican periodical, a well known priest, in defiance of the law which prohibits public religious processions, authorized such a procession, and blessed at the altar those who arrived with it. In many of the more remote districts the law requiring marriage ceremonies to be made by civil authorities is completely disregarded. The priests tell the people that the religious ceremony is all that is necessary. Although the Church upholds such marriages, in law they are absolutely null and void, and it is a deceit upon the contracting parties. Some priests go so far as to tell their people that the civil marriage is positively impious. And yet nothing is done to punish the above violations of the established laws. The government probably does not consider that these infractions of the strict letter of the law have reached a serious phase.

If the Roman Church of Mexico to-day, with its wealth confiscated, its public voice muzzled, its political powers annulled, has still power so that it can openly violate some of the fundamental laws of the country, we can have some faint idea of its power when it ruled the country with an iron hand. Those who see trouble ahead because of the avariciousness of some of the clergy, are fond of quoting the old Spanish proverb "The devil lurks behind the cross." Nevertheless, I believe that the clergy in Mexico to-day are superior to those who served prior to the change in status. Many of them are noble men striving to uplift the people and aid the government in its campaign for the enlightenment of the masses. The strife has purified them and they think less of the perquisites than the duties of their office. The well meaning priest no doubt suffers for the sins of his predecessors as well as those of his contemporaries who are blinded by the past glory of the Church. The Church as an institution is probably to some extent the victim of the ignorance and fanatical zeal of its early founders in Mexico. The Church will thrive far more when placed on the same footing as all churches are in the United States, and people and priest accept that condition. As one prominent American priest has recently said in commenting on the struggle in France: "Everywhere that church and state are united, the church is in bondage. Nowhere is the church so free and untrammelled, or so progressive, as in the United States."

The churches in all the cities are numerous and their capacity far greater than the number of those attending. Puebla, the City of the Angels, so called because of the many miraculous visits of the angels who even, on their first visit, measured off the city and fixed the site of some churches, is called the city of churches as it has the greatest number in proportion to the population of any city in the republic, many of them being erected in honour of the various angelic visitations. The City of Mexico contains the largest and most pretentious church building in the new world—the cathedral. It is also one of the largest church edifices in the world. This grand cathedral begun in 1573 was ready for service about three-quarters of a century later but the towers were not completed until 1791. It is four hundred and twenty-six feet long and almost two hundred feet wide with walls of great thickness, and reaches a height of one hundred and seventy-five feet in the dome. The towers are a little more than two hundred feet high. Then adjoining this building is another church, the Sagrario Metropolitano, which, to all appearances, is a part of the main structure, although of an entirely different and less beautiful style of architecture.

Within these two edifices were concentrated for centuries the pomp and ceremony of the Church of Rome and within their walls much of Mexico's history was made. It is still the headquarters of the church party while across the plaza is the National Palace, the official home of the government which conquered in the long struggle between the two forces. The estimated cost of the cathedral is $2,000,000, but that represents only a fraction of the actual cost if the labour is figured at a fair rate and the material had all been purchased at market value. There are some paintings by famous artists on the walls and dome. A balustrade surrounds the choir which is made of composite metal of gold, silver and copper and is so valuable that an offer of a speculative American to replace it with one of equal weight in solid silver was refused. Within the walls there are fourteen chapels dedicated to the various saints, and candles are kept constantly burning before the images, and in these chapels are kept many gruesome relics of these same saints. The remains of many of the former viceroys and some of the other noted men in Mexican history lie buried here. This, the greatest church in the western world, is also built on the foundations of the greatest pagan temple of the continent—the imposing *Teocalli* of the Aztecs. From the top of the towers we can look upon the same valley that Cortez viewed when Montezuma took him by the hand after ascending the great altar, and pointed out the various places of interest. The lakes have receded, the architecture is different, but our admiring eyes see the same majestic hills on every side.

Listening to the bells in the towers of this cathedral, once so powerful, one, who is a "dreamer of dreams," can almost imagine them lamenting the changed times in the words of the last poem written by the poet Longfellow:

"Is then the old faith dead,"
They say, "and in its stead
Is some new faith proclaimed,
That we are forced to remain
Naked to sun and rain,
Unsheltered and ashamed?

"Oh bring us back once more
The vanished days of yore,
When the world with faith was filled;
Bring back the fervid zeal,
The hearts of fire and steel,
The hands that believe and build.

"Then from our tower again
We will send over land and main
Our voices of command,
Like exiled kings who return
To their thrones, and the people learn
That the Priest is lord of the land!"

The very first movement on the part of Protestant organizations to evangelize Mexico was made by the American Bible Society when they sent out one of their representative with the American army in 1846. This man distributed several thousand copies of the scriptures between Vera Cruz and the capital which afterwards bore fruit. A few years later a woman, Miss Matilda Rankin, who had been engaged in missionary work in Texas, crossed over the border and held services in Monterey. In 1862 a Baptist missionary, Rev. James Hickey, also began work in Monterey. However, no organized effort was made by Protestant bodies until the years from 1869 to 1880, when missionaries were sent by the following denominations: Protestant Episcopal, Methodist Episcopal, Methodist Episcopal South, Presbyterian, Baptist, Christian and Congregational. Bishop H. C. Riley obtained an old church for the use of the Protestant Episcopal Church and Rev. William Butler purchased a part of the convent of San Francisco, in the heart of the city, for the Methodist Episcopal Church.

Dios y libertad had been the watchword of the reform movement, but it had not been put into practice until the time of President Juarez, who encouraged mission work, and exerted himself to protect the missionaries from fanatics. However frequent attacks upon these workers were made in provincial towns and one foreign missionary, Rev. J. L. Stephens, of the Congregational Church, was slain at Ahualuco in 1874. A number of native converts and preachers have met with serious, and even fatal injuries, but no other Americans have been killed. President Diaz has also encouraged these ministers when they were downhearted. Rev. William Butler quotes an interview which several missionaries had with him in which the President expressed himself as follows: "I have seen this land as none of you ever saw it, in degradation, with everything in the line of toleration and freedom to learn. I have watched its rise and progress to a better condition. We are not yet all we ought to be and hope to be; but we are not what we once were; we have risen as a people, and are now rising faster than ever. My advice is, do not be discouraged. Keep on with your work, avoiding topics of irritation and preaching your gospel in its own spirit." The president has no warmer supporters than the Protestant missionaries and their little bands of adherents.

Their numbers to-day after thirty years of aggressive work seem small, as the ten Protestant denominations who maintain missions in Mexico only claim about twenty-five thousand members, or about one hundred thousand adherents including those who attend the Sunday-school and other services. The Presbyterians are working in fourteen different states. They have fifty organized churches and two hundred and twenty-two outstations which are served by twenty-one foreign missionaries and one hundred and one native workers. The Methodist Episcopal Church has twenty-nine missionaries in the field and one hundred and twenty-two native workers, and is holding services at more than a hundred different places. The various denominations have divided up the field and are working together in harmony. The Methodists, for instance, are working in Guanajuato, Leon, Pachuca, Puebla, Silao, and Oaxaca. The Presbyterians have centred their efforts in Aguas Calientes, Zacatecas, Saltillo, San Luis Potosi and Jalapa. All denominations have missions in the City of Mexico. The Methodists, Baptists, Presbyterians and Congregationalists have their own publishing houses and issue periodicals and a great deal of printed matter in Spanish. There are in all about two hundred and fifty foreign missionaries in Mexico serving about seven hundred congregations. Many of these workers are medical missionaries who are doing a vast amount of good, and others are teachers who are instructing the youth. The Protestant bodies own property in Mexico valued at nearly two million dollars.

An era of at least tolerance toward Protestants is dawning in this land, and religious liberty is an actual fact. The Young Men's Christian Association has a strong organization in the capital. A fund has recently been raised to erect a splendid new building for the association. The President and his cabinet have also attended some special memorial services in the Protestant churches. This may seem a small thing, but a quarter of a century ago it would have been incredible. Some of the broad-minded Catholic clergy are even displaying a kindlier feeling toward the Protestant workers. It may not be many years before Catholic clergy and Protestant ministers may unite together in working for a common cause—the betterment of the morals and conditions of the people.

CHAPTER XVIII
PASSING OF THE LAWLESS

A rude wooden cross set up in a pile of stones is one of the striking features of Mexican landscape that is frequently seen. As the train whirls along through a narrow pass, high up on the mountain sides the cross is seen outlined against the sky; or, if you are pursuing your journey by horse or mule, in the remote districts away from the railways, your reverie is suddenly interrupted by coming upon one of these silent sentinels unawares. These crosses are mute reminders of an age that is passing away. Each one marks the spot where a murder has taken place in times past. It is an appeal for the good Catholic to mutter a prayer for the soul of the murdered one, who was thus without preparation thrust into the world beyond. There was a time, and that not more than a generation ago, when the murderous and lawless classes were numerous in Mexico. The Mexican bandit was so much feared, that, even to this day, some hesitate to travel in that country, and many more make walking arsenals of themselves before turning their faces toward our southern neighbour.

If the traditionary history that has come down to us is to be believed, these robber clans can trace their lineage back to the peregrinating merchants of the Aztecs, and Toltecs. The rich merchant of those days travelled over the country visiting the various cities with his wares. For self protection they were obliged to carry with them a large force of armed retainers. This knowledge of their own power led them to violence. If, for any reason, these merchants became angered at a town, or, if the people refused to trade with them, they would attack it, pillage it and carry off the inhabitants to be sold as slaves in other remote places, or hold them for ransom. This course generally proved far more remunerative than the more prosaic occupation of barter and trade. It was indeed a strong town in those days that could afford to refuse to trade with some of the powerful merchants. If one trader was not strong enough himself, he could easily enlist the assistance of another of his class, as the loot and slaves would be sufficient to remunerate both very well for the undertaking.

Later came the freebooters, who, in early Spanish days, had things very much their own way. Although many of these were well known, they would visit the cities armed to the teeth and no one would dare to molest them. It is even claimed, and with good reason, that many officials were in league with these knights of the road, and gave them information, and assisted them in their plans to waylay wealthy inhabitants. So long as the outlaws did not interfere with matters of government, their immunity was practically secure. There is one city in the northern part of Mexico named Catorce, the Spanish numeral for fourteen, because, for a long time, it was the stronghold of fourteen of the boldest, bravest and worst bandits that Mexico ever produced, who terrorized the country round about and could not be captured or subdued.

After independence, came a series of revolutions and uprisings for more than a half century. The bandits then became guerillas, fighting on whichever side offered the greatest advantage. They would loot a church, or rob the hacienda of some wealthy landowner, with equal cheerfulness. The place or person robbed depended upon whether the guerillas were enlisted in the cause of the clericals, or anti-clericals. By reason of the many turmoils and fights that took place, these guerillas became a numerous and powerful class with their rendezvous in the mountains, which, in no part of Mexico, are far distant. Before the advent of the railroads and telegraph it was a difficult matter to cope with these robber bands in Mexico because roads were lacking, and their haunts were almost inaccessible. This was one of the first problems attacked by President Diaz when he came into power, and he did it with the boldness, originality and dash for which he was noted.

This new leader found the army a disorganized band of guerillas led by a few men, not always over-scrupulous, and many parts of the country overrun by bands of outlaws with whom the local authorities were utterly unable to cope. Having some veteran troops after his many campaigns, Diaz sent them after the bandits whenever opportunity afforded. They were hunted and trailed into their mountain fastnesses. The soldiers were instructed never to take captives. A little heap of fresh dirt, or a few stones, marked the place where a living and breathing bandit had once stood. This war of extermination made welcome to many the proposition of Diaz. This was that he would furnish employment to those outlaws who should surrender, and would grant to them protection. The President being known as a man of his word, this proclamation had its effect and large numbers formerly under the ban of law, surrendered.

A *RURALE*

From this class of men the first companies of *rurales* were formed. Finding it was more profitable, or at least safer, to be in favour with this aggressive government than under its ban, they willingly entered this service. These men were brave and thoroughly familiar with all the mountain retreats and haunts of the outlaw bands. They hunted down their former confederates until a live bandit was a rare specimen. Travelling once more became secure, and now there are few places in Mexico where it is not perfectly safe for a traveller to journey. The companies of rurales, of which there are many, form one of the most effective forces for preserving order ever devised by any government. Like the famous *guardia civil* of Spain, the rurales patrol the remote mountain trails and great plains of the central plateaus, and are in reality a body of rural police. Many a lonely traveller has been made glad by the sight of the gray uniform of this band. They are generally kind hearted, and will do everything in their power for a foreigner. Their uniform is the typical riding costume of the country, and differs from the French appearance of the uniforms of the regular army.

They are fine horsemen, expert in the use of pistol and carbine, and form one of the most picturesque cavalry bodies in the world.

There is no sickly sentimentality wasted upon law breakers, and the highwayman, or robber, gets little sympathy. Few criminals get a second opportunity to commit their outrages through the pardoning process. The old *ley fuga*, or law of attempted escape, which was in force under Spanish rule, under which Indians or slaves attempting to flee were shot, was revived. Orders were promulgated to shoot highwaymen on sight, and all other prisoners if escape was attempted. Few attempts to escape are now made by prisoners, for the guards have a reckless way of sending bullets after fleeing prisoners, so that no chains are needed to secure them. The bullets are swift and any one in custody, even though held as a witness, will be followed by the quick, death-dealing messengers, if an attempt to escape is made. Gangs of convicts may be seen in various places working on the streets, or on the roads, under military guard but without shackle. The only report necessary in the event a prisoner is killed is that he attempted to escape. It may be a harsh proceeding, but it saves the state a great deal of money, and conviction is sure. Furthermore, it relieves judge, jury and prison officials of much hard work and annoyance.

A few years ago the Mexican army consisted of a few thousand irregular, nondescript soldiers so common in Spanish-American countries. Such men it was who placed Porfirio Diaz in power in 1876, the same year that we were celebrating the first centennial of our independence. In promoting peace this man of Mexico has not forgotten the arts of war. The army has been improved until it has ceased to be made up of the comic-opera type of the barefooted, half-naked soldier, and is now a well fed, well equipped, and well clothed organization to which Mexicans can point with pride. To the American eye the soldiers appear rather indifferent and insignificant, because of their smaller stature and brown skin, which reveals the fact that the regular soldier is generally drawn from the lower classes of Mexicans.

Although Mexico might be termed a military nation, as military service is made obligatory by the law of the country, yet in times of peace this service is not enforced. It is said that the majority of the enlistments are not even voluntary, but that recruits are drawn from the ranks of those who are persistent law breakers—those guilty of petty criminal offences which we would term misdemeanours. Many of these peon soldiers who before enlistment never knew what it was to have regular meals and wear clean clothes every day, leave the service after a few years much better citizens, and possessing a better education, for schools are maintained in connection with all the barracks where instruction is given in reading, writing and mathematics. The pay is about forty cents per day, in Mexican silver, and is good pay for that country when you take into consideration the fact that the soldier has absolutely no expenses except for such luxuries as he may want.

The standing army of Mexico consists of thirty thousand men and three thousand two hundred officers. Of this number the infantry number twenty-two thousand six hundred, cavalry five thousand five hundred, artillery two thousand, engineers and other branches of the service making up the remainder. This gives a soldier for every five hundred inhabitants, as compared with one for every fifteen hundred inhabitants in the United States. Both infantry and cavalry are equipped with the Spanish Mauser rifles and carbines. The headquarters of the army are in the City of Mexico, and several battalions of infantry and regiments of cavalry are stationed there at all times. The country is divided into a number of districts, at the headquarters of each of which are stationed large bodies of troops. Nearly every town of any size has a *commandancia* where a few troops are quartered. This general distribution of the military forces has been made with a prudent foresight in order to prevent any local uprising.

ARMY HEADQUARTERS, CITY OF MEXICO

In addition to the regular standing army, there are a number of armed forces which would swell the number of available troops in time of war. First and foremost are the *Rurales* who number about three thousand five hundred by actual count, but double that number in effectiveness. The Fiscal Guards number about one thousand and are in the revenue service. The police of the states and cities are compelled to undergo military drill also, and could be drafted into the army as trained soldiers. These several forces would constitute another army almost equal in number to the regular standing army. Militia organizations have been provided for by law similar to those organizations in our own country, but as yet little has been done. When these plans are perfected, it is designed to have the total war footing number a force of one hundred and fifty thousand drilled and disciplined men.

The President of Mexico is the commander-in-chief of the army and navy. The "West Point of Mexico" is located next to the presidential residence and is called the Chapultepec Military Academy. It was founded in 1824. During the war of 1847 Chapultepec was successfully stormed by the American forces, but heroically defended by the cadets. A monument now stands at the foot of the hill in memory of those cadets who fell in that engagement, and a graceful tribute is paid to the memory of those youthful patriots on each fourth of July, when wreaths are placed on the monument by the American residents of the capital at the same time that they decorate the graves of American soldiers who are buried near the city. This school now ranks high as a military school, and more than one-third of the commissioned officers of the army are graduates of this institution. The graduate leaves this school with the rank of lieutenant. The student must bind himself to serve seven years in the army, if he takes the technical courses, and, if he is discharged, or refuses to serve, must repay to the government $16 for each month he remained in the academy. If war should occur, all retired graduates would be compelled to report for service.

Not a generation ago the capital itself was the home of innumerable thieves. In fact, a goodly percentage of the people were either thieves, robbers or beggars. These were drawn from the *mestizo* class, and formed a picturesque but filthy group of blackguards. They would make love to any one's pocket, and argue with one another at the point of a long, sharp knife. Each one carried a knife and revolver. "Unfortunate men, women and children, the legitimate heritage of wrong, oppression and misgovernment, thronged the streets begging in daytime, and committing petty robberies by night. They slept by hundreds in doorways, on benches in public parks, in ruined houses, and in the dirtiest of apartments. A score or more of filthy beings of all ages and both sexes would sleep together in one small room reeking with the miasma that rose from sewers and unclean cobble-stone pavements."

Vice was the natural outcome of such conditions. All natural feelings of delicacy and shame were deadened. Morality was unknown, and they lived like animals rather than human beings. Marriages were unthought of, and children knew not their parents, for even their mothers deserted them. If not deserted, they were frequently maimed and turned out into the street to beg. Pulque and mescal added its touch to the picture. Disfiguring diseases were added, and the name *leperos* attached to them. Brantz Mayer, a writer on Mexico, has given the following definition of the *lepero*. "Blacken a man in the sun, let his hair grow long and tangled and become filled with vermin; let him plod about the streets in all kinds of dirt for years, and never know the use of a brush, or towel, or water, even, except in storms; let him put on a pair of leather breeches at twenty and wear them until forty without change or ablution; and over all place a torn and blackened hat and a tattered blanket begrimed with abominations; let him have wild eyes and shining teeth, features pinched by famine into sharpness, and breast bared and browned; combine all these in your imagination and you have a recipe for a Mexican *lepero*."

These *leperos* were the thieving class. They frequented all parts of the city. Even the churches were not exempt and you were just as likely to be robbed by some apparently devout, kneeling worshipper saying his *ave marias* in a sacred edifice as on the street. In the less frequented streets many hold-ups took place, and the bodies of those murdered would be found on the pavement in the morning. It was hardly safe to move about the street after night had fallen. The thieves' market was well known and did a thriving business. Here were the pawn-brokers who did a profitable business acting as "fences" for the thieves. Many instances are told by foreigners who were robbed, and, in a few hours, found their property exposed for sale in this market. They were obliged to pay considerable sums to recover their own property.

All these types are now disappearing, and even the beggars are less numerous. The former lawless *leperos* are now seen in the poor venders of lottery tickets who crowd every public place. Begging is forbidden in most parts of the city. Vice has not disappeared, it is true, nor has it in American cities. The poor peon still gets intoxicated and is dirty, but he is more law-abiding than formerly. Conditions, which are the result of neglect and misrule of centuries, can only be overcome entirely by education, immigration and the infusion of saner ideas, and this is a gradual process. A whole city, or a whole country, can not be plowed up and re-sown in a season, as the corn fields of last year were transformed into the waving fields of golden grain this year. A generation is even too short a time. The change actually wrought has been almost a miracle. Work can now be had by all who are willing to work, and the government is making strenuous efforts to get rid of the idle classes. It is a long and hard task, but another decade under present conditions will work wonders.

An excellent police system is found in the capital and all the other cities. A policeman is not hard to find. One is stationed at nearly every street intersection. During the day he stands like a statue, occasionally leaning against a door post. At night the policeman brings a lantern and a blanket, and sets the lantern in the centre of the crossing, while he stands beside it or not far away. The joker says the lantern is intended to aid the thief in avoiding the officer of the law. Sometimes after the people quit passing, he may lean up against a building and fall asleep, but you can locate his vicinity by the lantern. As the windows are all heavily barred, and the doors are heavy oaken affairs that it would take a stick of dynamite to move, and as fires are infrequent, his lot is not a very hard one. The police are very numerous, however, because the government wants to keep informed in order that a revolutionary movement may not gain any headway. One seldom hears of knock-downs now, and pocket picking is about the only kind of robbery.

These guardians of the peace are generally called *serenos*. This name clings to them from the old Spanish watchman whose duty it was to call out the time of the night and state of the weather. As this was usually clear, the watchman would say *"tiempo sereno"* meaning "weather clear." From the frequent repetition of this term the watchmen were dubbed *serenos*. The Mexican *sereno* is generally a faithful and reliable official and is obliging to a stranger. They have made the streets in the City of Mexico as safe as in Paris. The senses of sight and smell may be offended more often, but purse and life are just as secure.

CHAPTER XIX
THE STORY OF THE REPUBLIC

There is a strange fascination about the history of Mexico, and no one can thoroughly understand the country or the people without a little insight into those stirring events that preceded the establishment of the present republic. With the increasing friendly regard and the growing commercial intercourse between the two countries, a few pages devoted to this subject will not be amiss; and the prospective traveller, as well as the one who has already travelled in that country, will find an additional interest in Mexico and the Mexicans.

However we may feel inclined to criticize Cortez, the fact remains that he thoroughly subjugated the country, and presented to Spain the fairest jewel of her domain. Having been made the first governor of New Spain, he was too busy with fresh conquests and the task of keeping order to make a successful ruler. In order to reform the various abuses that had grown up, and represent in every way possible the person of the king, King Charles V sent the first viceroy in the autumn of 1535. This first of a long line of viceroys, reaching down to the year 1821, was named Antonio de Mendoza, himself of noble descent, a man of ability, and one who had at heart the best interests of the colonists and the welfare of the Indians. The latter had been subjected to many humiliations and hardships all of which were removed by him, and they were encouraged in the cultivation of the lands.

The colonists themselves were a source of great trouble for they were mostly adventurers and were not, like the early American colonists, men who were seeking religious liberty. The arm of the church was stretched just as strongly in new Spain as in the land of their birth, and to the religious orders was due in great measure the firm foundation upon which the Spanish government was established. During the rule of this man and his successor, Velasco, the country prospered, agriculture was stimulated and a number of industries suitable to the climate of the country encouraged.

At the close of the sixteenth century, Spain underwent great changes. The line of able rulers had passed away, and the government fell into the hands of profligates who were favourites of the reigning sovereign. The line of viceroys continued in rotation, and most of them were fair men who probably governed the best they knew how, but their knowledge on that subject was not very great. They were poor rulers when compared with the first two above mentioned. The church retained its firm grasp. As one writer has put it, during the first century of Spanish rule the church was a blessing to the country, during the second an indifferent quantity and during the third an actual menace. The inquisition—that terrible institution—had been established in Mexico as early as 1570. The first *auto-da-fé* was celebrated in 1574, when "there perished twenty-one pestilent Lutherans." Indians were exempt from this institution and it was only aimed at heretics of other nations. Large numbers were burned in the capital and other cities. In Puebla, the old house of the inquisition was remodelled within the last half-century, and a number of walled-up cells opened in which skeletons were found—no doubt remains of victims who had been buried alive. The inquisition was not formally abolished until the beginning of the last century, just prior to the beginning of the movement for independence. Even this concession, and the promise of correcting other abuses, did not stop the growing discontent, for generations had grown up who had few ties linking them to the mother country; who had intermarried with native races; and who would be satisfied with nothing but complete severance of their relations.

The beginning of the nineteenth century opened with a feeling of unrest in all European nations and their colonies. When Napoleon overturned monarchies, the idea of the divine right of kings received a shock. Among the countries thus affected was Spain, which had dropped down from the high pedestal it had formerly occupied. The eyes of the people of Mexico were opened by the events in Europe, and also by the successful revolution of the American colonies. All the offices of profit in Mexico were held by Spaniards, and the policy of the mother country toward her dependents was well expressed by one of the viceroys as follows: "Let the people of these dominions learn once for all that they were born to be silent and to obey, and not to discuss nor to have opinions in political affairs." The spirit of revolution and liberty was in the air and restraint became more and more galling. The events leading to the independence of Mexico, and the stirring times subsequent thereto, can best be treated by a glance at the men who were in the limelight during the various periods.

When Miguel Hidalgo, curate of the little village of Dolores, sounded the "grito" of independence by ringing the bell of the parish church early on the morning of the 16th of September, 1810, a struggle for independence was started that lasted for eleven years, and during which much of the soil of Mexico was crimsoned with the blood of those slain in battle or executed by the authorities as traitors. At the outset no people were less prepared for such a contest. They knew nothing of military tactics; their weapons were primitive and their leaders were without military training. No more righteous cause ever existed for rebellion against tyranny and usurpation. The first two leaders were consecrated representatives of the church that had assisted a despotic government in bringing about such an unfortunate state of affairs. These two martyrs who were excommunicated by the church, and executed by the government as traitors, are now honoured with resting places in sacred ground by a grateful nation.

The first revolt was headed by a picture of the patron saint of the country, and shouts of "Viva Nuestra Señora de Guadalupe" and "Viva la Independencia" were intermingled. Hidalgo and his compatriots were compelled to begin their movement before thoroughly prepared, because their plans had been discovered and betrayed to the government. On the morning of the memorable day above mentioned, Hidalgo addressed the people from the pulpit of the church where he had so often celebrated mass, and, leading his followers forth, released the prisoners in the town, and captured the principal Spaniards. Soon afterwards this priest-warrior patriot, who had been named Captain-General, followed by a few hundred of human beings (they can not be called soldiers), marched forth to conquer Mexico and give "death to the Spaniards."

It was a motley crowd armed with stones, lances, *machetes*, arrows, clubs and swords, whose numbers and enthusiasm were ever increasing as they marched across the country without meeting resistance. San Miguel and Celaya, Irapuato and Querétero, yielded, and the army which by this time numbered tens of thousands marched towards Guanajuato. The governor of that province assembled the terror-stricken populace in the now famous Alhondiga de Granaditas, built for storing grain but now a prison, as noted in that city as the Bastille of Paris. Upon a refusal to surrender, Hidalgo and his followers attacked this fortress with fanatical zeal, and captured it by the mere force of numbers. This supplied him with plenty of food and a million dollars in money which furnished the sinews of war.

Terror struck the hearts of the Spaniards and every town yielded to this new leader, who now bore the title of Generalissimo, as the army approached the City of Mexico. One terrible battle occurred at Monte las Cruces and both forces withdrew. Hidalgo—and this was probably his greatest error—retreated, and his fortune immediately turned. The volatile nature of the people asserted itself and his followers deserted by the thousands. He started for the United States, but was betrayed and captured, and was executed at Chihuahua on July 31st, 1811. For ten years his head was suspended by a spike from one of the corners of the Alhondiga de Granaditas, once occupied by him as conqueror, as a warning to revolutionists, but was afterward buried with great ceremony in the cathedral at the capital.

It was around a disciple of Hidalgo that the forces of discontent and patriotism rallied upon the death of their first leader, and that man was also a priest, Jose Maria Morelas. Of low birth and poor, this man drove mules until thirty years of age before an opportunity presented itself for education to fit himself for the priesthood, which was his ambition. In that time he had acquired the qualities of patience and cool calculation from the animals he drove. A student under Hidalgo, he had imbibed a love for independence, and leaving his church upon the sounding of the "grito," offered his services to the Generalissimo. He was an abler leader than Hidalgo and showed great military skill, winning a series of victories clear across the country from Acapulco, on the Pacific Coast, to Cuautla not far from Vera Cruz. At Cuautla he was besieged for over two months, and then successfully withdrew with all his forces by night. Returning to Acapulco he summoned the first Mexican Congress, which met at Chilpantzingo, a small town near that city. This congress met on the 14th of September, 1813, and on the following day issued its famous declaration of independence, as follows: —"The Congress of Anahuac, lawfully installed in the city of Chilpantzingo, of North America, solemnly declares, in the presence of God, arbitrator of kingdoms and author of society, who gives and takes away according to the inscrutable designs of his providence, that, through the present circumstances of Europe, it has recovered the exercise of its sovereignty, hitherto usurped, its dependence upon the throne of Spain being thus forever disrupted and dissolved."[5]

This congress provided a form of government with a military executive called Generalissimo, and Morelas was elected to this position for life, or "so long as he was worthy." Shortly after this his forces were defeated at Valladolid, now called Morelia, and his power began to wane, though resistance was kept up for some time afterwards with varying success. Spanish troops had arrived, and stronger leaders were in charge of the government forces and the cause of independence looked dark. The plans of Morelas were betrayed to the enemy and he was captured. The ecclesiastical tribunes covered him with ignominy. He was then sentenced to death by the military authorities, and shot in the little village of San Cristobal Ecatepec, near the capital, on December 22d, 1815, dying the death of a hero. This muleteer-priest-warrior was an able leader, an honest man and a patriotic citizen. He seemed devoid of personal ambition, although accepting title for the sake of the cause he fought for. He was possessed of restless energy and great piety, for he always made confession before entering battle. To-day, he is second only to Hidalgo in the affections of the people, and worthily fills that position. Over the door of the house once owned by him in Morelia appears the following inscription:—

> "Morelas the illustrious
> Immortal Hero.
> In this house honoured by thy presence
> Salute you the grateful people of Morelia."

The revolution was seemingly crushed at the death of Morelas but a few patriots retired to the mountains, and there kept alive for better days the sacred fire of liberty. Guerrero was one of those heroes who showed an unwearying activity, and kept up a constant warfare upon the government forces. The next prominent name in succession among those leaders of the movement for freedom was Agustin de Iturbide, a former active and able officer of the royalist forces, and to whom more than anyone else was due the failure of Morelas. Deserting the cause of Spain, because he thought injustice had been done him, General Iturbide issued the "Plan of Iguala" on the 20th of February, 1820, composed of three articles: preservation of the Roman Catholic church; independence of Mexico under a monarchical form of government with a prince of the royal house of Spain as ruler; union and equality of Spaniards and Mexicans. From this proclamation his army became known as the army of the three guarantees. His act was full of duplicity, for he had obtained the largest force possible from the Viceroy Apodaca in order to turn them over to the new scheme.

Before the viceroy could recover from his surprise, Iturbide, who had been joined by most of the insurgent leaders, had started on his victorious campaign. Valladolid, Querétero and Puebla succumbed. The viceroy tried by suppressing liberty, and enforcing enlistments in the royal army, to stem the tide but in vain, and he was deposed. O'Donoju, the sixty-fourth and last viceroy, arrived about this time at Vera Cruz, but was intercepted by Iturbide and entered into the treaty of Cordoba in which the independence of Mexico was recognized with a sovereign to be selected from the royal house of Spain, and a provisional Junta formed. Iturbide was selected as president of this Junta, and made a triumphal entry into the City of Mexico on the 27th of September, 1821. This ended three hundred years of Spanish rule in Mexico. Iturbide had accomplished in a little more than a year, and with little bloodshed, what ten years of strife had failed to do. He can not be classed with Hidalgo and Morelas as a pure patriot, but he has been officially designated as the "Liberator of Mexico."

The rejection of the treaty of Cordoba by the Cortes of Spain gave new impetus to the smouldering ambitions of Iturbide. The second Mexican Congress having been called, Iturbide at a packed session was declared Emperor by a majority of four to one of those voting, but not a constitutional majority, and he took the office as Agustin I. When he was crowned and anointed in the cathedral with much form and solemnity, on the 21st of July, 1822, the ambition of this self-made emperor had reached its full. The saying that uneasy lies the head that wears a crown never had better application than in this instance. Other leaders in the cause of liberty felt that they had been slighted, and every discontented person made common cause against the Emperor. A republic was proclaimed at Vera Cruz in December of the same year by Santa Anna, who was commander of a regiment stationed there, and he issued a *pronunciamento*. This plan failed, but it encouraged Bravo, Guerrero and other revolutionary leaders, and rebellion sprung up in a number of places. Iturbide had dissolved congress and this increased the dissatisfaction. A more formidable revolt arose, and on March 19th, 1823, Iturbide abdicated without attempting to retain his position by force of arms.

A few weeks later the ex-Emperor left Mexico and sailed for Italy, having been granted an annual sum of $25,000 for his services. He soon went to England and wrote the government from there that the republic was in danger, and he would come back to help fight the battles of his country. He did not know that his death had been decreed by congress, and so he set sail upon his last voyage. When he arrived at Vera Cruz he was captured, and after some delay was executed at Padilla on the 19th of July, 1824, as a traitor, in his forty-first year. His body was buried in a roofless old church and lay there until 1838, when it was removed to the Cathedral.

Opinion is very much divided as to the rank that should be accorded Iturbide. He was able, brave, honest so far as is known, and probably fell a victim to his ambition like many a man before him. The relative regard in which he is held is shown in the fact that the town which gave both him and his former vanquished foe, Morelas, birth, is now called Morelia, and a state is also named Morelas. In contrast to this there is neither city nor state named after Iturbide, and the famous Iturbide Hotel in the capital city, once his residence, is the only institution perpetuating his name so far as I could learn. The only things accomplished by him during his brief reign were the settlement of the titles by which he and his family should be addressed, the succession to the throne, order of precedence among the dignitaries, allowances of himself and family, and the creation of the Order of Guadalupe to bestow honours upon his followers.

At last a so-called republic was established, and Guadalupe Victoria was inaugurated as the first president on the 10th day of October, 1824, and served until 1828. When the fort of San Juan de Ulua at Vera Cruz lowered its flag, in 1825, the last vestige of Spanish power was gone, and the red and yellow striped banner of the Iberian peninsula was not to be seen on Mexican soil. And Mexico, as then constituted, was a big country, containing almost twice as much territory as to-day. From the end of the administration of President Victoria until after the death of Maximilian, there was not a year of peace in Mexico. Revolutions, *pronunciamentos*, "plans" and restorations followed each other in quick succession. Generals, presidents and dictators sprang up like mushrooms, and their position was as evanescent. The congress unwisely decreed the expulsion of the

Spaniards, and their departure took much of the wealth of the country. Revolutions were an every-day affair. A man in position of authority did not know when his time to be shot might come. A sudden turn of fortune might send him either to the national palace, or before a squad of men with guns aimed at his heart.

A good illustration of this uncertainty of affairs is seen in the treatment and fate of the grim old patriot Guerrero. Born of very low Indian parents he had climbed to the front and borne many of the burdens of the struggle with Spain. He cheerfully yielded his command to the renegade Iturbide, and fought valiantly under that leader for liberty. By a turn of fortune he became the third president in 1829. A few months later he was compelled to flee, but was soon afterwards betrayed and captured at Acapulco. At a farcical trial he was condemned to death as "morally incapable" to act as president, and shot on the 15th of February, 1831, at Cuilapa. Soon afterwards he was declared a martyr and his body removed to the capital with honours. Two monuments to this martyr now adorn that city, and a state has been named after him. Under his short rule slavery was abolished by statute.

Elections eventually became a farce. The unfortunate habit was acquired of appealing to arms instead of submitting to the result of the ballot. The trouble was that the people had copied the letter, and not the spirit of the American constitution. Liberty was interpreted as license, after their exaggerated ideas of the former. The scheming politicians would hesitate at nothing—revolution or civil war—to attain private ends or personal aggrandizement. A general indolence of character, and the hindrances to the acquirement of property among the masses, made the people more willing to yield to disturbing and designing politicians. They are impetuous by nature, impatient of restraint and easily fired up. The rapid changes in government can be seen when you read that there were five different presidents in each of the years 1846 and 1847, and four in 1855—not an evidence of tranquillity at least. The two leading parties constantly at war were the "progresistas" and "retrogrados."

During this period a few prominent names are constantly recurring, and by far the most prominent one is that of the notorious Santa Anna, who, for more than fifty years, occupied a prominent, but not always honourable, place in Mexican affairs. Earlier in life his restless energy was expended in a fairly commendable way, and he fought some battles in defense of the rights of the people. During the war of intervention with France in 1838 he lost his leg in the defense of Vera Cruz. Ever afterwards, when in trouble, he would flourish his severed limb and remind the people how he had been mutilated in the defense of his country, with the effect of restoring himself in public favour. As he grew older his naturally quarrelsome disposition increased, his vanity knew no bounds, and when at the height of his glory, he declared himself dictator and ordered all people to address him as "most serene highness." Never honest except as a matter of policy, his cupidity became more pronounced, until, near the close of the war with the United States, he offered to appoint commissioners and confirm a treaty of peace for the sum of one million dollars. First elected president in 1833, he was again either chosen to, or assumed the office, in 1839, 1846, 1847, 1853 and 1855, but did not serve long at any time. On one occasion his amputated leg was buried with great ceremony, but afterwards fickle sentiment changed, and the martyr part of this hero was brought forth by the rabble, dragged through the streets of the capital, and insulting epithets heaped upon the former idol.

Santa Anna led the forces against the Texas insurrectionists, and was the man responsible for the Alamo slaughter, when one hundred and forty brave Texans were trapped and slain. Visitors to that place are still shown the stains made by the blood of that brave frontiersman, Davy Crockett, and the cry of "Remember the Alamo" still has potency. This insurrection was soon followed by the war between Mexico and the United States.

Franklin says, there never was a good war nor a bad peace. The United States can not be justified in warring upon Mexico, though the results have perhaps been for the best with both nations. Bancroft does not mince words in his treatment of the subject for he says: "It (the Mexican War) was a premeditated and predetermined affair; it was the result of a deliberately calculated scheme of robbery on the part of the superior force." The result was a foregone conclusion, for Mexico, torn by internal dissensions, impoverished by the expense of revolutions and official robbery, and with a government changing with every change of the seasons, had neither armies, money nor supplies for such a conflict. The people were used to the smell of powder but were not trained soldiers, and the "generals" were simply a few of the twelve thousand recipients of military commissions that had been distributed by various presidents in the preceding three years. "Plans" promulgated by one party were bombarded with "pronunciamentos" from another. This was the condition of affairs when General Taylor assumed the offensive and fought the battle of Palo Alto.

Mexico might have sued for peace at this time, but no government was in power long enough to negotiate a treaty. A special envoy sent from Washington at the request of one president was refused an audience by a new one, who had usurped the office before his arrival. Generals Taylor and Fremont subdued Northern Mexico, and General Scott later began his memorable march toward the ancient Aztec capital, from Vera Cruz, like Cortez of old. Santa Anna, who had been "recuperating" from public unpopularity at Havana, returned and state after state immediately "pronounced" in his favour. He issued a manifesto assuming the executive control and took the field against the invaders. He first tried to secure $15,000,000 from the Church, but although the priests hated the "northern heretics" they were loth to give up the coin, and little was secured. Vera Cruz fell after two weeks' bombardment, and Puebla yielded to the Americans. Patriotism was finally aroused to save the City of Mexico, but the victories of Chapultepec, Chorubusco and Molino del Rey were followed by the triumphal entry of General Scott into the capital. The treaty of Guadalupe-Hidalgo ceded to the United States more than six hundred thousand square miles of the Mexican domain, including some of the richest mineral lands of the republic. Disgraced and humiliated as Mexico had been, it was, I believe, the beginning of better things for that country.

Santa Anna went into voluntary exile to Jamaica. The first president after the war, Herrera, actually served the appointed time of his office, but disorder soon began under his successor. "Pronouncing" became popular again, and Santa Anna returned. He was made dictator for a short time by his favourites. This was the last office held by this selfish politician. He exiled himself to St. Thomas again, and afterwards in Elizabethport, New Jersey. During the second empire he tried to curry favour with both sides, but neither would listen to him. Discouraged and disheartened he lived abroad, until, burdened by the weight of eighty years, he sought and obtained permission to return to the capital, and died on the 20th of June, 1876. Thus passed a man who had lived in stirring times, was most intensely hated, had been president six times, military dictator four times, had upset fifteen governments, had been marked for the assassin's bullet many times; and yet he lived to a ripe old age and died a natural death. However, all his glory had faded, and, blind, lame and infirm, he spent his last days in extreme poverty.

Here is a picture of this man drawn by Rev. William Butler,[6] who visited him about a year before his death: "Santa Anna was living in an obscure street, neglected and forgotten by all parties. On entering the apartment we found the old man sitting on a sofa, behind which hung a picture of his wife 'her serene highness, Dolores Tosta de Santa Anna' arrayed as a vice-queen. The magnificence of the painting contrasted sadly with the poverty-stricken aspect of the room and furniture. To him, however, this could make but little difference, as we soon saw that he was totally blind as well as feeble and broken in spirit, with a tendency to mental weakness." He was buried in the cemetery at Guadalupe without honours or recognition by the government, and his remains still rest there. As I gazed upon his tomb I could not help thinking what a contrast between his career and that of the patriots Hidalgo, Morelas, and Juarez.

The early constitution had declared that the Roman Catholic religion should perpetually be the religion of Mexico. Nevertheless a struggle had been growing up between the clericals and liberals for many years with increasing intensity. It finally centred in a struggle over the sequestration of the church property, and became wider and wider until the whole country was involved and divided into two great parties. The liberals were probably just as good Christians as the others but thought the Church had too much wealth.

A VILLAGE CHURCH

At this juncture there arose a pure Indian, of lowly parentage, who never saw a school until he was twelve years of age. His name was Benito Juarez. Although ever professing devout faith, he early espoused the cause of the anti-clerical party. He was banished by Santa Anna and fled to New Orleans, but opinion changed and his sentiments became the popular views. The new constitution of 1857 declared the separation of church and state. Juarez had been elected President of the Supreme Court under Comonfort.

The latter was compelled to flee the country and Juarez became president under the constitution, in 1857. Congress passed a law confiscating church property and civil war was begun. Juarez took the field in person and did not reach the capital until three years later. These three years have been called the years of horrors. The liberals were excommunicated by the church, and the papal delegate and several bishops were ordered out of the country in turn by Juarez. Ministerial crises and resignations became chronic. Guerillas and robbers were bold and attacked many aliens, and foreign obligations were unpaid because of the impoverished condition of the country.

Juarez alone remained cool in the midst of all these disturbances. The convention entered into between France, England and Spain for a joint intervention in Mexican affairs on the 31st day of October, 1861, brought new embarrassment to the Indian reformer. Underneath these acts of the convention the crafty hand of Napoleon can be seen. The man who had accomplished one *coup d'Etat* was a sworn enemy to all republican institutions. The pretext for this intervention was the collection of some money claims and reparation for alleged offences. Spain no doubt looked forward to a little revenge. The Spanish fleet occupied Vera Cruz on the 14th of December, 1861, followed by the other armies. A conference took place at Orizaba with Juarez who acknowledged the money claims, and Spain and England withdrew their forces. The French remained, secretly supported and encouraged by the extreme church party, and advanced to and captured Puebla. Distracted and disheartened by the state of affairs, the prospect of a stable government made the way easy to place Maximilian upon the throne as Emperor of Mexico, and this was done. He and the empress arrived on the 28th of May, 1864. Maximilian was a liberal ruler and the Empress Carlotta won the people by her charming personality and benevolences.

As long as the French forces remained his throne was secure. The prompt and decisive action of Secretary Seward sounded the death knell of Maximilian's ambitions. Napoleon withdrew his troops, and Maximilian might have easily escaped had he not wavered between ambition and discretion,—the former eventually winning. He met death with dignity and said "May my blood be the last spilt for the welfare of the country."

During all of these years Juarez maintained a semblance of authority and kept a cabinet under appointment although he was finally driven to the American border. Yet he could wait, for he had inherited from his dusky ancestors the qualities of patience, endurance and imperturbability. He also had executive ability and an abundance of good sense. After the execution of Maximilian he made a triumphal entry into Mexico. The country was impoverished. The short empire had added a national debt of $187,000,000. More than one thousand battles and skirmishes had occurred between 1863 and 1867, and a hundred thousand Mexicans had been killed or disabled. The people were still restless and an increasing element began to say that he had been president long enough. He was unmoved, but kept steadily on his way trying to better the condition of the people, improve the finances and bring prosperity to his country. The iron constitution finally gave way and he died on the 19th of July, 1872, beloved and honoured by his country. He deserves to be called the Washington of Mexico, for the real liberty of a republican form of government began with him. He had prepared the way for his successors to bring peace, prosperity and liberty to a country that for centuries had been groping and striving after such a condition. Juarez lies buried beneath a magnificent monument in the Panteon de San Fernando, in the City of Mexico.

Upon the death of Juarez the constitutional succession to the chief magistracy fell upon Lerdo de Tejada, who occupied that office for four years. The subsequent history of Mexico, however, centres around the personality of Porfirio Diaz, and the events of his long administration and final downfall are treated in the two following chapters.

CHAPTER XX
THE GUIDING HAND

"I should like to live fifty years to see the result of the seed I have planted," said Porfirio Diaz a number of years ago. It is not within the limit of human possibility that such a boon could be granted this amiable "republican despot" but he had lived long enough to see the good results of the policies established by him for the upbuilding of his country.

Succeeding to a government that had been in the throes of revolution ever since the patriot-priest Hidalgo first proclaimed independence on the 16th of September, 1810, President Diaz at once restored peace to the country that has lasted for thirty years. Inheriting a bankrupt treasury from his predecessors, and a large foreign debt that had on several occasions brought about foreign intervention, he succeeded in placing the finances of the country in a prosperous condition and has accomplished more for Mexico than had been done in three centuries of Spanish rule. He organized the army along modern lines and established the *rurales* which insured the safety of life and property. Railroads under the wise system of encouragement inaugurated by him have increased from three hundred and fifty miles to thirteen thousand five hundred miles; telegraph lines from four thousand five hundred miles to thirty-five thousand miles; the number of post-offices now number two thousand three hundred and fifty instead of seven hundred and twenty as it was in 1876. Imports and exports have doubled several times, and the annual balance sheet now shows a comfortable surplus instead of a deficit as in former days. All this has been done and old obligations met in spite of the serious loss in exchange due to the depreciation in silver, and the fact that the heavy foreign obligations had to be met in gold purchased with silver at a low and constantly varying valuation.

A COMPANY OF *RURALES*

The life of Porfirio Diaz is fascinating. It savours of the days of knighthood and romance. We are reminded of those heroes of old around whom time has cast a glamour, for he has had adventures as exciting, escapes as miraculous and a life seemingly as charmed as any hero created by the masters of romance, and his life may well be termed "stranger than fiction." One is naturally inclined to be rather eulogistic in his treatment of such a character.

The present President of Mexico was born in the city of Oaxaca in an unimposing house on the Street of La Soledad, that is now used as a sugar factory, on the 15th of September, 1830, a day already celebrated in Mexican annals. His father, Captain José Faustini Diaz, was of Spanish descent and followed the occupation of innkeeper, but died when Porfirio was only three years of age. His maternal grandmother was a Mixteca Indian. The church and law were the only two occupations open to an ambitious youth in those days, and this young lad was intended for the former. He chose the law much to the disgust of his relatives but never followed that calling. The fighting blood in him impelled him to the sanguinary conflicts on the field rather than the bloodless battles in the courts between contending counsel.

About this time the war with the United States broke out and the future president, a youth of seventeen, volunteered but saw no fighting, although he thus early in life showed his genius for organization by forming his fellow-students of the academy into a battalion for the defence of his home city. Benito Juarez, afterwards president, was attracted by this youth and invited him to read law in his office, which offer was accepted. Thus was begun an association between two men who were destined in later years to occupy such a prominent place in Mexican history. Through the influence of Juarez, the younger man was made assistant librarian and by the aid of the salary attached to this position, and money earned as tutor, he completed his course, and received his law degree.

Politics and war seem to have divided the attention of Diaz from the very first with a preference for the latter in early life. Diaz was a military genius. I can say this in all seriousness. Although he never commanded a large army yet, under his hands, the rawest recruits soon became valuable troops. He is possessed of a personal magnetism and the quality of *simpatica*, (which can not be translated into English) that draws people to him and, when once aroused, they become his enthusiastic partisans. In a land of lethargy and procrastination his movements were quick and decisive, and he soon became noted for night marches and early morning attacks. He never was overcome except by superior forces, and then only after his stores and ammunition were exhausted. Even when beaten and his army captured or separated, a few days of freedom would again place him at the head of a respectable force ready to take aggressive stand against the enemy. Had he been in command of a hundred thousand men, he would have met the situation with the same tact and ability.

The first of the many political offices held by Diaz was that of Jefe Politico, or mayor, of the little Indian town of Ixtlan when only twenty-five years of age. Here he devoted his time to organizing the Indians into a company of militia, and this little body of soldiers formed a nucleus that proved a great help to him in the troublous times which followed. Later he was made Jefe of Tehuantepec where he showed great administrative ability. Soon afterward, in 1861, he was elected a deputy to congress from

Oaxaca, but at that time would not sacrifice the excitement of war for the more prosaic duties of law-making.

Captain Diaz had seen his first military service in the revolts against the notorious Santa Anna, of Alamo fame. He had the courage to sign a remonstrance against this usurper, and was compelled to fly for his life. Later, in the campaigns against Santa Anna, he was so successful that he had become almost a hero in the eyes of his fellow Oaxacans. At the beginning of the French invasion, the rank of general of a brigade had been conferred upon him at the early age of thirty-two years, and he was assigned to the defense of Puebla under General Zaragoza. It was due to his tactics more than anything else that the way was paved for the great victory of *Cinco de Mayo*, 1862, when an inferior force of Mexicans defeated a numerically larger army of veteran French troops. It was nearly a year later before the armies of the allied French and Austrians, greatly augmented by new arrivals, were able to capture Puebla after a two months' siege, the ammunition of the Mexicans had been exhausted. General Diaz refusal to give *parol* and was made prisoner but escaped after a short confinement.

Because of the approach of the invading armies toward the capital, President Juarez had removed the seat of government to San Luis Potosi. He made General Diaz commander-in-chief of the armies south of the Valley of Mexico. Returning to his favourite haunts in Oaxaca, he soon gathered together an army and some money and marched forth on the offensive. By this time General Diaz had become such a formidable opponent that General Bazaine himself, later of European fame, leader of the French forces, took the field against this young leader with the determination to crush him. He finally shut him up in Oaxaca and captured that city in 1865. The French general had carefully laid his plans for this campaign, having transported a large number of guns, and was at the head of an army, Diaz claims, of sixteen thousand. The fame of this general and his large force created a panic among the troops of Diaz and his little army had dwindled to a few hundred. General Diaz was captured and taken to Puebla by his captors where he was prisoner for more than seven months in a former house of the Jesuits in that city. His escape is celebrated in Mexican annals, and his own account is as follows, although I have greatly abbreviated it:—

"After taps for silence had been sounded for the night, I went to a room which was roofless and which on that account was used as a yard. I had with me three ropes, wrapped up in canvas, and I threw them onto the roof. I also had another rope, and I succeeded in throwing it around a projecting stone spout which seemed to be sufficiently firm. When I had satisfied myself that the support was sufficient, I climbed up by the rope to the roof. My progress along the roof to the corner of San Roque street, where I had made up my mind to descend, was attended with much danger, for on the roof of the church a detachment and sentries were stationed to keep watch. Gliding on all-fours I made towards the point where I was to let myself down. I often had to stop to feel my way, for the roof was strewn with many fragments of glass which sounded when touched. Moreover, there were frequent flashes of lightning, which exposed me to being discovered.

"I finally reached the wall of the church. In order to arrive at the corner of the street of San Roque it was necessary to pass through a portion of the edifice which was occupied by the priest in charge of the church, and I was aware that shortly before he had denounced to the court martial some political prisoners who had bored a hole through their place of confinement into his dwelling, and as a consequence they had been shot the next day.

"I let myself down into an upper yard of the priest's house at the moment when a young man who also lived there had come in from the street; he had probably been to the theatre, for he was in gay humour and was humming an air from an operetta. He did not see me as he passed, and I remained quiet until he had entered his room. When I considered that sufficient time had elapsed for him to get into bed, and perhaps to fall asleep, I climbed to the roof of the convent on the opposite side to that by which I had descended and pushed forward to the corner of the street of San Roque, and I arrived there at last. There is at the corner, in a niche, a statue of St. Vincent Ferrer which I proposed using to fix the rope by which I was to descend. The saint wobbled when touched, but probably there was inside the statue an iron spike to hold it. In any case, in order to be more sure, I adjusted the rope around the pedestal of the statue which seemed to be quite firm. I resolved to alight in a vacant lot which adjoined and which was only fenced in. I did not know that there was a drove of hogs in this yard. As when I began the descent I turned somewhat with my rope, my back struck against the wall, and the impact caused a poniard which I carried at my waist to fall from its sheath among the hogs, probably wounding one of them, for they set up a grunting which grew louder as they saw me descending among them. I had to wait for some time for them to quiet down. I then climbed to the top of the partition separating the lot from the street, but I had at once to bob down again for just at that moment a gendarme was passing on his round, seeing if the doors were well fastened. When he had retired I sprang into the street."

In a few days he had rallied around him a few faithful followers and captured the small garrison of Tehuitzingo. From this time his career was a succession of victories until the capture and execution of Maximilian. These victories and the firm stand of the United States government re-established republican supremacy. Early in 1867 preparations were made to regain Puebla which city was defended by a force of several thousand French troops. On April 2nd he made a feint with a few hundred men on the convent of "El Carmen" which caused the army of the defenders to be concentrated there. Then a concerted attack followed from several points, and the soldiers of Diaz drove back the hardened troops of the third Napoleon, and the flag of liberty waved over the city in the early dawn. He followed up the fleeing foreigners and a series of engagements followed in which Diaz was victorious. The war was ended by the capture of the City of Mexico after a siege of several assaults.

From boyhood until the close of the empire in 1867, General Diaz had worked against great odds. He was by this time easily the most popular man in Mexico. One party at the general elections of that year nominated him for president, but he refused to run against his old friend and patron, President Juarez. He even refused an office and resigned his commission in the army. In search of rest he retired to the place of his birth, and his trip from the capital was a triumphal journey. The citizens of Oaxaca received him with open arms, and presented him with the estate of La Noria near that city. Hither he went with the wife whom he had married by proxy during the war and spent a few years in comparative quiet. In 1871 another presidential election was held. Juarez, who had failed both mentally and physically, had advocated a number of unpopular measures, but was determined to have himself reëlected to office. Diaz was also a candidate. When Juarez was declared elected, the "Porfiristas" declared a revolution with the slogan "less government and more liberty." However Juarez died in a few months and the executive power temporarily fell upon the president of the Supreme Court, Lerdo de Tejada, who was afterwards elected to that office to serve the unexpired term.

General Diaz refused reconciliation with this government, and, fearing trouble before the next presidential election, for Lerdo was an active candidate, he sold his estate and left for the United States after a *"pronunciamento,"* called the "Plan of Tuxtepec," had been issued to which he gave his allegiance, if he was not the author of it. This "plan" declared a president ineligible to succeed himself. By the time the revolution was well underway in several states, General Diaz had crossed the Rio Grande at Brownsville, Texas, with forty followers. These forty men increased to four hundred in a few days and they captured Matamoros on April 2nd, 1876.

Learning that a large force had been sent after him, General Diaz decided to return south. He went to New Orleans and took a steamer from there, called the City of Habana, sailing for Vera Cruz, and passed himself off as a Cuban doctor. He was not suspected until some of the troops he had captured at Matamoros a few weeks before got on board the ship at Tampico. They immediately made arrangements to secure him on arriving at Vera Cruz. Although the ship was four miles from land, Diaz jumped overboard and attempted to swim ashore. He was picked up after nightfall in an exhausted condition, and taken on board the ship again. However the purser was won to his cause and concealed him in a wardrobe, where he remained for several days on a diet of ship's biscuit and water. The purser, as a matter of policy and in order to disarm all suspicion, invited the Lerdist officers into his cabin, where they would spend hours in playing at cards. Oftentimes the chair of the one sitting in front of the wardrobe would be tilted back against the door behind which was the man they would have given almost anything to catch. From his cramped position General Diaz was in torment. He could not stand upright, nor was he able to sit down. When the *City of Habana* arrived at Vera Cruz the chief of the coast guard service, who was the fugitive's friend, managed to smuggle in to him a dilapidated sailor's suit and a very old pair of boots. At the same time the chief sent word that a rowboat, in charge of a man he would recognize by certain signals, would come alongside for him. When the ship began to unload bales of cotton into barges, this boat appeared among them, and the noted prisoner made his escape to land.

After several exciting adventures on the way, General Diaz again appeared at Oaxaca among his friends and ardent supporters. His popularity and prestige in Oaxaca have always been remarkable. Never did he appeal to his neighbours and friends of that state in vain. It was not long until he was at the head of an army of four thousand "Porfiristas"—men who would follow their leader to the death if need be, and many of whom had fought with him at Puebla and elsewhere. The news of the escape of Diaz brought gloom to the "Lerdistas." Lerdo immediately marched his army southward. The two armies met on the 16th of November, 1876, at Tecoac, and for a few hours the battle waged hotly and bitterly. The Lerdist army, which was considerably larger, began the engagement with every prospect of success. At the last moment Diaz led a charge in person which routed the enemy, and the result was a complete triumph for the "Porfiristas."

Flushed with victory, and determined to press his advantage to the utmost, General Diaz promptly proceeded toward the capital with his augmented army. Panic seized Lerdo and his followers. He took all the public funds available, and, with his ministers, fled to Acapulco. Upon arriving there he embarked for San Francisco, and made no further effort to impede the progress of the Diaz forces. Iglesias, President of the Supreme Court, upon whom the succession legally fell upon the death or resignation of the President, established headquarters at Guanajuato and issued a proclamation assuming the office of chief executive. Diaz at once marched upon Puebla, which he entered without opposition. City after city sent representatives announcing their adherence to his cause. The onward march was continued without a halt until Guadalupe, about three miles from the capital, was reached. Here he halted for a day in order to get his forces into presentable condition to make a triumphal entry into the historic capital.

It was on the 24th of November, 1876, that General Diaz made his memorable march into the City of Mexico. Riding at the head of an army of several thousand armed men he made a triumphal entry into that ancient capital, while thousands gathered along the route to see this new adventurer —as he was styled by his enemies. The Plaza was packed with the populace. This son of an innkeeper, this man with the blood of the Indian in his veins, this hero of many battles passed through the portal of the National Palace and became master of Mexico. From there he issued a proclamation assuming the provisional presidency of the republic, until an election could take place in regular form and a constitutional ruler should be chosen. This was held in December. With the government in his hands the result of that election was never in doubt. After a three months' campaign his authority was recognized over the entire republic. Since that time Porfirio Diaz occupied that high office continuously, except for an interval of four years from 1880 to 1884, when Manuel Gonzalez held that title, until May 25th, 1911, when he resigned. Diaz himself became a victim of the "Tuxtepec Plan," forbidding two consecutive terms, and gracefully retired at the end of his first term, although urged by a large following to remain at the head of the government. For the first time in Mexican history was seen the spectacle of one President voluntarily relinquishing the sceptre to his successor, and returning to private life without an effort to retain himself in power. Gonzalez entered the office one of the most popular men in Mexico, having been elected by an almost unanimous vote. Four years later he left it under a cloud of almost universal execration and contempt. During the four years of Gonzalez's administration Diaz was not idle, but served in the cabinet, as governor of Oaxaca and senator from Morelas. Isolated disturbances have arisen at times, but no formidable opposition arose against him until 1910. This revolution is treated in the succeeding chapter. The law limiting the succession was revoked during his second term, and the length of office was subsequently extended to six years. At the various elections the reported vote was almost unanimous for Diaz. On December 1st, 1910, he was inaugurated President for the seventh consecutive term, or eighth term in all.

Immediately upon first assuming the executive office after the flight of Lerdo, Diaz issued a statement in which he set forth in clear terms his intention to restore constitutional order and institute reforms. He invited all factions and cliques to coöperate with him. This soon won the regard of the intelligent and honest partisans of all factions, and he early showed his impartiality by selecting his advisers irrespective of party. It was not long until most of the Lerdistas and Juaristas were won to his cause. By this skilful handling of the leaders, he secured the good will of Congress in furthering his plans for reforms, and in organizing the finances on a better basis. New treaties were negotiated with foreign nations and able diplomatic representatives sent abroad.

It has been said that the best peacemakers are those who have made war. Those who detest powder most are generally those who have smelled it on the field of battle. To them—more than all others—are known the horrors and hardships of war, and what it entails upon the innocent and guilty alike. Even though a battle-scared hero may have profited by the advantages gained by military success, the tragedy of empty homes and nameless graves is known to and acknowledged by him. General Sherman said: "The main thing is to deal as hard blows at the enemy's forces as possible, and then cause so much suffering to the inhabitants that they will long for peace." A similar belief animated President Diaz. He himself has said in explaining his actions in suppressing brigandage: "Sometimes we were harsh to the point of cruelty. But it was all necessary to the life and progress of the nation. If there was cruelty, the results have justified it. It was better that a little blood be shed that much blood be saved. The blood that was shed was bad blood; the blood that was saved was good blood." Almost before they knew what was happening the professional malcontents found themselves in the grip of this masterful new leader. It was to this quality of firmness that he owed his pronounced success during the first years of his presidency.

Several scattered uprisings occurred during the first term, most of them being fostered by the "Lerdistas." Lerdo issued a proclamation on the 24th of February, 1877, from New York, claiming to be the constitutional President, and, a few months later, Iglesias did the same thing from New Orleans. Neither of these manifestos were looked upon seriously by the Mexicans, but they were in a great measure responsible for the tardy recognition of the Diaz government by the United States and other foreign powers. One revolt is worthy of mention because of its novelty. A part of the crew of the armed vessel *Trinidad* mutinied during the absence of the commander at Vera Cruz. They headed for a Campeche port, where they seized several thousand dollars of public funds. While the leaders of the mutiny were ashore enjoying the money, a counter mutiny was led by the boatswain, who took the ship back to Vera Cruz and returned it to the government.

Judging this man at a distance, we, who live in a country where even a third term is a "bogie," are inclined to smile at these successive elections to the presidency, and dismiss the matter with the charge of "dictator" and "republican despot," with all the odium that those terms imply. President Diaz was both. But, above all, he was, I believe, a true patriot. Whatever may have been his original motives in seeking this high office his later actions prove the statement. Responsibility will often develop a man, and that may have been true with Diaz. In securing the control by driving out Lerdo, and assuming the provisional presidency over Iglesias, who was the official designated by the constitution in case of a vacancy, he only did what many had done before. Whether his retention of the office for so long was a good or bad thing for the country, the historian of the future will be a better judge.

The accomplishments of Diaz were many. It would require a long enumeration to give them in detail. The very fact that he succeeded to a government which had seen fifty-four different rulers, including two emperors and a number of avowed dictators, in the fifty-five years preceding his own accession, and ruled the country for more than a generation, is in itself sufficient to stamp him as an extraordinary man. Those were indeed troublous times in Mexico while we were celebrating the centennial of our independence. The strong spirit of Juarez had been broken by the long strain from 1857 to 1872, during which time he was nominally President. His successor was a weak, ambitious man who accomplished little. Disorder everywhere, the country overrun with bandits and a worse than empty treasury were the conditions when Diaz grasped the reins. It was not until nearly two years afterward that his government was formally recognized by the United States. Few men could have steered the country through such a state of affairs so successfully. He did it without repudiating any valid claims. He established credit by paying foreign obligations rather than the salaries of government employees. He surrounded himself with an able cabinet, and started the machinery of government in a business-like way.

I do not subscribe to the doctrine of Shakespeare that all the world is a stage, and that each person is a player, for that would take away sincerity. Porfirio Diaz has been accused of only acting a part. He could not always be acting, for his course was too consistent under many and diverse circumstances. As a young man he refused pay for military services because the government was so poor. He declined promotion over the heads of men older in the service for fear of jealousies. He refused remuneration after the close of the war of intervention, although not a rich man at that time. He turned a deaf ear to the emissaries of Maximilian, who wanted to place him in command of the Mexican army when that ruler abdicated, which would practically have made him President. He was a humane adversary, as is shown by his treatment of prisoners of war. He disregarded ceremony as much as is possible in a Latin country. He declined to live in the National Palace, but resided in a private house the most of the time, and at Chapultepec a part of the year.

It is not to be wondered at that the man who rules with a strong arm will make bitter enemies as well as warm partisans. Likewise such a policy will always have its defamers as well as its supporters. Opinion is still divided upon Napoleon, and whether his high-handed methods wrought more good than evil. Hence it is that some can see nothing in Diaz but a tyrant, an enslaver of his people, and a man unfit for even life itself. They forget that peonage was not originated by Diaz, but was inherited from the Spaniards and supported by the voters of the country. They do not look into the conditions faced by Diaz when he first became President, nor the bloody history of the republic before that time. I believe that Diaz would have been permitted to serve his term had it not been for his efforts to control the vice-presidency, and the fact that his choice fell upon a man who was very unpopular. Knowing that at his age the President's span of life was uncertain, the politicians wanted to control this office because of the succession. For this reason discontent and jealousies had been growing for several years. Diaz had publicly declared his intention not to seek another term, so that those ambitious for that office took him at his word and began their wire-pulling. This was in February, 1908. Then, in the spring of 1910, he announced that yielding to importunity he would accept another term. This was the one great mistake in his political career. Had Diaz adhered to his previous declaration, he would have retired from the office of chief executive full of honours. As it is he resigned under pressure, and left the City of Mexico unannounced and accompanied only by his family and a few friends. He boarded a steamer in the harbour of Vera Cruz and sailed for Spain, where he has quietly resided since that time.

The personality of this dictator-president, who has filled such an important place in the world's history, is most interesting. As I sat in the great salon of the National Palace, awaiting the appearance of President

Diaz, I spent the intervening fifteen or twenty minutes in examining the room. On the high walls were pictures of General Washington, the father of liberty in the whole of the two Americas; of the patriot-priest Hidalgo, who first raised the standard of revolt in Mexico, and of Diaz himself. Then Diaz appeared—a man tall for a Mexican, solidly built, with white closely cropped hair and white moustache. He approached with an elastic, graceful and springy step entirely belying his almost eighty years. The Indian blood could easily be traced in his complexion and features. The most striking feature of this man is his eyes, which seem to look into the very soul of all he meets. It is probably this intuitive perception that has been one of the key-notes of his success. He has always been a democratic sort of man and easy of approach, and impresses his sincerity on all those who talk with him. Diaz was always a tireless worker and methodical in his habits. He is abstemious, and it is probably due to this characteristic and his methodical habits, that at eighty years of age he remained as active and energetic as the average man twenty years younger. He kept in touch with the most remote parts of the republic, even to the most distant village. His advisers were often surprised at the vast knowledge he displayed in all matters of state. The private life of Diaz has always been above reproach. He has been twice married. His first wife was Delfina Ortega y Reyes, who died in 1880 before sharing in the full greatness of her husband, leaving a son and two daughters, all of whom are still living. Three years later he was married to a daughter of Romero Rubio, whose full name is Señora Doña Carmen Romero Rubio de Diaz. She is a woman who by her sweetness of character, kindly disposition and charities won a warm place in the affections of the Mexican people.

The end of the political career of Diaz is not without a touch of pathos, as well as an element of personal dignity. Broken in health, and deserted by many of his former friends, he resigned the office of President in the following letter addressed to Congress:—

> "Señores: The Mexican people, who have generously covered me with honours, who proclaimed me as their leader during the international war, who patriotically assisted me in all works undertaken to develop industry and the commerce of the republic, to establish its credit, gain for it the respect of the world and obtain for

it an honourable position in the concert of the nations; that same people has revolted in armed military bands, stating that my presence in the exercise of the supreme executive power was the cause of this insurrection.

"I do not know of any facts imputable to me which could have caused this social phenomenon; but acknowledging as possible, though not admitting, that I may be unwittingly culpable, such a possibility makes me the least able to reason out and decide my own culpability.

"Therefore, respecting, as I always have respected, the will of the people and in accordance with Article 82 of the Federal Constitution, I come before the supreme representatives of the nation in order to resign, unreservedly, the office of Constitutional President of the republic with which the national vote honoured me, which I do with all the more reason, since in order to continue in office it would be necessary to shed Mexican blood, endangering the credit of the country, dissipating its wealth, exhausting its resources and exposing its policy to international complications.

"I hope, señores, that, when the passions which are inherent to all revolutions have been calmed, a more conscientious and justified study will bring out in the national mind a correct acknowledgment, which will allow me to die carrying engraved in my soul a just impression of the estimation of my life, which throughout I have devoted and will devote to my countrymen.

"With all respect,

"Porfirio Diaz."

CHAPTER XXI
THE REVOLUTION OF 1910

The year 1910 marked the completion of one hundred years of Mexican independence. In September of that year this event was celebrated with all the pomp and pageantry customary in Latin countries. Nearly the whole month was given up to public functions in various parts of the republic, and especially in the City of Mexico, the national capital. Representatives of all the great nations of the world were sent there to assist in the ceremonies incident to the celebration. Dedications of public buildings, magnificent balls, public fêtes and exercises commemorative of independence and of the national heroes, who led the struggle against the Spaniards, were numerous. The 15th and the 16th of September were the great gala days of this centennial anniversary. The further fact that added lustre to the event was the eightieth anniversary of the birth of President Diaz, who had established a substantial government after the many years of strife through which the country had passed between the years 1810 and 1876. In all the speeches made by foreign representatives the great work of this man was extolled, as well as the progress that had been made by the nation itself.

The culmination of the centennial ceremonies was on the night of the 15th, just a little while before midnight. By half past ten o'clock the immense Plaza, which faces the National Palace, was filled with an immense crowd of Mexican dignitaries, distinguished foreigners and the population of the city. It was a mass of living, breathing, expectant humanity. The many coloured lights formed veritable rainbows of colour, and this added an additional attraction to the teeming, seething crowd. The door leading to the central balcony on the front of the National Palace opened, and President Diaz appeared. An intense stillness fell upon the crowd. In his right hand the President carried the national flag of Mexico, and immediately on his appearance the red, white and green lamps (the national colours) surrounding the old bell with which Hidalgo first sounded the call to liberty, and which has found a permanent resting place here, flashed into a radiant glow. As the strains of the national anthem floated out on the breeze, the President waved his flag, rang the bell and shouted "Viva

Mexico!" The great crowd went wild with excitement. The cry of "Viva Mexico!" was taken up by the crowd near to the President, and then by those farther away, until the great shout might have been heard all over the capital. The bells of the grand old cathedral pealed forth their loudest tones, the factory whistles shrieked, sky-rockets were sent up in the air and every noise-making device was turned loose. Pandemonium reigned. "Viva Diaz!" and "Viva el Presidente!" were mingled with the cry of "Viva Mexico!"

In the light of later events this wonderful celebration seems to have been a sham, or at least only on the surface. At that time a political volcano was simmering all over the republic, and was just ready to break forth into violent eruption. Diaz had already been re-elected for the eighth term, but the inauguration was not to take place until the fifth of December. In November the first outbreaks against the civil authorities occurred. An abortive rising occurred in Puebla in which blood was shed. Armed bodies appeared in the states of Chihuahua and Sonora, in the northwestern part of the republic. These bodies attacked the outlying *haciendas*, robbed the owners of horses and foraged at will to secure supplies for themselves and their horses. The country in which these outbreaks occurred is ideal for the guerilla warfare that followed. Both of those states are mountainous and thinly settled, so that it was comparatively easy for even a small band of armed men to make a great deal of trouble and escape from a much larger force that might attempt to pursue them.

Government troops were promptly dispatched to the scene of trouble, but it was difficult to catch up with the marauders and engage them in battle. Their outbreaks would first be heard of in one neighbourhood, and a few days later reports of trouble would be received from sections quite remote. Additional armed bodies appeared in other sections, and it was not many weeks until the trouble began to present a serious aspect. Many of the government troops sent against the insurrectos were either cowardly or were in secret sympathy with those opposed to the government. Whenever actual engagements did occur the outcome was generally in favour of the Federal troops, but the defeated ones were always able to escape into the country, where it was difficult for them to be followed. The first battle of any note was fought at Mal Paso, when the Federals were routed, but a battle at Ojinaga a few days later was a decided defeat for the revolutionists. The failure of the government to stamp out the trouble promptly gave encouragement to all the disaffected ones, and the old spirit of lawlessness that once prevailed seemed about to break forth with all its animus and disregard of the rights of private property.

The predominant figures among the insurrectos were the Maderos, a wealthy family that owned great estates near the city of Torreon. In the presidential campaign that had just passed, Francisco Madero had been a candidate for the presidency. He was thrown into prison, as that family asserted, simply because he dared to oppose the dictator who had held power for so long. The reason given out by the government was, of course, far different. Nevertheless all the disaffected factions of the republic rallied around this family, which did the principal financing of the revolutionists. A propaganda was conducted in the United States by the Maderos, and they obtained a great deal of encouragement from the majority of the newspapers of the United States, which had recently taken a position extremely antagonistic to the Diaz government. Francisco Madero established a revolutionary junta in El Paso, and large quantities of ammunition were sent across the border. A warrant for his arrest having been issued because of violation of the neutrality laws, Madero with a handful of followers crossed into Chihuahua and entered actively into the campaign.

"No re-election" and "effective suffrage" were the two catch-words of Madero. It was very similar to that of Porfirio Diaz when he swept everything before him. At no time were there, according to the best reports that can be obtained, more than a few thousand men enrolled under the Madero banner. These troops were scattered throughout northern Mexico, from Ciudad Juarez to the Pacific Ocean. Into their ranks were drawn many soldiers of fortune from the United States, as well as from Europe. A part of these men were no doubt really patriotic in their motives, while others simply grasped the chance of engaging in an exciting campaign because of the freedom of action which was offered, and also partly because of the rewards that were promised by those at the head of the revolution. An eye-witness of the engagement at Tia Juana says that not over ten per cent. of the insurrectos who captured that town were Mexicans, the remainder being made up of Americans, including some negroes, Germans, English and other nationalities. This engagement occurred on May 8th and 9th, 1911. The Federals threw up breastworks of bags of sand, and the women and children were sent out of town to the American side. The fighting was severe and many were killed on both sides. On the second day the government forces yielded, and the rebels immediately pillaged the town and stores.

Most of the engagements took place at towns near the border, at Ciudad Juarez, Nogales and Douglass, as well as Tia Juana. Two reasons were probably responsible for this fact. One was that it gave the insurrectos, in case they were defeated, an easy escape across the border, and another was that they were anxious to capture the custom-houses in order to secure the revenue from that source. This would also enable them to set up a *de facto* government, which might secure for them recognition from countries that looked upon them with favour. Because of these fights on the border, and the reckless shooting by the combatants, no fewer than twenty citizens of the United States were killed and twice that number wounded upon the American side, including men, women and children, none of whom had taken any part in the conflict. The camps of the Maderistas at all times contained numerous American correspondents, and the reports of the majority of them were favourable to the cause of that faction. The battle of Casas Grandes was all but decisive. In this engagement Madero took part and was slightly wounded, while the opposing leader lost an arm. But Madero was soon in the field again at the head of his forces. The movement had likewise spread, and the government faced trouble in the country even as far south as the Isthmus of Tehuantepec.

The aim of the Maderistas was to secure recognition as belligerents from the government of the United States, and it was also the desire of the government to put down the insurrection in order to prevent action by the United States to suppress the trouble because of the complaint of many Americans whose property had been destroyed, or was in danger of destruction. Railroad tracks were torn up, mines were tampered with and much other interference with the property of foreigners followed. European governments did not dare to interfere because of the Monroe Doctrine, and pressure was brought upon the government at Washington to restore order. On May 8th there was great excitement in the United States following orders issued by the Department of War for the mobilization of American troops along the Mexican border. Almost twenty thousand troops were sent to Texas and centralized at San Antonio. From there they were sent to various places along the international border, but with positive instruction to take no part in the trouble on the other side of the Rio Grande. The press looked upon this action as preliminary to armed intervention, but no such result followed. This movement of troops was no doubt actuated by the motive of showing what the United States could do, and of impressing both sides to the conflict that foreign property must be left undisturbed and the rights of neutral parties carefully observed.

Several attempts were made by the Maderistas to capture Ciudad Juarez, the prosperous city directly opposite El Paso. The Federal troops in the city were under the command of General Navarro, while the insurrectos in the final siege were commanded by Gen. Pascual Orozco. After a battle of several days, including considerable street fighting, General Navarro surrendered his command of fifteen hundred men to General Orozco on the 10th of May. Shortly after this Madero himself entered the city as victor, and immediately set up a provisional government, giving himself the title of Provisional President. This gave the insurrectos control of the important custom house at Ciudad Juarez, and was a great victory for their cause. "On to Mexico" then became the popular cry, and preparations began to be made for that long march. Torreon had fallen, and Pachuca, only forty miles from the capital, had been taken possession of by the revolutionists. Chihuahua and a number of other cities were besieged by them.

At this stage Diaz and his advisers asked for an armistice in order that negotiations might be conducted. Each side appointed commissioners, and efforts were made to agree upon terms for settling the trouble into which the country had been plunged. The Maderistas refused to consider any terms which did not involve the resignation of President Diaz, Vice-President Corral and the entire cabinet. President Diaz, in order to avoid further bloodshed, the outcome of which would be very uncertain, finally acceded to these terms and agreed to resign before the end of the month. His resignation was delayed, however, for some time, and disorder again broke out in several places. Even in the City of Mexico mobs formed, and practically took possession of the city on the 24th and 25th of May. Before the close of the latter day President Diaz handed in his resignation, as the Vice-President had previously done, and the government was turned over to Francisco de la Barra, who had been agreed upon as the Provisional President until a new executive could be chosen at a special election.

President Diaz secretly left the City of Mexico, and embarked on a vessel at Vera Cruz for Europe. A new cabinet was selected by Acting-President Barra, the majority of whom were suggested by Francisco Madero. A wiser selection than Dr. de la Barra it would have been difficult to make for such a troublesome position. He had represented Mexico at Washington just prior to the troubles of his country, and commanded great respect among the officials in that city.

With the downfall of Diaz the real troubles of the Maderistas began. It is almost always true that the victorious are impatient to secure the fruits of their victory. Extravagant promises had been made by the leaders of the revolution, which included free land, lower taxes, higher wages and a decreased cost of living. It was impossible for the leaders to do these things at once, as it would take several years to work out such a program. Although Francisco Madero held no office, he had been designated as an adviser of the new government, and no appointments were made by the Provisional President without his approval. This brought about jealousies among the ambitious leaders, and there has been more or less fighting in various sections of the republic in which much blood has been shed. A few generals deserted the standards of Madero and have kept up fighting on their own account. A serious outbreak occurred in the city of Puebla in which many were killed. Many political parties followed, as it had been many years since there was a definite party organization in Mexico. Some of these were very small, being made up simply of factional groups. The Church party again became prominent and started to take an active part in the approaching election. Bernardo Reyes, who had been sent on a mission to Europe by Diaz in order to get him out of the country, returned, and a strong party known as the Reyesistas arose and wanted to nominate him for the presidency. He left the country, however, before the final elections, claiming to be in fear of his life. This voluntary expatriation of General Reyes on September 28th, when, disguised as an invalid, he walked up the gang-plank of a steamer at Vera Cruz, bound for New York, removed the only obstacle in the path of Sr. Madero. The election, which was held on Sunday, October 1st, 1911, was as peaceful as such an event could be in most parts of Mexico. It does not necessarily mean that they were not inclined to fight, but there was nothing to fight about. The result was that the electors chosen were almost unanimous for Francisco Madero.

To an American this election would seem almost farcical. For the purpose of the election the country was divided into districts, with one presidential elector for every five hundred inhabitants. Before election day two officials were appointed in each district. One of these officials compiled a list of the voters in his little subdivision. When he had looked up the voters in his district, and the names were printed and posted on some convenient street corner, this official's duties ended. Any one whose name did not appear on the printed list had a right to go to the proper authorities and state his case. All those qualified to vote received a ballot on which they were to write the names of the electors they wished to vote for. The second official appointed took charge of the election booth on the morning of the election, and these booths were generally placed at the entrance to business houses or even in the parks. The voting places were supposed to open at 9 o'clock. The first seven voters who appeared, with the one commissioner appointed, constituted the election board. In American cities one could imagine a great rush of voters to be among the first seven, but in many of the Mexican booths that number did not arrive until half an hour or an hour after the time the booth was supposed to open. The commissioner in charge sat at the table with a list of the voters beside him, and, as the voters appeared, they indicated the names of the electors for whom they wished to vote, and the commissioner then communicated this information to the other members of the board in an audible voice. As a general rule there was no closed ballot box, but the ballots were merely laid in an open pasteboard box with a paperweight on top to hold them down. Of secrecy or an attempt at secrecy there was none. Some citizens sent their wives to vote for them with the information that they themselves were indisposed, and these ballots were accepted. It is claimed that the peons generally abstained from voting, partly because of pride because they were not able to write, but more likely because of indifference since they had never been allowed such a privilege before.

SR. DON FRANCISCO I. MADERO.

Courtesy of the Bulletin of the Pan-American Union.

The only real contest in the election was over the choice of a Vice-President. Dr. Vasquez Gomez, who had been the principal aid of Sr. Madero in the revolution, had been cast aside by him in favour of José Maria Pino Suarez. The cause of the disagreement between these two leaders of the revolution was in part over the name of the party. Dr. Gomez insisted upon the original name of the revolutionist party, which was Antireelectionista, while Sr. Madero decided upon the name of Constitutional Progressive. Dr. Gomez continued as a candidate under the name chosen by him. Many also voted for the Acting-President, although he was not an active candidate. Other names of parties with tickets in the field were Pure Liberal Party, Red Liberals, Evolutionist Party and Reyesistas. An active campaign was carried on by several of the candidates, and Señor Madero visited many of the states in a speaking tour. Everywhere he was received with respect and at many times with real enthusiasm. Soldiers were present at the voting booths in many places on election day to prevent trouble, but there was very little disturbance in any part of the country.

On the 6th of November, 1911, Francisco Indalecio Madero was inaugurated President of Mexico with elaborate ceremonies, and Pino Suarez was inducted into the office of Vice-President. The new chief executive of the republic was born on the Hacienda del Rosario, in the state of Coahuila, on the 4th of October, 1873, and is still a young man. He is the eldest of a family of thirteen children, and both of his parents are members of wealthy land-owning families. It is estimated that the revolution cost the Maderos more than a million dollars, but they could well afford it. He married Señorita Sara Pérez, the daughter of a prominent Mexican, in 1900. For several years President Madero has been the leader of the opposition in the republic. His appearance is not that of a leader, for the new President is barely five feet four in height and weighs less than one hundred thirty-five pounds. His figure is slight, with small hands and feet, and he wears a full beard. By way of preparing for his campaign Madero wrote a book entitled "The Presidential Succession in 1910," which created such a tremendous sensation that it was finally suppressed by the Diaz government. It was a fearless arraignment of what he considered to be the evils of that administration. On June 7th, 1910, he was arrested at Monterey and imprisoned for several weeks, not being released until after the election had been held. It was then that he published his political platform known as the "Plan of San Luis Potosi," which was issued from that city on the 5th of October. Among the reforms advocated by him were a more equitable distribution of the lands of the republic, free restitution of lands wrested from the Yaquis and a return of that tribe to their native state, and an abolition of the practice of admitting malefactors into the national army.

It is impossible to predict the outcome of the Madero administration. If the people stand by him many needed reforms may be accomplished. The main difficulty to be overcome will be that personalism enters so much into Mexican politics. If parties backed by real and genuine principles and not dependent for their strength upon a single personality, shall arise, then peaceful conditions will return and President Madero will be permitted to work out his program. He showed himself humane and considerate during the revolution, although he did not distinguish himself especially as a strategist or military leader. He broke all precedents in yielding the provisional presidency to Dr. de la Barra, instead of seizing that office himself as he might easily have done. In his speeches he has counselled moderation among his followers. He has a difficult task before him, but it is the hope of the writer that he will not disappoint those who have raised him to power.

President Madero has been accused of being anti-American in his sympathies. As an answer to this I quote from an authorized statement by him in an American newspaper:

"I am glad at this time to have the opportunity to assure the American people of my great friendship and regard for them, and to assure them that I will do all in my power during my administration to strengthen still more the already strong friendly relations existing between the two nations. I feel very sure that during my administration the bonds which unite the sister republic will become far stronger than they have ever been. I am a great admirer of the American people, for I went to school in the United States and I have travelled much in your country. I will welcome Americans to Mexico at all times. I want to see American energy, American brains and American capital come to this country and assist in its development and progress, and Americans will always find a friend in me and my government."

CHAPTER XXII
THE SIERRAS AND BEYOND

"Las Madres," says the Mexican, whenever he is asked the name of the lofty range of mountains that runs through the western part of the northern half of Mexico, and which separate the lofty interior plateaus from the Pacific Ocean and the Gulf of California. This range of mountains effectually cuts off the west coast from the best developed part of Mexico, and for that reason this section is not so well known as those parts which are visited by travellers. At the present time no railway has been completed across this range of mountains, but it will not be long until this disadvantage will exist no longer. This district includes the great states of Sonora and Sinaloa, the territory of Tepic, and a large part of the states of Chihuahua and Durango. To-day it is almost a counterpart of what California was before the gold rush of 1849—little known, isolated and undeveloped—but with just as great natural advantages. Dense jungles cover the lower levels along the coast, where water is plentiful, while great areas in the north are semi-arid. In the higher altitudes vast forests of pine and oak crown the serrated peaks. The population is generally sparse and scattered.

In the future the main gateways to reach this part of the country from the United States will be El Paso, and Benson, Arizona. From El Paso it is a distance of a little more than two hundred miles to Chihuahua. The traveller has no sooner crossed the Rio Grande than the change is seen in the Mexican town of Ciudad Juarez, formerly Paso del Norte. This city was the objective point of the revolutionists in the late trouble in that country, and was the scene of a great deal of fighting before it was finally captured. After its capture it was the seat of the temporary government of the Maderistas. For several hours on the journey southward there is nothing to be seen but the chaparral and desolate-looking hills, with just enough novelty in the little towns that may be passed to make the trip strange and rather old-fashioned. Big-hatted, shiftless peons stare at you from their leaning positions against the station walls. The "hee-haw" of a lone burro or the "cough" of a gasoline engine will be the only sounds to break the silence.

The train rolls along through a narrow valley which is quite level, and with high tablelands all about. Then the route reaches the land of *haciendas*, where herds of cattle, sheep and goats may be seen. It is a land of deep valleys, with glimpses of majestic mountains, and sometimes with broad spreading plains as well, but the mountains are always in view. At length, after a ride of a little more than half a day, the train reaches Chihuahua, which is the principal city and metropolis of this section of Mexico. Chihuahua is not a very beautiful city; nor is it as attractive as many of the other Mexican cities, for its location and the climate are not such as can greatly be recommended. It is destined to be a much larger city than at present, however, by reason of the mineral wealth surrounding it, and also because it is the starting point for what will ultimately be the principal trade route between the United States and northwestern Mexico. Like Monterey this city has become very much Americanized, and that influence is noticeable in both people and architecture.

Chihuahua is on the line of the Kansas City, Mexico and Orient Railway, which, when completed, will form a direct route from Kansas City, Missouri, to Topolobampo, a new port on the Pacific. At the present time trains are running from Wichita, Kansas, almost to the Mexican border, and two detached sections are in operation in the Republic of Mexico. One of these starts from a point near the Rio Grande and runs to Chihuahua. From Chihuahua westward this railroad, in conjunction with the Mexican Northwestern Railway, traverses one of the finest grazing sections of the republic. Broad prairies which are covered with grass stretch out on either side to the foothills, and form rich grazing lands. The vast ranges, the temperate climate and a fair average rainfall makes this almost an ideal country for cattle. Upon them are fattened the beef that feeds the country, and many animals find their way to the markets of the United States. It is a region of immense *haciendas*, which form almost empires in themselves, for they are larger than some of the principalities of Europe. One estate near Chihuahua would make a commonwealth as large as the states of Massachusetts and Rhode Island combined, with a small farm of a million acres besides. The Zuloaga family own a *hacienda* directly on this line of railway, which is thirty-five miles wide and nearly one hundred miles long, and includes about two million acres. Most of this estate consists of fine grazing land, and it ships about forty thousand head of cattle each year, as well as from three to six thousand mules and horses. A few years ago the late proprietor of this estate bought an adjoining farm for two hundred thousand dollars, and his method of paying for it is a good illustration of Mexican business methods. He secured silver coin for this amount, which weighed nearly six tons, and hauled it over to the seller in two great carts.

A GROUP OF PEONS

The buildings of the Zuloaga *hacienda*, which I visited, lie about fifty miles west of Chihuahua, in one of the most beautiful locations that could be found anywhere. They are near the foot of a range of low mountains, and in front projects out a plain that gently slopes down to a lake a couple of miles distant. Beyond the lake is another range of wooded hills which seem to complete the picture. Within the walls are the home of the *hacendado*, the church, the stables and a store. The church is a beautiful structure, artistic in its details, and all of the materials used in its construction were secured upon the plantation; and all of the work, including some magnificently carved woodwork and some creditable paintings, was done on the premises and by those living there. The buildings are all one-storied in height, with walls thick enough to withstand any earthquake. The rooms are large and airy, with extremely high ceilings, through which you might drive a carriage, and the parlours are nearly as large as public halls. More than three thousand peons are employed on this *hacienda,* most of whom live in buildings arranged in big hollow squares just outside of the walls of the family's quarters.

TARAHUMARI INDIANS.

There are a number of small towns along this trans-continental line of railway, the principal of which is Miñaca, a quaint little old-fashioned place. The inhabitants would rather attend a chicken fight than work or go to mass. From Miñaca this road begins the real climb over the divide on its way to the Pacific coast. For scenic beauty it equals any railroad in Mexico, not excepting the ride over the Mexican railway from the City of Mexico to Vera Cruz, hitherto described. Deep cuts, high hills, and tunnels succeed each other, as the railroad climbs up on its way toward the line of perpetual snow. It passes through one of the best timber sections of Mexico, where tall pine trees, straight as an arrow, rise up for a hundred feet or more without a limb. Huge crags of fantastic outline, tall pines silhouetted against the low-hanging clouds and the mysterious depths of the barrancas combine to form scenes of awe-inspiring grandeur. At dangerous points crosses on the trail tell the story of tragedies—of riders who have probably stumbled into eternity without a moment's warning.

This Sierra region of Mexico should appeal to the sportsman, for much game abounds. At nearly all elevations may be found the white-tail deer. The mountain lion, called *tigre*, lurks in the fastnesses of the mountains. The bear may be found wherever there are good feeding grounds. The wild turkey is plentiful in many sections. The Mexicans do not hunt much, so that there are many game birds. Quail are numerous in the foothills, and wild duck, snipe and curlew are exceedingly numerous on the lagunas and marshes of the coast, as well as in the lakes of the mountain region. Hunting is inexpensive, and it is strange that more Americans do not visit this unhunted region.

One of the strangest of the many tribes of Mexican Indians inhabit the valleys and barrancas of this part of the republic. These are the Tarahumaris, a timid race who rather shrink from contact with the white people to any greater extent than is necessary. Occasionally these Indians may be seen on the streets of Chihuahua, whither they go to buy some things, or, perhaps, to carry a message for a Mexican or American. But they do not linger any longer than is necessary. They can always be distinguished from the other Indians because the men almost invariably have their legs absolutely bare in all kinds of weather. They also wear their hair long, and it hangs down over the shoulder like our red men, while the Mexican Indians usually wear their hair short. Their features are coarse, but their bearing has a kind of native dignity about it that attracts. One of their medicine men once cut his hair to get some new ideas. While the new hair was growing he kept his head tied up to prevent his thoughts from escaping. I mention this to give an idea of the primitiveness and simplicity of these strange people.

The Tarahumaris pay no taxes or tribute to the Mexican government. They are quiet and inoffensive, however, and for that reason they are allowed to inhabit the mountain slopes and inhospitable barrancas in peace. Their houses are very simple. They are usually made by setting up forked poles across which other straight poles are laid, and then roughly-hewed boards are set up along the sides. Sometimes they are made entirely of small rocks. Many of them live in the natural caves which abound in that region, and of which I have seen scores. They are nomadic and change their domicile frequently, although the new location may be only a few hundred rods away from the old. Store-houses may be seen in which the family stores its surplus supply of corn and beans, which are the only food supplies cultivated by these people. Upon the mountains the men kill deer and squirrels, and these, together with fish, rats and little ground animals which abound in that region, constitute their principal meat supply.

The Tarahumaris are not a sociable people, nor are they industrious, for they like too well to lie on their backs or breasts in the hot sun. They are great runners and have been known to run day after day, stopping only to eat and secure some necessary sleep. When they are travelling across the country one will seldom see them walking. Even on a mountain trail they usually keep up a trot. I have seen them running up a steep path where most of us would not want to walk very long without stopping to rest. The chief men of the tribes carry canes as their emblem of authority. If a man is charged with an offence a messenger is sent to him, armed with a cane made of red Brazil wood, and the person summoned would not dare to disobey the order. No writ issued by any court in a civilized land commands greater obedience. It is generally the older men who are entrusted with this badge of authority, and they are very jealous of the privilege. This method of designating authority is quite common among the aborigines of the Americas. The Tarahumaris are very superstitious. They are afraid to travel after night because the dead are supposed to be abroad at that time. The *shaman*, as the medicine man is called, is a man of great importance among these superstitious people. He is always present at all family celebrations, such as weddings and funerals, and he is generally called in when there is sickness in the family.

About one hundred and fifty miles southwest of El Paso, in the state of Chihuahua, is a colony of considerable interest to Americans. After travelling that number of miles of semi-desert land over the Rio Grande and Sierra Madre Railway from Ciudad Juarez, as dreary a landscape as one could imagine, the appearance suddenly changes as one approaches the lands of the Mormon colony that has settled here. Fearful of the results of the anti-polygamy agitation in the United States a few hundred followers of Brigham Young banded together, and sought a new "promised land." They travelled in caravans that contained all their worldly goods until they crossed the border into Mexico. Here they were welcomed, for farmers are what northern Mexico needed, and religious or ethical questions did not disturb the Mexican government. The colonists were exempted from taxes for ten years, and their implements were allowed free entry. Each colonist was granted a certain number of acres at low interest and on easy terms.

The original colony has expanded into several settlements numbering more than five thousand persons. The principal colony is named Colonia Juarez, and it is a few miles from the station of Casas Grandes. The Mormons are splendid agriculturalists, and they sell large quantities of alfalfa, grains, potatoes and dairy products. They use the very latest of American agricultural machinery on their farms. Every village has a graded school supported by a voluntary tax, and a large central academy is also maintained for higher education. They are devout followers of the Mormon prophets,—these colonists across the Rio Grande,—although they claim that no open polygamy is practised. Each man will deny the possession of more than one wife. The excess of women with families over the men, however, and the fact that the Mormon man is thoroughly at home in more than one house would easily lead one to a different conclusion. To this must be added the knowledge that these Mormons left good homes in Utah for a tract of almost desert land in Mexico, mainly because of the efforts of the government of the United States to stamp out plural marriages.

The other main route to the Sierra regions is an extension of the Southern Pacific Railroad, which is known as the Sonora Railway. This railroad extends from Nogales, and it is destined to run to the city of Guadalajara, a distance of about eleven hundred miles. Nogales is a city of about three thousand inhabitants, half of which lies on either side of the border line. A simple glance without any explanation would show the visitor which part of it belongs to the United States, because of the difference in the buildings and the energy of the inhabitants. From there the railroad runs south through Magdalena and across some fertile plains until, at a distance of almost three hundred miles from the border, it reaches Hermosillo, the capital of the state of Sonora, which is the second largest state in the republic. Much of this state is useless for agriculture, as it is dry and arid, and a part is very mountainous. In other sections the soil is extremely fertile, and irrigation would render it invaluable. Such projects could be carried out if there was as much enterprise on that side of the border as on the northern side. Near the Yaqui River the soil and climate are as well adapted to fruit culture as southern California. There are many large mining enterprises, the largest being at Cananea, and nearly all are American enterprises. The trouble with the Yaqui Indians has greatly hindered development in Sonora during the past decade. Several parties of American prospectors and miners were attacked and a number of Americans killed. The government finally deported thousands of the Yaquis to other sections of the republic, and their depredations then ceased.

Hermosillo is situated on the Sonora River, in the midst of an agricultural district and surrounded by rugged mountains, where there are many mines of gold and silver. It is the seat of a Catholic diocese, for which a fine new cathedral has been built, and also has some very creditable buildings. It is a city of perhaps ten or twelve thousand people, and is the largest city in the state. From Hermosillo this railroad runs to the port of Guaymas, which is quite an important commercial town, and less than a hundred miles from the capital. The Bay of Guaymas is one of the best on the Pacific coast, and the marine trade is quite important. For a long time this town was the terminus of this railroad, but it is too far up the Gulf of California to ever become a very important ocean port. Within the last few years construction work has been rapidly pushed southward at a little distance from the coast, and through trains are now running as far as the city of Tepic, on the way to Guadalajara.

Not a great distance south of Guaymas the Sonora Railroad enters Sinaloa, a state nearly as large as Indiana. This state is destined to be a great agricultural state, as it is well watered and contains a number of fine rivers. Besides the Fuerte, Sinaloa, Culiacan and Elota Rivers, there are a hundred or more smaller streams traversing it. It stretches along the Pacific coast for a distance of nearly four hundred miles, and has an average breadth of eighty miles. One-half of the state is little known, and is traversed only by obscure and difficult trails. Cane and corn culture have been the chief industry, but it offers good inducements for the raising of almost all kinds of grains. In undeveloped natural wealth, both agricultural and mineral, and in its splendid water powers, Sinaloa is unsurpassed by any Mexican commonwealth. An American land company has recently opened up a tract of two million acres, and is establishing a colony that promises good results. The capital is Culiacan, a short distance from the coast. Heretofore the only outlet for this city of fifteen thousand has been a miserable railroad to its port, Altata, but the new line enables passengers to go by Pullman cars to all points in the United States. It is an old city, for the Spaniards found a considerable settlement there. They immediately established a town which was well fortified. The present city is quite attractive and possesses a little manufacturing. It is the residence seat of quite a colony of rich and cultured Mexicans, and a number of Americans interested in mining also reside there.

Mazatlan, a little further down the coast, is the largest city and principal port of Sinaloa. It is a picturesque place, with its cathedral spires outlined against the sky, and cocoanut palms and thatched roofs below. The blue Cordilleras in the distance complete the picture. A lighthouse at the north entrance is said to be the highest lighthouse in the world, with the exception of the one at Gibraltar. It is a city of about twenty thousand inhabitants, and the largest city on the Pacific coast. Although a great deal of shipping is done in Mazatlan, the harbour is poor and offers no protection to vessels. Plans have been approved for a safe harbour, to cost several million pesos, in order to prepare it for the anticipated increase in business. Whether the internal troubles will stop the building of this much-needed west coast railroad improvement remains to be seen. Its completion will not only give an outlet for this rich region to the United States, but also to the City of Mexico, and the stimulus can already be seen wherever the railroad is in operation. There is not a richer section in the whole republic than these coast lands, but because of their isolation everything has been backward, and all work has been done in the very crudest and most primitive ways. The only development that has taken place is in mining, and most of the mines are even yet operated in the old-fashioned ways, because of the difficulty of transporting machinery and fuel.

The territory of Tepic is almost as large as the states of Massachusetts and Connecticut combined. In natural resources it will compare with Sinaloa, for it is well watered and affords fine opportunities for agriculture. Some day the jungles will be transformed into orange groves and banana plantations, while the higher lands will produce rich harvests of grain and coffee. The water power could be utilized to turn the wheels of factories or to run the railroads which are so much needed.

The capital city of Tepic, a municipality of fifteen thousand people, has been asleep, but will now be awakened daily by the noise of the locomotive. At an elevation of three thousand feet the air is fresh and invigorating. The climate is pronounced almost ideal by those who live there, and it is free from the fevers that prevail in the low coast lands. It does not differ in general appearance from many other Mexican cities, but is a quaint and interesting town.

Separated from the mainland of Mexico by the Gulf of California and the Colorado River, lies that little known territory of Baja (lower) California. It is a long narrow peninsula that projects about eight hundred miles southeasterly from the southern border of California. Its width varies from about thirty to over one hundred miles, with an irregular coast line over two thousand miles long bordered by numerous islands, and in size is a trifle larger than the state of Iowa. Lower California is mainly mountainous, with irregular plains along the Pacific coast, and smaller plains and valleys along the north coast and in some parts of the interior. In climatic and other physical features the northern part of the peninsula is very similar to southern California, with some local modifications. The southern end of the Colorado Desert crosses the border, and continues down along the northern coast for some distance. Along the Pacific coast a low range of mountains recedes a short distance inland, and continues for some distance. In the southern part of the peninsula they become higher, forming the San Pedro Martir Mountains, which reach a height of over ten thousand feet above the sea. Vast desolate plateaus of black lava, which surround little gem-like valleys, are succeeded by extensive stretches of desert upon which nothing but the cactus will grow. The western coast is bathed by cool waters and fogs, while the eastern shores are washed by the waves of a warm inland sea, and have almost continuous sunshine.

Lower California was one of the early discoveries of the Spaniards, and was promptly placed in charge of the Jesuits, whose missionaries were quite successful. They explored all parts of the peninsula and established missions among the Indians, and at the same time introduced many of the crops and fruits of the Old World. They established three main trails throughout the length of the peninsula, one following each coast and the other running near the centre. These roads are to-day the only routes of travel, and, except for short distances, can only be pursued on mule-back. Most of the Indians who formerly inhabited the peninsula have disappeared, and the population to-day is very small. Some of the old mission churches are still in use, while others are represented simply by fragments of ruined walls and choked-up irrigating ditches.

Agriculture has never flourished to any great extent in Lower California. Numerous colonies have been practically failures, with the exception of some recent ones near the international border, where water for irrigation has been obtained from the Colorado River. All of the peninsula has been traversed many times by prospectors in search of gold, silver and other minerals, and a number of valuable mines have been located in various places. The general climate is hot and arid, as is evidenced by the vegetation, although in the southern regions there are districts which have regular summer rains. As a consequence of the arid conditions the surface water is scarce, and is limited to isolated waterfalls or to springs from which small streams sometime flow for a short distance, and then sink into the earth.

The country is divided for administration into the northern and southern portions, with Ensenada, a small port on the west coast as the capital of the northern part, and La Paz, on the eastern coast, the capital of the southern portion. La Paz is the only city of any particular size, and is a place of about six thousand people. The streets are well laid out, and there are some excellent stores and many comfortable houses. The gardens are filled with palms and various tropical trees, so that the city has quite a decided tropical appearance, although it is surrounded by an arid district. It is the seat of the pearl fisheries, which are quite flourishing in the Gulf, and the output of pearls is quite an important item. Tia Juana (Aunt Jane) is a small town on the border not far from San Diego, and it is, perhaps, better known than any other town on the peninsula. Several skirmishes took place within its borders during the recent revolution led by Madero, and many of the participants were Americans.

Magdalena Bay, concerning which there has been considerable talk of the United States trying to secure as a coaling station, is the finest land-locked harbour on the Pacific coast, with a narrow entrance which is protected by the high headlands. The bay is about fifteen miles across, with low sandy shores, and would furnish a fine protection for scores of the largest vessels. It is also within sight of the regular sailing route of steamers bound for Panama. For that reason it would be a very advantageous possession of the United States, if it could be obtained by negotiations with the Mexican government.

The plant life of Lower California is different from that of any other part of the world—so naturalists say. There is a veritable riot of strange forms of cacti and other plants which manage to live without rainfall. The cacti vary from giant forms, which raise their massive fluted trunks to a height of fifty to sixty feet, to little straggling species which are too weak to stand upright. Another peculiar form is the creeping devil cactus, as it is called, which has the appearance of gigantic caterpillars crawling in every direction. These plants do actually travel away from a common centre, as the stem sends down rootlets every little distance, and then the older stems in the rear die about as fast as it advances in the front. There are not many species of birds or animals, and only such kinds as can live where water is scarce will be found. It is said that some animals have been found that never drink water, and even in captivity can not be taught to drink, as it does not seem necessary to their existence.

Owing to its desert character the peninsula is very thinly peopled, and there are extensive sections where not a single inhabitant will be found. The most populous section is that south of La Paz, where the rains are more regular. A few small towns or villages will be found scattered around the coast, with a limited number of prospectors and miners gathered in the interior. The effort to colonize Lower California has been a tale of unbroken failure for more than fifty years. A few rainy years will cause apparent prosperity, but the succeeding years may be rainless and disaster follows. Those who have studied Lower California say that it is not all a hopeless desert, but that there are possibilities of agriculture through irrigation in many parts.

CHAPTER XXIII
THE RUINED CITIES OF YUCATAN

The Mayas (pronounced My-yah) were an ancient people of whom little is known. They dwelt on the broad plains of Yucatan and Central America, and built many cities, or governmental centres, for no ruins of private dwellings have yet been found. The groups of buildings resemble in no way our cities of the present day. They consist everywhere of temples and palaces of the reigning princes or caciques, of public buildings scattered about apparently at random, covering a vast area, with cemented roads and gardens intervening. The centres of the towns were occupied by the public squares and temples; around these were the palaces of the priests and lords, and the outskirts were evidently allotted to the lower classes. Religion and government seem to have gone hand in hand among these primitive Mexicans. The Maya civilization had reached a height unexcelled by any people of the western hemisphere prior to the coming of the white man. They were skilled in architecture, in sculpture and in writing. The priests had developed the science of astronomy to a considerable extent. They had studied with some success the solar system. They had developed a calendar system and created a chronology. So far as these chronological accounts have been worked out they run back three thousand years or more. They reckoned time much as we do, from a fixed date, namely, the birth of Christ. The later dates of the Quirigua inscriptions are generally believed to be somewhere about the beginning of the Christian era.

The oldest of the ruins of the Maya race is said to be that of Copan, which is situated in Honduras, just across the border from Guatemala. It also seems to have been the southernmost point of their migration, as Tula was the northerly terminus of their wanderings. Then comes Quirigua, in Guatemala, which is one of the most remarkable and inexplicable of all the ruins. Tradition sheds no light whatever on these ruins of Copan or Quirigua. The mysterious silence that surrounds these forms a void in the history of the human race. There are doubtless other ruins awaiting the traveller and explorer in the wilderness around Lake Peten, in the northern part of Guatemala. The founder of the race was Izamat-Ul. "To him were brought," says an old writer, "the sick, the halt and the dead, and he healed and restored them all to life by the touch of his hand." Hence he was generally known as the Miraculous Hand, and in inscriptions is frequently represented by a hand only.

CRUMBLING RUINS OF THE ANCIENT MEXICAN CIVILIZATION

In the extreme southeastern part of Mexico, on a small peninsula known as Yucatan, is a section which was at one time the abode of this progressive and migrating race known generally among anthropologists as the Mayas. This distant province deserves far more mention than it usually receives from passing travellers. Though possessing few natural attractions Yucatan is a never-ending source of interest for the anthropologist and archeologist. The whole peninsula is a vast limestone formation, with little or no surface water. Rain is infrequent in most parts, and one might travel for miles without crossing a river or brook, or even chancing upon a spring. In most sections of this peninsula the water is at least seventy feet below the surface of the ground. At the present time windmills aid the inhabitants of that section where the henequen, from which binder twine is made, is raised, but centuries ago such facilities were unknown. There were, however, in some places natural wells which reached down to the depth of what seem to be underground rivers, and it was near these that several ancient cities were located. At least a score of these ancient cities have been explored, of which the best known and most important are Palenque, Uxmal and Chichen Itza. It is known that since the Spaniards first set foot on this peninsula many monuments and practically entire cities have disappeared. At one time, a contemporary writer asserts, there were destroyed in Yucatan five thousand idols of various forms and dimensions, thirteen huge stones which were used as altars, twenty-two smaller stones of various shapes, one hundred and ninety-seven manuscripts of all kinds, including twenty-seven written on deer skins.

Chichen Itza, which is generally interpreted to mean "the mouth of the wells of the Itzas," seems to have been the leading city, and it was located near two of the largest natural wells, which are immense natural pits with perpendicular sides. It is probable that these phenomena attracted the Mayas in their northern migration. As the tribes quarrelled different factions separated from the original body and established new cities as capitals. Thus Chichen Itza came into being. On this desolate soil,

" ... buried 'mid trees,
Upspringing there for sunless centuries,
Behold a royal city, vast and lone,
Lost to each race, to all the world unknown,
Like famed Pompeii, 'neath her lava bed.
...
At every step some palace meets the eye,
Some figure frowns, some temple courts the sky."

Before Cortez landed on Mexican soil the star of these ancient peoples had already set. Their oldest cities had their birth so far back in the twilight of time that not even tradition was able to tell the history of the tribes, the causes that led to their decay or the time of their disaster. Some traditions were told to the Spaniards, but they are of such uncertain origin that very little credence can be placed in them. Upon the walls are sculptures which speak to us in an unknown language; hieroglyphics, and the chiselled types of a people long since departed. The hieroglyphics would probably explain all, but no interpreting key has yet been discovered to give an explanation to the writings. Some authorities assert, however, that Chichen Itza was inhabited at the time of the Conquest. A Spaniard by the name of Aquilar was wrecked on this coast and lived with a powerful cacique for several years, but he left behind him no written memoirs. At any rate, it is known that the Spanish forces occupied this place for at least two years. At first the submission of the natives was complete, but after a time they rallied from their stupor, tiring of ministering to the insatiable wants of their conquerors, and much severe fighting followed.

Of the two great wells at Chichen Itza one was used for the general water supply, the *cenote grande,* and the other was reserved for religious use exclusively, the *cenote sacra.* Picturesque indeed must have been the throngs of white-robed women who peopled the steps of the *cenote grande* at all hours of the day to fetch water for household purposes. They probably carried double-handled urns on their hips or shoulders just as their descendants do at this present day. From far and near all over Yucatan pilgrimages were made to the sacred well, which was on the outskirts of the city, just as pilgrimages are made to-day to holy shrines by Catholics and Mohammedans. It was this that gave the city its holy character. Offerings of many kinds were made to the deities. It is said that in time of drouth offerings of precious stones and other valuables were thrown into it, and in specially protracted cases human beings were thrown into it as sacrifices. Even after the time of the Spanish conquest there are recorded instances of pilgrimages to the sacred well for the purpose of sacrificing slaves to relieve a drouth. These victims were supposed to live even after they had disappeared beneath the sacred waters. A Spanish writer of the time asserts that this was done as late as 1560.

The Chichen Itza of the olden times, filled with pilgrims from far and near, would scarcely be recognized in the place of to-day. The jungle has gradually crept its way into the very holy of holies. Columns have been overthrown, and some of the structures have been almost lost in a tangle of thorns and creepers. Even in the last half century the destruction and disintegration has been very noticeable. To reach the place it is necessary to ride about fifteen miles over a rough and wearisome road. All around lie buried in thick jungle ruins of palaces and other buildings. Pyramid-like structures seem to have been one of the favourite forms of building. The most imposing of these on this site rises sixty-eight feet above the plain, and each side is almost one hundred and seventy-five feet in length, the whole covering about an acre of ground. This structure is called the Castillo, although it was really a temple. It is made up of nine terraces of faced masonry, narrowing toward the top, each one elaborately panelled to relieve the monotony. On each side there is a broad stairway, with a flight of ninety steps, with stone balustrades, which are generally carved to represent reptiles. A stone building almost forty feet square crowns the summit. The northern façade must have been very striking before time and the destroying hand of man wrought their work. There were no doors on any of the buildings, and no traces of hinges have been found. At the western base of the pyramid is the walk that leads to the sacred well. It is believed that on the top of this pyramid the sacred rites of the priests of their faith were performed, and it is said that the sacrificial victims were led down these stairways, then along the causeway and finally cast into the sacred well. It is easy for the imagination to picture the scene in all its splendour of white-robed priests, smoking censors, and—saddest of all—the victims bedecked with garlands of flowers.

There are ruins of colonnades, courts, buildings and other structures of which many columns are standing at Chichen Itza, and it has been called "the city of a thousand columns" by some writers. One of the most important monuments is the Nun's Palace, as it is called. It is not so large as others, but contains a greater number of apartments. It is said to have been the custom of these people to educate girls of noble birth to the service of the gods, on their attaining the age of twelve or thirteen. Their service was similar to that of the Vestal Virgins, although the vows were not always perpetual. It was their duty to keep the altar supplied with fresh flowers and to sweep the temples. One group of structures is called the Ball Court, as it is believed to have been used for a game similar to the modern basket ball. It consists of two perpendicular parallel walls from north to south thirty-two feet high, three hundred and twenty-five feet long and one hundred and thirteen feet apart. The ends of this quadrangle are each occupied by a small temple. In the centre of each wall, about fifteen feet from the ground, there are two stone discs with holes through the centre, which seem to have had a part in this or some other game. The vast proportions of this court, or tlachtle, would seem to indicate that this game was very popular with the Yucatecos. Some of the well preserved ruins present beautiful sculptured façades, to which names have been given because of the fancied resemblance to something. For instance, one has been called the ruins of the

"House of the Tigers," because of a frieze of stalking tigers divided by richly fringed shells; another round building, known as El Caracol, "The Snail," is the best preserved building at Chichen; "The Red House," and the "House of the Dark Writing," are still other structures. In all directions for several miles the bush is strewn with ruins. Crumbling walls and courts overgrown with jungle growth are encountered on every side, but because of the disintegration these once splendid palaces and temples are now little more than shapeless masses of crumbled masonry. The human figures seen on these monuments have the usual types of the Toltec carvings on the plateaus of Mexico. The total area covered by these ruins has been estimated by some investigators as high as ten square miles.

The next largest and most interesting city of ruins is known as Uxmal, which was the capital of the Tutal Xiu branch of the Mayas. This city is located between low ranges of hills, perhaps one hundred miles from Chichen Itza. When seen from an eminence a dozen or more imposing structures of white limestone are presented to view. This city, no doubt, supplied a very important part in the early history of Yucatan—at least if one is to judge from its size. It is believed that this was the original city of the Toltecs. A dozen or more imposing structures of considerable size still stand here that can be identified, in addition to the large numbers of ruins which can scarcely be outlined. The most notable sanctuary of Uxmal, which is now known as the "House of the Dwarf," is over fifty feet high, and also surmounts a steep-sloped pyramid one hundred feet in height. Two stairways on opposite sides lead to this building. It is so named because the natives say it was built by a savage dwarf in a single night. Long after the city was abandoned this temple was held in especial veneration. The Spanish priests used to find offerings of cocoa and copal on it, and they attributed this to devil worship. Two lines of parallel walls, parts of which are still standing, enclose a court or quadrangle, which is similar to the Ball Court at Chichen. The group of buildings around it encloses more than one hundred rooms. All of the buildings seem to have been built on low platforms or terraces. There is also at this place a high terrace, or platform, that covers over three acres of ground, and on which is a second and a third terrace, upon the latter of which is the ruin of a building known as the Governor's Palace. This building is one of the finest samples of early American architecture still extant. It stands at an elevation of forty-four feet above the plains, and commands a splendid view of the city. Its exterior walls are decorated with sculptured masonry, in the making of which it is estimated there are upward of twenty thousand sculptured pieces of stone. The building is three hundred and twenty-two feet long, and is divided into three parts by two arcades which pass clear through. It is built entirely of stone without ornament to a height of ten feet, then comes a cornice, above which is a wall that is a bewildering maze of beautiful sculpture. This frieze has a row of colossal heads, and is divided into panels which are alternately filled with grecques in high relief, and diamond or lattice work. All the lintels of the building here are of wood in an excellent state of preservation.

AN OLD CHURCH

At Uxmal there is a building called the "House of Turtles," because of a row of turtles used as ornaments in the upper cornice. It is the freest from ornamentation of any of the structures. The turtles are found sculptured at various places along the cornice. The "House of the Pigeons" is the name of another building, because of the fancied resemblance to a dove-cote. The crest of the roof is perforated with many rectangular openings—but the resemblance for which the name is given is very fanciful. At this site there were none of the natural wells described at the other city, but these people constructed some natural reservoirs a short distance from the town in which the rainfall was collected, and which gave the necessary water supply for the people. Furthermore, some of the buildings seem to have had subterranean cisterns of large size under them. Heavy rainfall occurs here for about one-half the year, but during the other half there is practically no rainfall, and water becomes very scarce and valuable. The so-called "House of the Nuns" is the largest building and bears the richest and most intricate carving at Uxmal. It is composed of four buildings, the largest of which is two hundred and seventy-nine feet in length. The four buildings enclose a great court, with sides two hundred and fourteen and two hundred and fifty-eight feet in length, the entrance to which is through a high triangular-arched gateway. This building originally contained no less than eighty-eight apartments of various sizes. A number of writers believe that many of these buildings at Uxmal are comparatively recent, because of the appearance of the stone and the well-preserved character of the wood used in the construction.

These structures are only a part of the ruins that still remain, for the jungle on either side hides the remains of what were once imposing buildings. Many of these have been literally torn asunder by trees, whose roots have forced themselves between the stones and pried them apart. No doubt this city once housed many thousands of people, but to-day it is without inhabitants. The pomp and glory of former times have disappeared; and all is silent save for the birds that nest in the trees and bushes.

The third city of ruins, Palenque, is situated at a considerable distance south and west of the two just described, and not far from San Juan Bautista. Palenque, according to Charney, was a holy city—a place for pilgrimage. In the carvings neither sword, spear, shield nor arrow appear. The representations are all of peaceful subjects, usually a personage standing with a sceptre and with prostrated acolytes at his feet. From the expression one would judge that they were worshippers, and not slaves or captives. Their expression is always peaceful and serene and that of worshippers and believers. The city is built in the form of an amphitheatre, on the lowest slope of the lofty Cordilleras beyond. Its high position affords a magnificent view over the forest-covered plain below stretching as far as the sea. In all the structures the builder levelled out the ground in narrow terraces, on which artificial elevations of pyramidal forms were reared, and the hillside was faced with hewed stones. At Palenque there are in all ten buildings in view, each one crowning an elevation artificially made. As one enters the grounds there are several buildings to the right and left, but directly in front are the remains of the Palace. At one time this building has been very large and imposing. Remains of a broad flight of steps that led to the imposing entrance corridor are in plain evidence. Flights of steps led down to the first patio, which was surrounded by lofty corridors with roofs of pointed arches and which led into small apartments. There were two of these patios in the Palace of irregular size. Double galleries which made a sort of cloister surrounded them. Gloomy entrances from these corridors lead to underground chambers, where there are tables which are called altars, beds and dining tables by different writers. A lack of system seems to prevail in the building of the Palace. On top of one of the walls two immense forest trees are now growing. In the central portion are the ruins of a tower, of which three stories are still standing, with many windows. It is a square tower ornamented to the north with pointed niches; otherwise it is almost devoid of ornamentation. On the contrary the galleries are richly ornamented with medallions, probably representing priests and priestesses. Many human figures are sculptured in low relief representing priests with mitres on their heads and in uncomfortable attitudes. The faces are oftentimes defaced in order to give an appearance of ferocity. Some of the figures of the deities are fantastic, monstrous and even terrible.

The Temple of Inscriptions stands on a hill about fifty feet high. A magnificent view of the ruins is afforded by this elevation, as well as the broad tablelands surrounding. There are three large mural tablets covered with picture writing and hieroglyphs, supposed to be copies of the laws of these ancient people, in the building. Across a little valley over which an aqueduct leads the land rises in terraces, and is surmounted with artificially made hills on which are the ruins of more buildings—two Temples of the Cross and the Temple of the Sun. The Temple of the Sun is almost perfectly preserved. The interior is one large room with a sanctuary at one end. In each of these are mural tablets which contain what is known as the Cross of Palenque. The cruciform shape, such as the swastika and other forms, is not uncommon among aboriginal people, but this is what is known as the Latin cross. Whether this arose by chance through the invention of the artist, or the cross had some religious significance among these people, still remains an absolute mystery. Charney asserts that it is one of the symbols of Tlaloa, the god of rain, but other writers differ with him. The body of the cross, which rests on a hideous head, is sculptured in the centre, and at the upper end are two human figures. On one there is an inscription of sixty-eight characters, which doubtless explain the ceremony represented by the sculpture. Again it is surmounted by the sacred bird of the Mayas, the quetzal. In another this place is taken by a representation of the sun with its spreading rays. Where did the Mayas get their idea of the cross so sacred among Christian people? No one has yet been able to answer this question satisfactorily.

Who built these structures? For what purpose were they reared? Various are the theories, and many are the speculations covering them. But authentic information is absolutely wanting, and the passing years shed little light. The modern Yucatecos are an attractive people. No people in the world are pleasanter or have more delightful manners than they. The young women have a winning grace and charm that is peculiarly their own. Their costume is not greatly unlike that of the Tehuanas—and it is fully as unique and becoming. It is quite probable that their customs and characteristics have not changed much since the Spanish occupation. They have always been an independent people, and have caused much more trouble than the majority of the aboriginal tribes of Mexico.

CHAPTER XXIV
THE PRESENT AND THE FUTURE

The old-fashioned Don, accustomed to ox-carts, wooden ploughs, and a horde of men ready to serve him, no doubt views with dismay the changes being wrought by steam and electricity. The younger generation has been educated abroad, or in the States, and rather welcomes the innovations. The spirit of revolution and political unrest that prevailed for the first sixty years of the republic has lessened, even if it has not entirely passed away. Education and immigration have worked wonders in the country; and, above all, the establishment of a government that for almost a third of a century commanded obedience at home and respect abroad is responsible for the mutation in Mexico. It was an absolute republic and under a strong controlling hand. It was the family government applied to the state, for it was very paternal in its rule.

PRIMITIVE TRANSPORTATION

Mexico is a human country and is not without its faults. The greatest of these are, however, the result of conditions for which the present generation of nation-builders are not responsible. A transformation can not be wrought in a decade, nor in a generation. And yet the real accomplishments of the past twenty-five years in Mexico are marvellous. Americans who have lived there during that time wax eloquent in describing the great change for the better. Whereas formerly people hesitated to invest money for fear of political changes, investments in that country are now looked upon as safe, and Mexican securities are given a fixed value on the bourses of the world.

Modern luxuries and conveniences are being introduced everywhere. The people are simply installing in a hurry the things that other countries have been acquiring for the half of a century. Every city is bestirring herself, and electric light plants, modern sewerage systems and water works are being constructed as rapidly as things can move in this land of procrastination. Old and crude methods of power are being replaced by up-to-date machinery in mines and manufactures. Electric railways are replacing the mule tram lines, and the merry hum of the trolley is fast succeeding the bray of the long-eared motor just mentioned. Mexico lagged behind so long that she has had quite a distance to go, and it will be a long while before she can entirely catch up with the head of the procession. Material wealth is increasing. Better wages are paid, and the surplus is being expended for more and better goods. The wants of the great bulk of the people are so few, that it must be a long time before there will be a great change in their method of living; but their children are being educated, and that in itself works wonders in their uplifting.

For more than twenty years the finances of the government have shown a surplus. What a contrast to all the years of the republic before that time. In 1876 the total revenue of the government was but $19,000,000 silver. For the fiscal year ending June 30th, 1910, this had increased to $53,164,242 United States gold. From a yearly deficit a surplus has been evolved which annually amounts to several million dollars. The total cash in the treasury at the date of the above report amounted to $37,042,857 gold. This statement shows a healthy condition of affairs. The government now finds willing buyers for its bonds, and all its obligations have been met promptly for a number of years.

Finance Minister Limantour, who held that position for many years, proved himself to be a Napoleon of finance, and his reputation extended to every financial centre in the world. Establishing the gold standard was a great achievement. Just a few years ago Mexican silver varied from $2.05 to $2.40 for a gold dollar, and all business was unsettled as a result. Now the government has established a rate of exchange of two silver dollars for one of gold, and all this was done without any friction or disturbance. It is to be hoped that the new administration will maintain the same high standard of financial integrity that has been handed down by its immediate predecessor.

The foreign trade of Mexico runs into big figures. The total extra-territorial trade of the republic for the year ending June 30th, 1910, amounted to $227,456,025 in United States gold. Of this amount $130,023,135 represented exports and $97,432,890, imports. Of the exports $78,260,037 were of mineral products, while vegetable products were less than half that amount. An analysis of the imports shows by far the largest items were included under manufactured articles, such as machinery, textiles, chemical products, etc. Arms and explosives imported exceeded a million and a half dollars in value, thus showing that the government and people were even then preparing for the struggle to follow. By far the largest proportion of exports and imports was with the United States. Imports from the United States amounted to the tidy sum of $56,421,551, an increase of twelve million dollars over the preceding year, and the exports to the United States were $98,432,859, an increase of almost an equal amount. The United Kingdom is the nearest competitor in the foreign trade with our neighbouring republic. While the imports from the United States showed an increase of twenty-four per cent. over the preceding year, the increase from the United Kingdom and Germany was only twelve and eighteen per cent. respectively. Imports from the mother country, Spain, were less than three per cent. of the whole.

In the matter of trade, as is shown by the trade statistics, the United States is easily the predominant factor. The proximity of the country has probably been the cause of this, as it has led Americans to investigate the natural resources and invest money in railroads, mines, public works and many other enterprises. The same influence can be seen in the banking interests. There are a number of very strong banks in Mexico, of which the

Banco Nacional, or National Bank of Mexico, is the most influential. This bank was established in 1881, at a time when the financial condition of the country was anything but prosperous, and its growth has been continuous and at times almost phenomenal. This bank and one other are the only institutions that have the privilege of issuing bank notes in the Federal District, although some banks in other parts of the country have the same privilege. The Bank of London and Mexico, originally a British concern, but now owned by French capital, ranks next in importance, although it is very closely followed by the United States Banking Company, an American enterprise with a number of branches throughout the republic. There are many other banks, some of them under the banking laws of the republic, and others private enterprises, which gives Mexico very good facilities for the transaction of all kinds of banking and commercial business. In 1893 there were only eight banks in the entire republic, but now there are more than sixty. They have a circulation of nearly $100,000,000, and a capital in excess of that sum. The American influence, and the banks controlled by Americans, have aided greatly in the development of business between the two countries, and it is the writer's belief that similar establishments throughout the rest of Latin America would be one of the greatest aids to the extension of American influence and commerce that could be devised.

The increase of manufacturing has been quite noticeable in recent years, and eventually will cause a diminution in the imports of certain articles. Quite a number of cotton factories have been established in certain sections of the country, and the labour has been found quite well adapted to that class of manufacturing. Establishments for the preparation and curing of meats have also been built under government concessions, while tobacco factories, which work up the very excellent tobacco grown in the country, and breweries have been established in many sections of the country. The Mexican tobacco is said by those who pose as experts to have a very excellent flavour, and by many is claimed to be superior even to the Cuban article. The product grown in the state of Vera Cruz has the best flavour, but a number of other states produce large quantities of the weed.

The greatest enterprise now operating in Mexico, excepting only the railroads, is the Mexico Light and Power Company, a Canadian corporation. This group of men own the electric light and gas plants and the tramways of the City of Mexico, Puebla and a number of other cities. As a part of their enterprise they have built a great dam by means of which the waters of the Necaxa River are utilized for the production of the electricity. This is distant ninety-six miles to the northeast of the capital. Fed by springs this river becomes a good sized stream before it plunges over a precipice of four hundred and sixty feet, and a short distance beyond is one of a still greater fall. The main dam is one hundred and ninety-four feet high and about thirteen hundred feet wide, and contains an immense amount of material. It is built of stone and concrete. By means of this and the auxiliary dams a valley has been made into an immense reservoir, so that the dry season might be provided for when the natural flow of water would be insufficient. It is claimed that enough water can be stored to run the power plant through two years of continual drouth. The water is carried to the turbines by means of pipes which pierce the mountain, bringing to each turbine a stream of water six feet in diameter and carrying all the force of a drop exceeding one thousand feet. The total transmission lines reach a length of more than two hundred miles, and the capacity of the plant is two hundred and fifty thousand horse power. At the present time this company supplies all the electric power in the capital, as well as several mining enterprises, and as soon as the plant is wholly completed, will supply Puebla and other cities. Its franchise is from the Mexican government and is in perpetuity. This simply gives an indication of what can be done in the development of the natural resources of Mexico. In a country where fuel is scarce and high priced, the value of the water power is accordingly increased. There are many other waterfalls awaiting development, and it only needs the necessary capital, and a combination of far-sighted men, such as those who compose the Canadian corporation above mentioned, to supply the great need of Mexico for cheap and satisfactory power.

PRIMITIVE PLOUGHING NEAR OAXACA

It is unfortunate for Mexico that mining has absorbed almost all of her energies, and agriculture has been allowed to drop into a secondary position. One cause for this has been the Spanish characteristic, as represented by the original conquerors, of seeking quick wealth instead of attempting to coax out of mother earth the treasure that she possesses. There are labourers in plenty, if they are properly instructed, but the *hacendados*, as well as labourers, adhere to the most primitive methods. It has been said that "earth is here so kind that just tickle her with a hoe and she laughs with a harvest." This is not true of all parts of the country, of course, for much of it is mountainous and of a broken character, but the statement will apply to large portions of the republic.

The government of Mexico has endeavoured to improve agricultural conditions by disseminating information as to scientific methods of cultivation, irrigation and fertilization, but very little of it has had a noticeable effect. The government has also distributed large quantities of seeds and plants with little effect. In most parts of the republic the land is tilled just as it was four centuries ago. It is really surprising that, in spite of these antiquated methods, the results have been so good as they are. As mentioned heretofore the wooden plough with a small iron shoe, which merely scratches the surface of the earth, is still used; men may be seen cutting wheat with the sickle, and much of the threshing is done by driving horses and mules around a ring covered with grain, just as it was done in the old Biblical days. The winnowing is accomplished by tossing the wheat and the chaff into the air, and then the grain is hauled to the *haciendas* or markets in clumsy and ponderous two-wheeled carts.

A *hacienda* run upon modern American methods would certainly be a much more profitable enterprise than when conducted after this style. In a few sections of the country, one will find a plantation here and there where some new methods have been introduced and American machinery employed, but these are rare. Even in the Valley of Mexico, not far from the City of Mexico, the most antiquated methods will be seen employed at all times. The richness of the land and its cheapness has caused the floating of many land companies in the United States. They can show great prospects on paper, but the trouble is that many of them have been floated by unscrupulous men, who care nothing for the interests of the stockholders, but are looking simply for promoters' profits. When the real buyers reach the land they discover that things are not as represented, do not find conditions of living to their liking, and in a very short time the whole enterprise is dropped. Many have probably lost practically all of their savings. These things, of course, cannot be entirely guarded against, and they certainly fail to prove that Mexico is not a rich agricultural country. They simply demonstrate what fraud can be perpetrated upon people in a country where the land is teeming with fertility. Land values have undoubtedly advanced in the past few years, and some enormous tracts have been purchased by Americans, which are already showing profits for the owners.

There has been much criticism heaped upon the Mexican courts, and a great deal of it has been deserved. The judicial system of Mexico is copied rather after the French and Spanish than the Anglo-Saxon system. In recent years the procedure has been improved greatly, but it still needs other changes in order to bring it up to the twentieth century standards. In years past American railroad engineers, who were unfortunate enough to run over some one, received harsh treatment in Mexican jails. The law of *incommunicado,* by which an accused person is locked up for three days, is still in force. It used to be that a wounded person could not be touched or moved before the arrival of the authorities, which caused much suffering; but this at least has been abolished. The judicial system, which includes supreme courts, district courts, circuit courts, police courts and other minor courts, is intended to give justice to the defendant in a criminal action, and to both parties in a civil action, but in many cases—to an American—the result does not seem to be satisfactory.

The jury system is in use in Mexico, and nine persons compose a jury. The jurymen may consist of both natives and foreigners, but the members must have some occupation, education or independent means. The law provides that the accused must be acquainted with the names and number of his accusers, and must be confronted with the witnesses who testify against him. The testimony is all taken down in longhand writing, which is a tedious process, as followed out in Mexican courts. In criminal cases it is generally read over to the witness and signed by him, which method, although it is cumbersome, sometimes gives a degree of certainty and correctness to the testimony. It is true that in many cases the points that are raised by the accused are treated with very little consideration. This is not the fault of the law, but is the result of its maladministration by the officials, just as similar instances are the world over. Arrests of natives are made for all sorts of offences, many of which are trivial, and they are generally kept in jail for several days before they are finally given a hearing. Foreigners are usually treated with great consideration and substantial justice is done them. It probably is not good policy for citizens of another country to criticise Mexico, when there are so many blots upon the administration of justice in every civilized country, and the United States is not an exception. Local conditions, public clamour and other things influence the action of courts in Mexico, just as they do in every other country.

In addition to the railroad connections the steamship lines form a very important part in the national transportation of Mexico. The long coast line on both the Pacific Ocean and Gulf of Mexico provides many ports. The national traffic between these ports is quite a considerable item, but the foreign commerce is still greater. At the present time Mexico has direct steamship connection with the United States, Canada, Europe, South America, Central America, the West Indies and the Orient. The principal ports are Tampico, Puerto Mexico (formerly Coatzacoalcos) and Progresso on the Gulf, and Salina Cruz, Acapulco, Manzanillo, and Mazatlan on the Pacific. There are in all more than twenty steamship lines that have contracts with the government for carrying the mails, and nearly all of these enjoy subsidies of large or small amounts or enjoy certain privileges or concessions.

The most important company operating is the one known as the Ward Line, which conducts a weekly service between several Mexican ports, Havana and New York. This company has some very good boats, and does a large business between all of those ports. The Mallory Line, the Mexican-American Line and the Munson Line have regular service between Mexican ports, Galveston and New Orleans. There are also several companies that make regular trips between Vera Cruz, Tampico and European ports. On the Pacific coast the Kosmos Line, operated by the Hamburg American Company, have a regular service from Seattle down the west coast of the United States, Mexico, Central America and South America to Europe by the way of the Straits of Magellan. The Pacific Mail Steamship Company operate about three boats a month from San Francisco to Panama, where connections are made for New York and West Coast ports of South America. The American-Hawaiian Company have boats which sail between Hawaii and Salina Cruz. There are also, in addition to these mentioned, a number of coast lines on both the Pacific and Atlantic side, which do a considerable traffic between the various ports. The Canadian-Mexican Pacific Steamship Company recently began to operate boats between Victoria, British Columbia and Salina Cruz, and gives a monthly service between those ports. In order to develop and facilitate this coast traffic the Mexican government has spent a great deal of money in providing harbours and docks at a number of the smaller ports, in addition to the larger enterprises that have heretofore been described.

Mexico has not a great number of navigable rivers. On the Pacific side the Mayo, the Yaqui, the Balsas, the Rio Grande de Santiago and one or two others are classed as navigable streams, but because of bars and other obstructions they can be used only by boats of comparatively light draft. On the Atlantic side, just below the Isthmus of Tehuantepec, is the Grigalva River, which is a broad and imposing stream. Large boats ply regularly up this stream to San Juan Bautista, a distance of about seventy-five miles. Small boats go up still farther, the boat traffic extending clear to the mountains. The Usumasinta River is an affluent of this stream, and is navigable for small boats even beyond the Guatemala border. The Coatzacoalcos River, which flows into the Gulf at the town of the same name, is quite an important stream, and furnishes an outlet to a considerable territory. The Papaloapan River, which flows into the Gulf of Mexico near Vera Cruz, has been dredged and made navigable for a considerable distance into the interior. It has proved a great benefit to many small towns and plantations there situated.

North of Vera Cruz are the Soto La Marina, the Tuxpan and the Panuco Rivers, all of which are navigable for a hundred miles or more. As an adjunct to the navigable streams and the deep water ports the government is now building an intercoastal canal, which is similar to the one proposed along the Gulf coast of Louisiana and Texas to connect the Mississippi and Rio Grande Rivers. There are a series of lagoons and small lakes that lie just a short distance within the coast line, and which can be connected and deepened. They will then form a convenient and safe waterway for navigation. The government is spending several million dollars on the first link of this system, which will connect the ports of Tampico and Tuxpan, a distance of about a hundred miles. Half of this section is already finished and in operation, and it is estimated that in three or four years more this part of the canal will be finished. This waterway has a width of seventy-five feet and a uniform depth of ten and one-half feet, and will connect the mouths of the Panuco and the Tuxpan Rivers. The Panuco, near Tampico, is fifty feet deep, and the deepest draft ocean vessels can come in and unload at the docks of Tampico. The section of the canal already opened is constantly filled with long and narrow boats, manned by natives, which are propelled by means of long poles when the wind fails.

The opening of this section of the canal has worked wonders in the development of this part of the coast land, because it places the products of the plantations and ranches within easy reach of the markets. It has also served to drain thousands of acres of land, which were formerly considered to be of no use whatever. On this route the canal passes through Lake Tamiahua, which is seventy-nine miles long and from five to twenty miles wide. Lake Tampamachoco, a much smaller lake, will also be traversed by this canal. The water in these lakes is comparatively shallow, and it has been necessary to deepen them considerably in order to make the canal of uniform depth with the other portion. The distance between Tampico and the mouth of the Rio Grande is about three hundred miles, but a number of salt water lagoons, which lie near the coast, can be utilized as a portion of the canal. If this project, and the similar one planned by the United States, are completed, it will furnish a very long inland waterway for the coast region. It will serve the double purpose of draining and making more healthful that portion of the country, and likewise giving an outlet for the development that will surely follow. The land when once drained has been proved to be of unusual fertility.

The influence of the Anglo-Saxon in Mexico has been very marked. What the English have done in Argentina and many parts of the world, the Americans have done in our neighbouring republic. It is a significant fact that the Spanish influences have been perceptibly disappearing, while that of the Anglo-Saxon has been in the ascendency. This change can be noted in a great many ways, both in thought, customs and foreign relations. This transition has not been promptly recognized, and in some quarters it has been strongly objected to by the extreme conservative elements; but, nevertheless, it has been steadily marching on. Many of the Mexicans prominent in the political and business life recognize this trend and encourage it, for they feel that Mexico needs Anglo-Saxon methods and ideas in order to develop the country, and give it the prestige that its importance deserves. There are perhaps twenty or twenty-five thousand Americans who permanently reside in Mexico, and, in addition, there is the effect of the many millions of American money invested in the country, and the thousands of tourists and business men who annually cross the borders.

There is, doubtless, a strong prejudice against the American and his methods in many parts of Mexico, and this feeling seems to have been somewhat intensified in the recent revolution. It is not to be wondered at that such a feeling exists. From first to last Mexico has ceded to the United States almost one million square miles of territory, which is almost one-third more than the present size of the republic. First came the separation of Texas, which was undoubtedly due to the intriguing of Americans who had crossed over into that section of Mexico. These pioneers and adventurers brought about the declaration of independence by the Lone Star State. A few years later that territory was admitted into the United States as one of its integral parts. Then came the Mexican War, which most of us admit was an unjust war, and which resulted in the cession of more than half a million of square miles of territory. A few years later, by the Gadsden Purchase, which was due to disputes over the boundary line, another block of territory, as large as the state of Ohio, was added to the domain of the United States.

In the revolution of 1910 many Americans crossed the border, joined the forces of the revolutionists, and aided in the troubles of the then existing government. Furthermore, very many American tourists who visit Mexico make themselves disagreeable by their actions and their criticisms, which also add to the anti-American feeling. So many include all Mexicans under the general title of "greasers," and can see no good in anything that is not American. It is a fortunate thing that the good people of Mexico understand very little English; otherwise they would frequently be excited to anger, if they could hear the remarks that are made by Americans in visiting their churches, battle fields and other places surrounded by sacred associations. They are not fools, however, and even if they do not understand the words they can catch the trend of remarks by the gesture and laugh that accompanies them. As the Spanish race are exceedingly sensitive this lack of sympathy and almost open contempt cannot result otherwise than do injury to a general good feeling. Some Americans grumble at everything, get mad because all the waiters and porters do not understand English, complain about the hotels because they cannot obtain everything just like they would in a Fifth Avenue hotel, and, in fact, find fault with everything that they see. As a contrast to this one might consider the attitude of Mexicans. It is difficult to do justice to the innate courtesy of officials and people when Americans show them so little. You can murder his beloved Spanish in attempting to address a Mexican, and he will listen with infinite patience and never a smile of amusement or expression of vexation on his face. The Mexican is polite not only to his superiors and equals, but to his servants as well.

The republic of Mexico has passed through dark days. It has suffered from the evil government of foreigners and from the reckless ambitions of its own rulers. The burdens of former mistakes still remain, and there is a lingering distrust of the powerful republic to the north in many places. This distrust has been fanned into greater intensity by recent political agitators. The good sense of the leaders will quickly reassert itself, however, and a more perfect understanding will surely result. American intelligence and capital have done too much in bringing about the material prosperity of the country for such conditions to exist permanently. Mexico needs capital for the development of her resources, and American capital is most available for that purpose. Americans will even be interested in the moral and material advancement of their neighbours across the Rio Grande.

To the reader who has followed this narrative to the end, I give my valediction, *a la Mexicana*:

Adios! Vaya usted con Dios.

THE END.

www.ingramcontent.com/pod-product-compliance
Lightning Source LLC
Chambersburg PA
CBHW080018130526
44590CB00045B/3435